LOCOMOTION PAPERS LP240

REDDITCH & EVESHAM LINE

by

Bob Yate

THE OAKWOOD PRESS

British Library Cataloguing in Publication Data
A Record for this book is available from the British Library
ISBN 978 0 85361 736 5

Typeset by Oakwood Graphics.
Repro by PKmediaworks, Cranborne, Dorset.
Printed by Berforts Information Press Ltd, Stevenage, Herts.

Front cover: Saltley shed's Ivatt class '4' 2-6-0 No. 43049 is just about to get under way with a southbound train from Broom Junction in the summer of 1960. The left-hand side of the island platform was signalled for working in either direction, a legacy from the time that trains for Stratford-on-Avon used this platform face. By this date, it was used for northbound services. The simplicity of the facilities and the relative isolation of the single platform in the surrounding countryside can be appreciated in this photograph.
J. Tarrant/Kidderminster Railway Museum

Rear cover, top: An Ivatt class '4' Mogul makes a smoky departure from Salford Priors with a northbound passenger train in the summer of 1960. The three-coach corridor set has been strengthened by the addition of a non-corridor brake second of LMS vintage. The goods yard still seems to be reasonably busy judging by the number of wagons therein.
J. Tarrant/Kidderminster Railway Museum

Rear cover, bottom: One of the earlier batch of Fowler 2-6-4Ts, No. 42340 runs into the branch platform at Barnt Green with a southbound train composed entirely of non-corridor stock in the summer of 1960. The locomotive is still carrying the early BR 'lion and wheel' emblem on its tank side. *J. Tarrant/Kidderminster Railway Museum*

Published by The Oakwood Press (Usk), P.O. Box 13, Usk, Mon., NP15 1YS.
E mail: sales@oakwoodpress.co.uk
Website: www.oakwoodpress.co.uk

Contents

Saltley's allocation of Ivatt class '4' Moguls were more likely to be seen on passenger workings, but for once we see here No. 43046 rolling northwards out of Redditch with a diverted class 'F' part-fitted freight on 2nd July, 1961. The primitive coaling arrangements for locomotives at Redditch shed are illustrated by the wooden coaling stage on the right. *Author*

Introduction

The line from Barnt Green via Redditch and Evesham to Ashchurch has been gifted several names over the years: the Redditch Line, the Redditch Branch, the Evesham Route, the Barnt Green to Ashchurch Loop, and the Birmingham-Gloucester Loop. This latter was first used by the Midland Railway to distinguish it from the Birmingham-Gloucester main line, and it was probably this title, shortened with usage to the 'Gloucester Loop' that came to be used in the latter years of the Midland Railway.

The country through which the line ran was mostly rural, and the towns it served whilst important, were not large. So the number and complexity of proposed lines in this area is somewhat surprising, and these will be examined as part of the chronological survey of railway developments along each part of the line. As no railway exists in isolation, the events and services on the connecting lines as far as they affect this line, are also examined.

At first glance the line appeared to have been constructed on a piecemeal basis, as it was built by three separate companies, and opened in four stages between 1859 and 1868. However, the Midland Railway had seen the potential, and backed both of the nominally independent companies. Furthermore, each section of the line was operated by the Midland Railway. Although the line was never originally conceived as a strategic route, it was developed gradually from a desire to keep competitors at bay into a useful diversionary route. Later, with the opening of the line promoted by the East & West Junction Railway from Stratford-on-Avon to Broom, further traffic patterns began to emerge. In the meantime, the line proved prosperous as it served the developing manufacturing towns of Redditch and Alcester, and the important fruit and vegetable growing area of the Vale of Evesham. Passenger traffic was normally fairly light, but the area served also brought a good deal of day trippers from the Birmingham area at weekends and holidays. In modern times, the passenger traffic from Redditch was at first roundly discouraged, until common sense prevailed and the now much shortened line was modernized. The growth of Redditch as a New Town created a level of passenger traffic never previously imagined, and the surviving line has a frequency of trains that are the envy of much larger towns. It now forms the southern end of the electrified 'Cross City' rail link from Lichfield through Birmingham. The corollary is that freight traffic on the branch is nowadays non-existent.

The spelling of various locations, towns and villages in the text are those in use at the time. Some vary from one era to another, and especially may be different from those in use today, for example: *Pigeon Bridge* and *Pigeon's Bridge, Winchcomb* and *Winchcombe.* Nowadays, *Stratford-on-Avon* refers to the District to distinguish it from the town, *Stratford-upon-Avon.*

Abbreviations

B&GR	Birmingham & Gloucester Railway
BR	British Railways (later British Rail)
BWSR	Birmingham West Suburban Rly
dmu	Diesel-multiple-unit
emu	Electric-multiple-unit
EWJR	East & West Junction Railway
GWR	Great Western Railway
L&BR	London & Birmingham Railway
LBSCR	London, Brighton & South Coast Rly
LMR	London Midland Region
LMS	London, Midland & Scottish Rly
LNWR	London & North Western Railway
LTSR	London, Tilbury & Southend Railway
LWLKR	London, Warwick, Leamington & Kidderminster Railway
MR	Midland Railway
OWWR	Oxford, Worcester & Wolverhampton Railway
SMJR	Stratford & Midland Junction Rly
WMPTE	West Midlands Passenger Transport Executive
WMR	West Midland Railway
WR	Western Region of British Railways

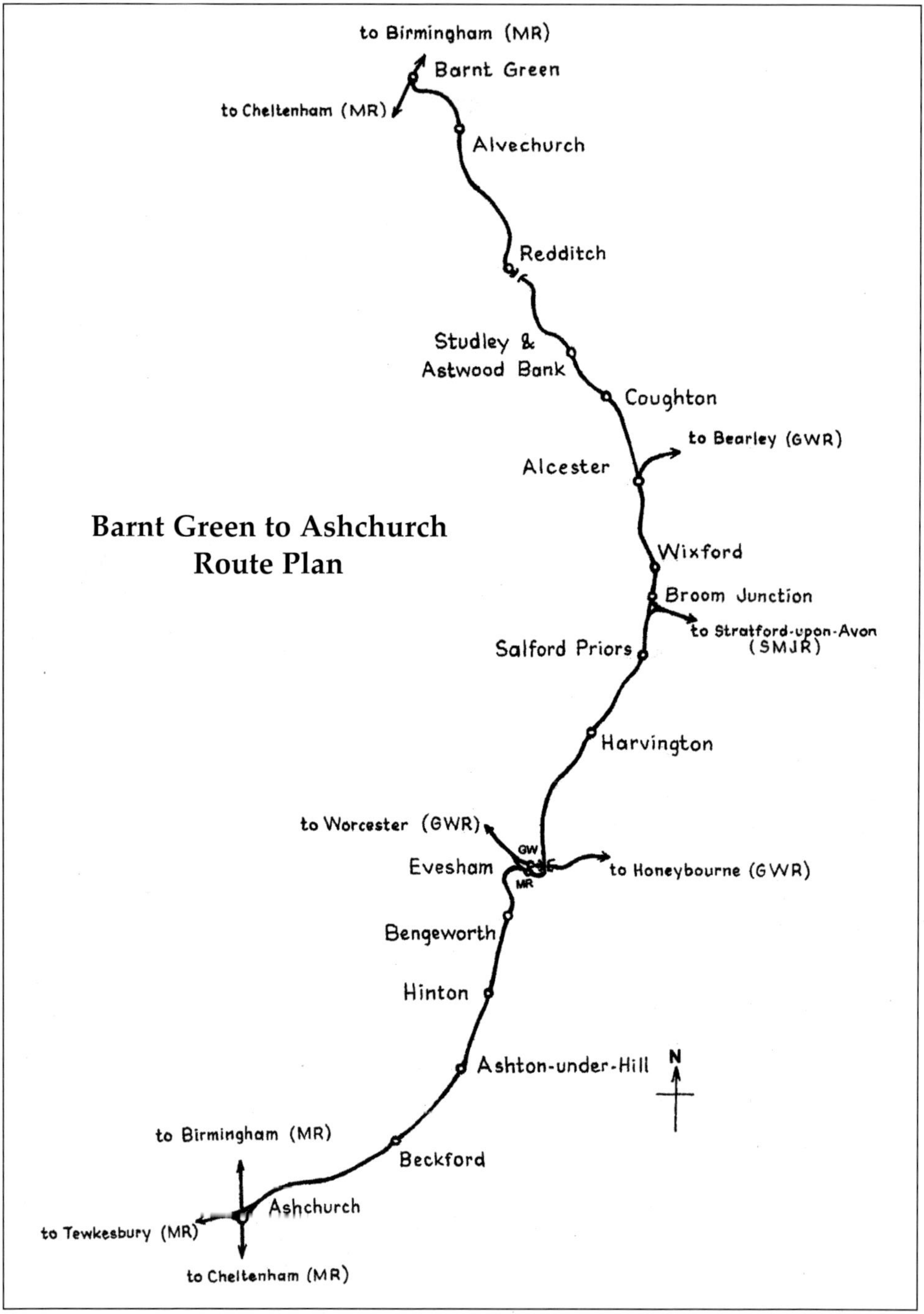

**Barnt Green to Ashchurch
Route Plan**

Chapter One

The Existing Railways

Before starting on the history of the line itself, it is perhaps useful to understand the railways that existed in the area immediately prior to the commencement of our line. These do have a bearing on some of the subsequent events, and so a brief history of them is appropriate at this point.

The Midland Railway

The original route southwards from Birmingham was constructed by the Birmingham & Gloucester Railway (B&GR), which was authorized on 22nd April, 1836 to build a 40 mile line from Birmingham to Gloucester. The line was originally surveyed in 1832 by Isambard Kingdom Brunel, who favoured a route to the east of that eventually constructed, and it is interesting to consider that had his route been adopted, a main line railhead for Redditch might have been nearer to the town, thus making the later railways unnecessary! However, that, as they say, is pure conjecture. The B&GR promoters were keen to avoid any towns, so as to keep down the costs of acquiring land. Their stated policy was to link Birmingham to the River Severn at Gloucester (and eventually Bristol) by the most direct route, in order that manufactured goods should be able to shipped promptly to the rapidly expanding export markets. Evidently, any potential traffic arising from placing the line convenient to additional users did not concern them. Adopting this directive, Brunel's route lay to the east of the line as built, and indeed passed within a mile of Redditch, to join the later B&GR route at Cofton Hackett, less than one mile north of Barnt Green. The route contained no gradients steeper than 1 in 300 but was considered by the promoters to be too expensive, and so not used by them, although they paid Brunel the princely sum of £100 for his trouble ! Other routes were surveyed in 1824, 1833 and 1835, all to the west of the eventual line.

The route, engineered by Captain W.S. Moorsom, was selected as most appropriate, being as straight as possible from Birmingham to Gloucester, even if this meant a formidable climb up the side of the Lickey Hills north of Bromsgrove. However, the resolute people of Cheltenham created such an outrage in being bypassed, that the B&GR demurred, and changed its route to serve that town.

It opened from Cheltenham to Bromsgrove on 24th June, 1840, and onwards to Cofton Farm (near Longbridge) on 17th September of that year. The route finally reached its southern terminus at Gloucester on 4th November and its northern terminus at Camp Hill in Birmingham on 17th December, and linked with the London & Birmingham Railway at Curzon Street station on 17th August of the following year. New Street station was reached by the Midland Railway (MR) in 1854. Intermediate stations were provided north of Barnt Green at Longbridge, Lifford, and Moseley. We shall look at the routes used by trains from the Redditch line into Birmingham in Chapter Seven.

Barnt Green station did not open until 1st May, 1844 and at that time provided a railhead for passengers from Redditch, who had the benefit of a horse-drawn omnibus connection. The small station at first comprised just two platforms, staggered in the fashion of the day, so that passengers could cross from the end of one to the end of the other. The village of Barnt Green was otherwise rather small, but did benefit from people wishing to visit the Lickey Hills for a day out from Birmingham.

A Johnson 0-6-0 pulls out from the down relief road onto the branch line at Barnt Green with a goods train around 1902. The original up main line platform and signal box can be seen on the left, with copious advertisements along the platform fencing. *R. Carpenter Collection*

Looking northwards from the footbridge at Barnt Green in 1949, the main line signal box is visible left of centre, and the four track section continues through to Kings Norton. The splitting bracket signal on the left has repeater arms at low level for better sighting, one of which is suspended by a 'doll' from the upper gantry and appearing to be very much of an afterthought. This signal was later renewed, eliminating the lower arms, and raising the upper gantry signals even higher. The signal box appears to be in the same position as the earlier photograph, but the trackwork has been considerably altered. *Joe Moss/R. Carpenter*

Worcester was eventually connected to the MR system in October 1850 when a new line was opened by the Oxford, Worcester & Wolverhampton Railway (OWWR) from the MR at Stoke Prior, south of Bromsgrove, to join their system at Droitwich and so run into Worcester. This line from Stoke Prior to Droitwich was always worked by the MR. South of the county town, an MR connection was put in at the same time, from the OWWR Evesham line at Norton Junction to the Birmingham-Gloucester line at Abbotswood Junction. From that date the MR began running trains that called at Worcester on their way south to Gloucester, although some services terminated at Worcester.

At the southern end of our line, Ashchurch station was opened on 24th June, 1840, being the same day as the section from Bromsgrove to Cheltenham opened. Meanwhile, the B&GR had been working on a 1¾ mile branch from Ashchurch to Tewkesbury, which had been authorized on 15th May, 1837 and opened shortly after the main line, on 21st July, 1840. Thus the station building at Ashchurch on the up side comprised the main line platform and the Tewkesbury line platform, and presented a unified and pleasing appearance. More than 20 years were to elapse before the nominally independent Tewkesbury and Malvern Railway was incorporated on 25th May, 1860 to construct a line linking the West Midland Railway at Malvern to Tewkesbury and Ashchurch. The line was eventually opened throughout on 16th May, 1864. This required a new station on the outskirts of Tewkesbury, as the original station was a terminus close to the town centre, but without any opportunity of being extended as a through route. As the original station was thereafter at the end of a short branch, this continued to be used for goods traffic, and also for access to the engine shed located part way along the branch. As from 1st July, 1877 the original company was vested in the Midland Railway, which had worked traffic along the entire line from the outset. On 1st December, 1952 all services were withdrawn from north of Upton-on-Severn to Malvern, although interestingly after that date through services continued from Birmingham New Street to Malvern Wells, via Worcester Foregate Street and the former West Midland Railway line to Hereford. Finally, passenger services were withdrawn between Ashchurch and Upton-on-Severn as from 14th August, 1961 and the line finally closed entirely from 1st July, 1963.

Stanier 'Black Five' 4-6-0 No. 44843 heads a northbound express through the main line platforms at Ashchurch station on 27th June, 1964. The smaller glass canopy on the down main platform is seen to advantage here. It will be noticed that with the withdrawal of services on the line to Evesham in June 1963 BR had changed the station running-in boards to read 'Ashchurch for Tewkesbury' (although that latter place was no longer rail served). *R.K. Blencowe Collection*

The GWR connection at Evesham

The Great Western Railway (GWR) line at Evesham was originally constructed by the Oxford, Worcester & Wolverhampton Railway which had been authorized to construct its main line from Oxford to Worcester and Hereford on 4th August, 1845. The section from Worcester to Evesham opened on 1st May, 1852, as a single line and was of standard gauge, mostly laid on baulk sleepers. Around 10,000 people turned out at Evesham to see the first official train on this day, which was composed of 21 four-wheeled carriages hauled by 'Engine A'. At this time, trains between Stourbridge and Evesham were worked under contract by C.C. Williams with David Joy as his locomotive superintendent. Their locomotive stock was entirely inadequate, and indeed this locomotive had only been delivered a few days before the opening, having been purchased second-hand from a firm of contractors in Pontefract. This engine was a 2-4-0 passenger engine built by E.B. Wilson at the Railway Foundry, Leeds in 1849 and was unusual in having mixed frames, with inside frames for the coupled wheels and outside frames for the leading wheels. It was later converted at the OWWR works in Worcester into a 2-2-2, becoming their No. 31, then West Midland Railway No. 31, being GWR No. 206 and finally withdrawn in May 1876.

From Evesham southwards the line was single and to be laid as mixed standard and broad gauge. However, when Captain Galton of the Board of Trade arrived on the day decided by the Directors to open the line, 7th May, 1853, he found that the broad gauge rails were incomplete in several places, and the junction at Wolvercot, just outside Oxford, had not been laid. He therefore refused to pass the line for passenger workings, and so regular passenger services were not allowed to commence. Nonetheless, as it was by then too late to cancel the festivities, the formal

Collett 'Castle' class 4-6-0 No. 7004 *Eastnor Castle* comes to a halt at Evesham with an express from Paddington to Hereford on 11th June, 1962. The large black building in the centre is the original OWWR goods shed, built to broad gauge specifications. The MR goods yard and signal box can be glimpsed to the upper right. *Author*

opening ceremony went ahead anyway! A special train consisting this time of no less than 26 four-wheeled carriages ran over the entire line from Stourbridge to Wolvercot, where the passengers had to climb down on to the ballast in order to reach a connecting train laid on by the GWR to the city of Oxford. At Evesham, the passengers were allowed a break and treated to a champagne luncheon before continuing their journey southwards.

A week later, on 14th May, Captain Galton again inspected the line, but once again refused to pass it for passenger workings, as there were still gaps in the broad gauge south of Evesham. Two weeks later he returned to the line, but this time refused to carry out an inspection when informed by the Chief Engineer that it would be unsafe to take a broad gauge engine over the line. Eventually, and after a great deal of night time working, the line was completed, and on 2nd June, 1853 the Captain travelled the line from Wolvercot to Evesham in a saloon attached to a broad gauge engine. He granted immediate permission to open the line, and services began two days later, on Saturday 4th June.

The line was doubled from Norton Junction, just outside Worcester, to Evesham in July 1852. Meanwhile, the OWWR was rather reluctant to continue northwards with the broad gauge line, and so laid mixed track between Stourbridge and Evesham on the *down side only*. The OWWR never owned any broad gauge locomotives, and it is doubtful if the lines north of Evesham ever saw any broad gauge workings. In fact any south of Evesham are similarly unlikely, although using GWR locomotives they may at least have been possible given the more complete set of rails. In any event, the GWR insistence on the OWWR to maintain its broad gauge lines was reversed by a tentative agreement in February 1858 that the OWWR could remove its broad gauge rails. This was formalized in an Act of February 1859 and the rails were removed soon after, and sold to the GWR for use elsewhere on their system.

The following year saw the OWWR being absorbed into a new concern, the West Midland Railway, by amalgamation with the Newport, Abergavenny & Hereford Railway and the Worcester & Hereford Railway on 1st July, 1860. The West Midland Railway (WMR) was, in turn, absorbed into the GWR as from 1st August, 1863.

The original station at Evesham was a standard OWWR wooden construction of only about 32 ft in length and with a small canopy; this design of station building was unusual in not providing urinals. A large single-road goods shed of brick and wood construction, and measuring about 67 ft by 45 ft, was provided. The original station building was replaced by the GWR around 1890 by a standard brick building, which at last provided much needed relief, as well as the usual waiting rooms and offices.

A single-road locomotive shed was sited on the north side of the up line, at the east end of the station, measuring some 111 ft by 17 ft, of which 37½ ft were actually beneath the road overbridge at this point. This shed is believed to have opened with the line in 1853, and was demolished in 1901, when the new shed was erected at the western end of the yards.

Chapter Two

The Redditch Railway

The origins of Redditch and its early transport links

The town of Redditch only appears to date from the mid-15th century, indeed the nearby settlements of Ipsley and Beoley are much older. The town stems from the establishment of a Cistercian abbey at Bordesley, which was begun in 1140, and which soon spawned a small settlement around it. This became known as 'Rubeo Fosetto' and later Redditch, due to the red colour of the water in a nearby stream, caused by iron oxide in the soil. This settlement does not appear to have grown much in the following two centuries, and indeed was wiped out by the Black Death of the 14th century.

The first mention of Redditch as a town was in 1461, although it does not appear on any surviving maps from around this time. At the direction of Henry VIII, Bordesley Abbey was dissolved in 1523, and subsequently destroyed. Under the monks needle making had prospered at this site, so with the disappearance of the abbey, the industry moved to nearby Alcester and Studley, where suitable sites for the water-powered mills were available.

Henry VIII caused further upset in the area in 1542, when, having stayed at Lord Windsor's estate at Stanmore (near to present day Heathrow airport), he decided he liked the estate so much that he would have it for himself. As compensation, he gave Lord Windsor the run-down Bordesley estate and some surrounding lands, formerly occupied by the Cistercian monks. No-one argued with the King in those days, much less as he was Henry VIII! So Lord Windsor could do nothing than accept the situation, and he visited his new property, staying at Hewell Grange, near Tardebigge. Here he eventually built his new manorial home.

The 16th century saw little development towards the town of Redditch, although there was a gradual movement of people from the Bordesley area to Redditch Common, which later became the centre of Redditch. In 1625 we learn that there was, unsurprisingly for the times, a serious plague in Redditch, so that by 1700 the town comprised no more than 700 people. Meanwhile, the needlemakers were gradually moving back from Studley and Alcester, so that by 1787 there were 400 in Redditch, out of a total of around 2,000 in the area. Nonetheless, it is true to say that most needle making was still carried on in Alcester. Earlier, in 1781, the Irish firm of Connolly had moved its fish hook making business from Ireland to Redditch. A fine reputation for needlemaking had been earned, and the area became known as 'The Needle District'.

This was characterized in a regular coach service to London by Clarke's 'Needle Coach' in 1821, and in the same year the first daily post service was inaugurated. Barry and Higgins of Stourbridge were also conveying passengers and goods on their cart service to London, once a week each way. In 1826 the Great South Road from Birmingham to Pershore was opened, enabling fruit and vegetables from the Vale of Evesham to be taken to the markets of Birmingham, although this road bypassed Redditch. Passengers from Redditch wishing to use the twice-weekly coaches from Alcester to Birmingham had to travel about three miles east to Branson's Cross to join the service, although by 1843 one of the coaches travelled via Redditch. The following year a regular omnibus service was introduced from

Redditch to Barnt Green, for passengers to join the newly-opened line of the Birmingham & Gloucester Railway.

The expansion of canals throughout the country in the 18th century similarly bypassed Redditch, with the Birmingham & Worcester Canal (authorized by an Act of 1791), opening from Birmingham to Tardebigge, about three miles west from Redditch, in 1807. This canal was engineered by John Woodhouse, and eventually opened to a total distance of 30 miles in 1815, having cost £610,000 and containing 58 locks. A lift was installed to replace many of these locks at Tardebigge, but this soon malfunctioned, and the potential cost of repairs was so great that the locks were reinstated. The canal company considered the possibility of a branch to Redditch, but the high cost of overcoming the topographical problems ruled out any construction. Instead, the waggon service for goods and passengers from Tardebigge to Redditch continued.

Returning to the needlemakers, between 1820 and 1830 many of the craftsmen of this trade from all over the country moved to the town, some along with their employers, as it had become an acknowledged centre of excellence for the industry. Established firms expanded rapidly, such as Richard Hemmings and Sons Ltd (founded early 18th century), Henry Milward & Sons Ltd (founded 1730, and later to become Needle Industries Ltd), Abel Morrall Ltd (founded 1785, and later to become part of Aero Needles Group Ltd). The fishing tackle industry was represented by Samuel Allcock (founded 1805, and later part of the Shakespeare Corporation), and J.W. Young & Sons Ltd (founded much later, in 1884).

Some early railway proposals

The growth of the town, its population and industries, can thus be seen as an attractive proposition for the introduction of a railway service in the area. Mention was made in the previous chapter that the Birmingham & Gloucester Railway had already considered several possible routes between its two centres, including one surveyed in 1832 by Isambard Kingdom Brunel that would have brought the line within a mile of Redditch. This was rejected as being too costly to build.

The 'Railway Mania' of the 1840s resulted in several further schemes that would have linked Redditch, Alcester and other districts with the outside world, but were all doomed to failure, mostly because they were lacking in finance. The London, Warwick, Leamington & Kidderminster Railway (LWLKR) was engineered by John Addison, and plans were deposited at Worcester on 29th November, 1845 for a line of 57½ miles from the London & Birmingham Railway (L&BR) at Weedon through Southam, Leamington, Warwick, Claverdon, Aston Cantlow, Great Alne, Coughton, Hunt End, Feckenham, Hanbury, Stoke Prior, and Chaddesley Corbett to Kidderminster, where, after passing beneath the proposed OWWR, it would link with the proposed Welsh Midland Railway, also never built. There was to be a branch of 8 ¾ miles from a point between Coughton and Sambourn, running north to Ipsley, then round the eastern side of Redditch to Pigeon's Bridge, then following much of Brunel's route to Callow Hill, round the south side of Bittell Reservoir to join the B&GR at Cofton Hackett, about ¾ mile north of Barnt Green. This route would have avoided the twisting, sharply curved route into Barnt Green, but there would have been no junction station with the B&GR.

The Midland Railway countered with a proposal of its own on 30th November, 1845, engineered by Robert Stephenson, for the branch line from Cofton Hackett to join the LWLKR near Coughton. This was principally similar to the branch line of the LWLKR, but passed through Alvechurch, and ran to the east of Pigeon's Bridge. Actually, both of these lines followed the general direction of Brunel's earlier suggested route for the B&GR in this area.

Another proposal was the Worcester, Warwick & Rugby Railway, engineered by W. Gravatt, and for which plans were deposited once more on 30th November, 1845. This ran from the L&BR at Rugby through Warwick, Claverdon, Wootton Wawen, Oldberrow, Studley, Ipsley, Feckenham, Hunt End, Fladbury, Hanbury and Huddington to Claines, in Worcester. There was to be a branch from Huddington to Droitwich. On the same day, plans were also deposited for the Warwick & Worcester Railway, whose Engineer was William B. Prichard, assisted by Sir John Macneill and James Thomson as Consulting Engineers. This shorter railway ran for 28¼ miles from Warwick, following the same general route as the LWLKR above, as far as Alcester where it turned more directly westwards to serve this town, then continued through Inkberrow, Grafton Flyford, Tibberton, and Broughton Hackett to Claines. A branch of 6⅞ miles was to run from near Grafton Flyford to join the OWWR at Droitwich.

At the same time, William Prichard engineered another line, the Rugby, Worcester & Warwick Railway which differed in that it started from a junction with the L&BR at Rugby before reaching Warwick, and after Grafton Flyford turned more directly westwards to reach Worcester via Bredicot and Spetchley.

One further proposal resulted from the competition suffered by the Worcester & Birmingham Canal as a result of the opening of the B&GR in 1840. The canal company decided in 1845 that its best course of action was to build a railway alongside its canal from Birmingham to Worcester, but with a branch to Redditch. However, the shareholders, who grown accustomed to generous dividends, were not attracted by the necessity for further funding and voted out the scheme, before the company even had chance to deposit plans for the line. This would influence the canal company's behaviour later, as we shall shortly see.

The lack of success of these proposals in attracting finance is hardly surprising when considering the number of other proposals being put forward at the same time, all over the country! It was left to local people to ensure that Redditch was put on 'the railway map'. In our story, we shall meet many of the people and places mentioned above in a context with the introduction and development of this railway route.

Formation of the company

The Redditch Railway was founded during 1857 by the enterprise of several local businessmen, who we shall meet later. The line was duly surveyed, and the Notice of Intention to Apply for a Bill, along with the plans, deposited at Warwick County Court on 30th November, 1857 at 3 o'clock by the solicitors Browning & Richards of Redditch, acting on the company's behalf. Unfortunately, the name of the engineer was not given, but this is assumed to have been J.B. Burke, who was subsequently appointed as Engineer. The total length of the line was given as 4 miles and 5 furlongs, although this was later to change. The Bill was presented before Parliament, achieving its Royal Assent after the third reading on 23rd July, 1858. The Birmingham & Worcester Canal had opposed the Bill, but was unsuccessful in its opposition, even if this did cost the railway company in both time and legal costs. The company was thus incorporated on 23rd July, 1858 under the Redditch Railway

Act, 1858 (Vict. 21 and 22, cap. 137), which also included powers for the acquisition of land and construction of the line from Barnt Green (junction with the Midland Railway) to Brock Hill Lane, Redditch. The Act specified the capital of the company to comprise a maximum of £35,000 in share capital and £11,500 in loans, which compared with the Engineer's estimate that construction costs including land acquisition would not exceed £35,000.

The news was greeted with much celebration in Redditch, as recorded in the *Worcester Herald* of 31st July, 1858:

REDDITCH, THE RAILWAY

At eleven o'clock on Friday morning news arrived that the railway bill had passed the House of Lords, and the bells immediately rang out a merry peal, and kept it up for two or three hours. At six o'clock in the evening a telegram was received, intimating that the bill had received the Royal assent, and again the bells gave out merry peals, which they kept until many good people were in bed. The Provisional committee met for the last time, the functions of that body having ceased with the passing of the bill. The solicitor's and engineer's report was received as to proceedings since the previous meeting, and several resolutions were passed, the most important being that the ceremony of the cutting the first sod should take place as early as possible, and Mr Osborne was deputed to wait on the Hon. R. Clive, and request his active cooperation in that direction. The Directors appointed by the set, viz. Messrs H. Millward, J. James, J. Osborne, J. Smith, and S. Thomas, met the same evening, when the minutes and proceedings of the provisional committee, and their various sets and agreements, were approved and confirmed; the engineer and solicitors to the company were severally appointed, and instructions given to them to take the necessary steps to obtain early possession of the land required for the line. We are glad to be able to state that Mr Osborne succeeded in inducing the Hon. R. W. Clive, MP, to consent to turn the first sod, which will take place on Thursday next with great rejoicing, and as stately a ceremony as circumstances will permit. As a matter of course there must be 'a bit of biting' about the business, but we have not been favoured with any information of the intention of the Directors in that respect.

As reported above, a meeting of the provisional committee of the company took place on this day, at the offices of their solicitors, now known as Browning & Son, in Redditch. Those present were Henry Milward (chair), John Osborne, John James, Samuel Thomas, James Smith, James Walton, William Smith, Dr J.R. Nicholson and C.B. James as promoters, J.B. Burke as Engineer and for the solicitors, Mr Richards and W.J. Manning. The meeting confirmed the appointed of J.B. Burke as Engineer to the line, and it was agreed to open an account with the Stourbridge & Kidderminster Banking Co. It was also agreed that the minimum number of daily trains on the line would be three. This was to be incorporated into a proposed agreement with the Midland Railway for them to run the trains, and this agreement was to be forwarded to the MR for their approval and comment.

The ceremony for the turning of the first sod was reported in some detail in the *Worcester Herald* of 7th August, 1858:

REDDITCH RAILWAY; TURNING THE FIRST SOD

The usually quiet town of Redditch was yesterday (Thursday) [5th August 1858] the scene of great festivity on occasion of the turning, by the Rt. Hon. Windsor Clive, MP, of the first sod of the railway from that town to Barnt Green station of the Midland Company ... At an early hour the town presented a gay and bustling appearance. The band of the Worcestershire Yeomanry was engaged, and played several pieces of enlivening music. At two o'clock a procession formed of the Directors, provisional

> committee, and shareholders, and headed by the Yeomanry band, playing appropriate music, walked from the Unicorn Hotel to a field situate a short distance from the town, on the Birmingham-road, in which the station is to be erected. Here a large circle had been formed, in which the ceremonial was to take place, and on one side of the area a platform was erected for the convenience of ladies, many of whom were present, and appeared to take great interest in the proceedings. ... The Rev. G. Fessey offered up a prayer to the Almighty ... The Hon. Robert W. Clive then came forward, and was received with loud applause. Having received the spade, he, in a craftsmanlike manner, turned the first sod, which he placed in a new wheelbarrow, provided for the occasion, and wheeled it a distance of several yards, and then overturned.
>
> The gentlemen then retired to a commodious and suitable tent, erected on the ground, in which a very excellent cold collation was provided, the edibles by Mr Mountford, of Worcester, and the wines, &c., by Mr Jesse Castree, of the Unicorn Hotel, Redditch.

The report contained the details of several, or more accurately, many speeches made during this occasion, but for the benefit of the reader these are not reproduced here!

The first shareholders' meeting took place at the National School Rooms, Redditch (where all subsequent shareholders' meetings would be held) on 20th October, 1858. The Directors were elected as follows: Henry Milward (Chairman), James Smith, Samuel Thomas, John James and John Osborne.

Construction of the line

Construction actually commenced on the same day as the turning of the first sod, 5th August, as the contractor had already been appointed. It is unclear whether any competitive bids were solicited from potential contractors, as no details have survived. The method and reason for selecting George Furness as contractor are therefore unknown. This is particularly unfortunate, as this information would have helped with an understanding of ensuing events, as we shall see. In turn, Furness appointed Messrs W. & R. Maxwell of Banbury as sub-contractors. They were later to comment that work would have proceeded much faster in 1858, but for the fact that no workers were available in the area during the harvest time.

In any event, the first recorded payment to George Furness was made on 25th August, 1858, for £235, no doubt to cover initial expenses. A further 14 payments were made to him until January 1860, totalling £20,601 9*s*. 0*d*. Work appears to have gone quite well, although considerable difficulty was experienced in excavating through a sandstone outcrop at the appropriately named Sandhills, about a mile south of Barnt Green. However, the behaviour of some of the navvies was fairly normal for the times, as one example, reported in the *Worcester Herald* of 1st December, 1858, shows:

> DRUNKENNESS – On Monday last, before Mr R.S. Bartlett, Esq., Charles Moor, of this town, a worker on the railway, was brought-up, after two nights and one day's solitary confinement in the lock-up (a place denounced by the bench as scarcely fit for a dog to be confined in), charged by F.S. Rowley with being drunk and incapable on Saturday night. Fined 5s. and costs.

The Birmingham & Worcester Canal was still unhappy about the construction of the line, and smarting from its lack of success in Parliament, managed to be particularly awkward as the contractors prepared to bridge their canal just outside Alvechurch. Delays were experienced here as the canal company used every means to complain of the most trivial detail, but their tactics only slightly delayed the inevitable completion of the line.

There were no major accidents to workers during construction, but at least one was injured, as this report, again from the *Worcester Herald*, a week later, on 8th December, 1858 reveals:

> RAILWAY ACCIDENT – One of the excavators on the line got hurt on Wednesday, through his own recklessness. He was going into the cutting, which is kept as narrow as possible for the tracks to pass along, when his comrades shouted to him to come back as a train of trucks was running in. Instead of taking their warning he proceeded, and where the trucks overtook him he thought to avoid the danger by squeezing himself hard up against the bank, but found, to his cost, that the space was not sufficient, and got crushed and bruised very badly. He was taken to Mr Smith, surgeon, who found that no bones were broken, and he is now doing well.

The implication here is that the trucks were being propelled. This is not something that would have occurred if they were being powered by horses, and so we must assume that a locomotive was in use here. The only known locomotive used on the line is one hired by Maxwell, the sub-contractor, and this was presumably the engine involved in propelling the wagons in this incident. He had hired LNWR 0-4-2 No. 117D during July 1859 for ballasting purposes, at the rate of £3 10*s*. 0*d*. per day, paid in advance, but 'exclusive of working expenses'. This engine had been built for the London & Birmingham Railway by Bury, Curtiss & Kennedy on 6th February, 1846 with 15 in. x 20 in. inside cylinders and 5 ft 0 in. driving wheels, and was first given the running number 117. This was retained when it became part of the LNWR Southern Division, but was replaced in May 1859 thereafter carrying the suffix 'D'. Eventually, after its hire to Maxwell, it was sold to the Clay Cross Company that November for £500, plus £50 for repairs.

On 25th May, 1859 the Directors agreed that Furness was to erect the station and engine house at Redditch, and 'all other buildings', which presumably referred to those necessary at Barnt Green and Alvechurch. At this time, the rails were due to be laid at the Redditch end, but the canal bridge at Alvechurch was still incomplete, although one of the abutments was 'beginning to show itself'.

By July 1859 one of the underbridges leading to Mr Reeves' farm at Butler's Hill showed some signs of weakness, and had to be reconstructed. Just prior to the opening it was reported in the *Worcester Herald* of 24th September, 1859 that Mr Maxwell, the sub-contractor, was 'about to construct several coal wharves contiguous to the line, and between the station and Mr Holyoake's mill, on the property of Baroness Windsor, which will be let out to dealers. The Redditch station will be covered in by a glass Paxton roof, for the comfort of travellers and others'. The glass roof for the station was never erected, but the coal wharves were almost certainly located in what became known as Dixon's coal sidings, west of the station, for at a shareholders' meeting on 4th July, 1860 it was announced that land had been purchased for a siding at Mr Dixon's wharf, near to the station.

The final costs of construction totalled £54,574 compared to Burke's original estimate of £35,000 which came as a considerable disappointment to the Directors, especially as the calls on paid up shares had only reached £27,120 plus the loan of £11,500, giving a shortfall of some £16,000.

A most regrettable affair with George Furness

Prior to the opening of the railway, some disquiet had been expressed at the standard of the work performed by the contractor, and that many of the payments had not been supported by certificates approved by the Engineer. This disquiet had reached the proportions of a dispute by January 1860, some four months after the line had opened, when it was found that one bridge was 'in a dangerous condition'. Furness claimed that the payments related to additional works, but at a shareholders' meeting on 30th April, 1860 the Directors stated that no more payments would be made until such certification was forthcoming, including one for £3,411 requested in March 1860. At another meeting on 4th July, 1860 the certificates were still not forthcoming. Meanwhile, the Directors were also becoming less than satisfied with the work of the Engineer, J.B. Burke. In February 1861, the Directors reported that they had asked the MR Engineer, a Mr Crossley, to examine the line and report on any shortcomings. The results of this examination are not recorded, even if was carried out, but on 12th June, 1861 a new Engineer had been appointed, John Underwood. He immediately prepared a report on the line, and on 30th September, 1861 copies of this report were sent to George Furness for him to complete the works regarded as unsatisfactory or incomplete. Needless to say, Furness did nothing, still claiming that he was owed money, and would do nothing until that was paid.

At this point it should be remembered that the company was in a serious financial position, with the costs far exceeding the original estimates, and that this situation may well have influenced the Directors' dealings with both Furness and Burke.

At a shareholders' meeting on 2nd January, 1862 the Directors proposed that a Bill in Chancery should be made against Furness, to compel him to finish his work. At the same meeting it was proposed that the company should apply for a Bill authorizing the raising of additional monies to cover those excess construction costs. This would entail the authorization of leasing powers, and the creation of preference shares, and debentures or mortgages, which could be used for other purposes too. The *Redditch Indicator* of 25th January, 1862 reported that the Bill for this purpose had already passed Standing Orders unopposed in the House of Commons. But Furness had acquired a number of shares, so as a shareholder decided to use his position to his advantage, and at a meeting on 4th June, 1862 requested a poll of the shareholders against the inclusion of leasing powers in the proposed Bill. He also demanded that the meeting should record 'that the Directors acknowledge that no charge of fraud rests on Mr Furness, in relation to his work on the Redditch Railway'. However, the Directors could not possibly agree to make such a statement, and decided to omit the leasing powers clause, thus rendering his opposition useless. He lost the poll, also standing to forfeit 788 shares within 21 days, as he had not paid calls on his shares. The amount involved was some £7,000, which he denied at the next meeting on 14th July, claiming that this represented costs outstanding to him.

The next element in this saga took place on Wednesday 16th July, 1862 in the House of Commons, when the company's Bill to raise further capital had already been passed in the House of Lords, and now came before a Select Committee. A petition had been recently presented by Furness in opposition to this Bill. The *Redditch Indicator* of 19th July, 1862 reported that the counsel for the company, Sir William Slade, Bart, opposed this petition as being unjust towards the general body of shareholders, and as Mr Furness was himself a shareholder, he had no right to be heard there. The court agreed with this argument, and the petition was denied. The Redditch Railway Act of 7th August, 1862 (Vict. 25 & 26, cap. 214) therefore permitted the company to raise additional capital to make up the shortfall of some £16,000 arising from the construction costs mentioned earlier.

Still Furness was not ready to give in. At the half-yearly shareholders' general meeting on 29th September, 1862, a Mr Baylis, employed by Furness as an overlooker or agent, required to make some comments as the meeting began. The chairman, Henry Milward, said that he did not know this person, or by what right he claimed to address the meeting. Mr Clift (now a Director) advised him that Baylis was in fact, a shareholder. Baylis then complained that the Directors' report before the meeting was incomplete, misleading, and had not been circulated to shareholders two weeks before the meeting for their consideration. He cited the lack of detail about two Chancery suits hanging over the company (the first was in fact the claim by Furness and the second had only arisen three days before the meeting), and that it did not contain one word concerning any dividend, amongst other minor matters. He moved that the meeting be adjourned until 27th October to enable the proper preparation of a report and its scrutiny by shareholders. This was seconded by a Mr Rixon, who it transpired was the attorney to George Furness, who had evidently spiked the meeting!

Another Director, Mr S. Thomas rose and explained this situation to the shareholders, and then became quite agitated in his anger against Furness. The *Redditch Indicator* of 4th October, 1862 describes his performance as follows:

> Mr S. Thomas rose, and begged the attention of the Shareholders for a few minutes while he explained who the gentlemen were who had just shown so much solicitude for the general interests and the welfare of the Shareholders of the Redditch Railway. First, Mr Rixon was the mere paid advocate – the solicitor; the other, the mere nominee - the servant - of the man who had made all the mischief of which both now impudently complained. To enable either to do this dirty work, in that room, shares had been put in their hands - given to them , maybe - within a month of the present time. These men, who pretended to have the interests of the shareholders at heart, had been made shareholders for the purpose, only, of acting as tools to the man who had (also for the welfare of the shareholders) made the line so bad that the Midland Company refused to take to it; had received much more for ballasting than he had ever put on the line; who had put in sleepers and posts already rotten; had charged for excavations never executed; and had done other work so ill as to swallow up a large portion of the earnings of the line in replacing their rotten sleepers and posts, and doing other necessary work to make the line in working order. (Mr Thomas became angry and excited toward the close of his remarks, and said) - To show what sort of man they represent - he challenged me to fight when I was in London. I, who was twice his age. If I were younger I would thrash not only him but these, also, the pair of them.
>
> The Chairman - 'Order', - 'Order'.
>
> Mr Harrison *(another shareholder)*, who said - Mr Chairman, and gentlemen, I cannot be silent under such impudent attacks from such a quarter. I had made up my mind to take no part in speaking, because I feel I have taken too prominent a part in railway matters; but who can sit and hear the Directors thus insulted - gentlemen who have bestowed so much time and suffered so much for the public? How dare these men accuse the Directors of 'shuffling', they, the victims of swindlers, I say that it is a disgrace for any member of the body to whom Mr Rixon belongs, to become the advocate of so bad a cause. Although Mr Thomas had been stirred up to warmth and excitement in his manner he had not made one charge which was not strictly true. He (Mr H.) for his part would sooner give up everything - money, position, all that he possessed, rather than be a party to such dishonourable transactions. How those two men could look on, much more insult, those honourable men whom their clique had so infamously wronged, he was at a loss to understand.

The redoubtable George Furness. *Brent Community History Library*

[The contempt hurled on the patriotic two seemed to sting Mr Baylis, at least, for he rose, gesticulated, and violently slapped his thigh, indignantly.]

After the excitement had calmed down somewhat, the Chairman put the amendment as his own substantive resolution from the chair, Mr Clift, at the same time observing that the Directors would not give the deputation from Mr Furness any trouble or time unnecessarily by going vexatiously into a poll, although their conduct was all of the obstructive kind.

The question of adjournment was then put from the chair and carried, and the proceedings terminated.

Mr W.T. Heming proposed a vote of thanks to the Chairman for his conduct in the chair. Mr C. Miles seconded it; and being carried, the meeting, which had been a very stormy one, broke up.

At the adjourned meeting held on 27th October following, further more detailed accounts were available to the shareholders, but Furness had planted another resolution, this time to 'adjourn the consideration of Directors' report and accounts' until 22nd December. The Chairman explained that this was another attempt by Furness to disrupt the business of the company until the Directors became tired or frightened into accepting his terms. Whilst his resolution was denied by the meeting, the shareholders were becoming a bit fed up with the whole affair, and could see that legal costs involving this dispute could well exceed the amounts involved (thus proving this not to be a modern phenomenon!). Consequently, it was resolved that the legal action be discontinued and that the Directors should seek other means to solve this dispute.

As a consequence, on 20th March, 1863, the Directors reported that the matter had been referred to arbitration. The final episode was reported in the *Redditch Indicator* for 1st October, 1864 that at the Ordinary Half-Yearly Meeting on 30th September,

> ... the Chairman , Mr Milward made a few remarks... especially alluding to the way in which the Arbitrator had dealt with Mr Furness' claim. He awarded him £1,500, the claim being about £4,000 and interest thereon for four years, at 5 per cent. This was very satisfactory, showing as it did, that the Directors were justified in resisting his claim.

So finally the matter had been laid to rest with regard to Furness' claim, but the claim from Burke was still outstanding, and at a meeting on 15th November, 1864, the Directors reported that a settlement had been attempted with Burke who claimed £250, in contrast to the company's claim against him of £751 9*s*. 0*d*. Nothing more is known of this claim, which it is thought likely was written off. It is perhaps fair to comment that the Directors had probably been somewhat naïve in their dealings with Furness, and that he had taken advantage of his position. It is nonetheless interesting to reflect briefly on the career of George Furness.

The life and times of George Furness

George Furness was born on 31st October, 1820 at Great Longstone in Derbyshire. As an established contractor he took offices in Westminster, and in 1856 bought Roundwood House in Willesden (north London), which had been built for Lord Decies about 1820. He became a personal friend of the renowned contractor Thomas Brassey, and also worked with other notable architects and engineers such as Sir John Rennie, Joseph Locke, Isambard Kingdom Brunel and Sir Joseph Bazalgette. He was elected an Associate of the Institute of Civil Engineers in 1864.

His first work was probably on the Paris to Rouen Railway, engineered by Joseph Locke, with Thomas Brassey as the main contractor. His overseas operations also saw him working in Brazil, on the 78 mile line from Pernambuco to Agoa Preta, which opened on 30th November, 1862. Around this time he was a Director of the West Somerset Railway, which ran 14½ miles from Taunton to Watchet harbour, and opened on 31st March, 1862, and may have been involved in its construction. He was also contractor on the early part of the Wallingford and Watlington Railway, but after a dispute with the company, relinquished his contract to Thomas White on 14th March, 1865. This railway eventually opened on 15th August, 1872. He completed the 11 miles of single track railway across the Isle of Grain from Hoo Junction to Port Victoria in 1882. The hopes for this to become a major cross-channel port never materialized, and the little-used pier closed in 1916. He was also involved with Robert Turner on the building during 1893/4 of the Birmingham and Henley-in-Arden Railway, which had lain uncompleted from the turmoil of the mid-1860s, and finally opened on 6th June, 1894.

His other civil engineering works included several extensive dredging contracts in Italy over a period of 30 years, at La Spezia, Ancona, Livorno and Palermo, for which he was decorated as a Chevalier of the Order of the Crown of Italy by King Victor Emmanuel. He also carried out drainage, paving and general restoration of services in Odessa, Russia after the Crimean War with an overall value of around £750,000.

In England he tendered for the major section of the Thames Embankment (Westminster to Waterloo Bridge), which involved building interconnecting sewers beneath the embankment. Although his was only the third lowest bid, his was selected and the work was finished by 1870. He was also awarded the contract for the Metropolis Main Drainage - Northern Low Level Sewer, Isle of Dogs branch in December, 1865 for £75,456. There was unsubstantiated speculation at the time of collusion between him and the engineers, Sir John Rennie and Bazalgette. This was partly fuelled by an unproven claim that Bazalgette was under some obligation to Furness as a result of work at Odessa.

He became one of the largest freeholders of land in the Willesden area, developing much of it between 1875 and 1899, including the building of houses, and creating his own brickworks, Willesden Brick & Tile Co. in 1875. Other activities lead him into leading roles in local government and church affairs. Although he lived in Willesden until his death on 9th January, 1900, he kept his original house in Derbyshire. His wife, Sarah Rebecca Green was also from Derbyshire, and of their eight children, two died in tragic circumstances. The youngest daughter was killed during 1899 in India by her husband of only one year, who then killed himself. His eldest daughter and her son, along with George's widow were killed in a boating accident on the lakes of Killarney in 1902.

The opening of the line

The *Worcester Herald* reported on 21st May, 1859 that it was understood that the line might be opened earlier than expected, and that 1st August was provisionally anticipated as the opening day. However, it seems that several works were unsatisfactory by this date, including the bridge at Mr Reeve's farm.

The anticipated opening date proved to be over optimistic, and the inspection by Captain Galton of the Board of Trade was not performed until Thursday 8th September. The *Worcester Herald* of 10th September reported that his inspection proved satisfactory, and that he was afterwards entertained to a luncheon at Redditch station by three of the Directors (John Osborne, S. Thomas and John James), provided by Mrs Castree of the Unicorn Hotel, and in the evening the party of Directors and Captain Galton dined with Mr Thomas. The opening day was fixed for the Fair Day of Monday 19th September.

In a supplement to the *Worcester Herald* of 24th September, 1859, the proceedings were reported at length. The following are extracts from this report:

> This line, which has been thoroughly described by us more than once, was on Monday last opened for passenger traffic under auspicious circumstances ... It commences close to the town and runs into the Midland Company's Gloucester line at Barntgreen [*sic*] station ... its length is 4 miles and 60 chains. Mr Barker was the engineer; Mr G. Furness, of London, contractor; Messrs W. & R. Maxwell, of Banbury, sub-contractor; Messrs Patterson and McDonnel, conductors of the works; and Mr Charles Lavey, resident engineer...The Birmingham and Worcester Canal did their best or worst to defeat the bill, but the landowners headed by Baroness Windsor, being entirely in its favour, it was eventually successful ... Although a single line at present, land has been purchased to make it a double one ... .The Midland Company have engaged to work the branch at 50 per cent of the produce ...
>
> At a very early hour on Monday morning the inhabitants of Redditch were on the *qui vive* in expectations of the joyous proceedings that were to take place during the day. It being a fair day also, the bustle was necessarily much increased, and the streets of the usually quiet town were filled with gay holiday folks, evidently waiting the opening of the line with much interest. Several of the Directors arrived at the station soon after seven o'clock, and not long afterwards a train, consisting of an engine and eight carriages belonging to the Midland Railway, was provided to convey them to Barntgreen to join the train from Birmingham. A very handsome arch of flowers, evergreens, and flags, was erected over the line near to the station, on which was inscribed 'Success to the Redditch Railway'. The station yard and approaches, together with the banks and hedges along the whole of the line, were lined with eager spectators, and a scene of more bustling activity had certainly never been seen in the neighbourhood. At length the shrill whistle of the engine announced that the first train was leaving the station, and a long protracted joyous shout betokened the pleasure experienced at the moment by all 'in presence there'. It was very pleasing and must have been gratifying to the Directors to find that the undertaking for which they had devoted much precious time and labour was so highly appreciated by all classes of their fellow-townsmen ... Masses of spectators were grouped along the line, who loudly testified their applause, and availed themselves of every means at hand to express their satisfaction. The distance between Redditch and Barnt-green [*sic*] was leisurely travelled in about fifteen minutes, or at the rate of twenty miles an hour, and the ride was most agreeably devoid of unpleasant oscillation ... We may here mention that it has been arranged with the Midland Company that they shall, on all days of the week, except Sunday, run three trains to and from Redditch, and each train will be Parliamentary. The hours of starting from Redditch during the week are 8.45 am, 1.20 and 7.45 pm, and on Sunday, 8.45 am, and 7.55 pm, and from Birmingham to Redditch at 7.15 am, noon, and 6.0 pm on week days, and at 7.30 am and 6.45 pm on Sundays. It is noticeable that with respect to passengers from Worcester and other stations below Barnt-green no increased facility of communication with Redditch is at present offered, but they must still have to wait a long time at the Barnt-green station. This shortcoming it is to be hoped will be remedied quickly.
>
> With much liberality the Midland company placed a train of seventeen carriages, first and second class, at the disposal of the Board of Directors of the branch line, for an excursion, free of cost, to Cheltenham; and Mr Needham, traffic manager of the company, attended personally to supervise the arrangements. The trip train started from Redditch at about ten o'clock, and called at Barnt-green and Bromsgrove, where the

numbers of passengers were increased, and in all exceeded four hundred persons. The route to Cheltenham was along the Midland Company's old line via Spetchley, and it was a most agreeable journey, the sun shining brilliantly during the whole distance. The company arrived at Cheltenham about a quarter before twelve, having performed the distance of about 40 miles safely in a little short of two hours. Flys and other conveyances were quickly engaged, and the excursion party proceeded into the town, where they amused themselves by admiring the numerous beautiful promenades and buildings, and some of them visited Pittville Spa and gardens. They returned to the station at a quarter before four. The engine of the excursion train, and also of the several trains that used on the branch line during the day, were profusely decorated with flowers, and bouquets of flowers were thrown to the excursionists by ladies standing on Clifton's-bridge, Sandhills [near Barnt Green]. The return train left Cheltenham at four o'clock, and arrived at Redditch shortly before six, where were assembled a large concourse of persons, who loudly cheered the arrival of the train. A band of music was waiting at the station, which played 'See the Conquering Hero comes'.

Returning to Redditch, the Chairman and Board of Directors, with other invited guests, to the number of about 30, were engaged at a sumptuous dinner by the contractor, Mr George Furness, who presided. The dinner was excellently served by the proprietors of the Unicorn Hotel, the trustees of the late Mr J. Castree, and the wines were of superior quality. Afterwards, the bowling green was brilliantly illuminated, and the pleasure grounds and gardens were well patronized by dancers to the music of the Bromsgrove sax-horn band.

Excerpts from speeches:
G. Furness: They shortened the time of travelling to Barnt Green from one hour, as it was formerly by omnibus, to a quarter of an hour.
John Osborne: Concerning the excursion to Cheltenham - the Cheltenham people had formed a very high opinion of them, for, on being told where Redditch was, they said that they had never heard of that place before, but they had had many excursion trains to Cheltenham, and never knew of one where the people were so respectable. (Laughter). Well, with truth they might say so, for generally speaking, the fares on excursion trains were so low that any person might travel by them, but this time every arrangement was made that the people should be respectable. The people of Cheltenham expressed a wish to again to see an excursion from Redditch. (Laughter, and a voice 'The Innkeepers'.)
Mr Tomson: The foolish and absurd opposition of the Birmingham Canal Company to the bill authorising the construction of the line. The canal company had not the slightest chance of defeating the railway, nevertheless they incurred great expenses themselves in legal proceedings, and also occasioned serious loss to the railway company.
Mr Maxwell: Difficulties which had occurred in the completion of the line were by no means the fault of the contractors, who had spared no money to get it completed by the time originally proposed, but there were unforeseen difficulties which threw the works back, and in harvest time they could not get workmen for love nor money.

There were also celebratory dinners and festivities held by the Brunswick Lodge of the Odd Fellows (about 60) at the Warwick Arms Hotel, Redditch furnished by Mr & Mrs Cheesman. At the Fox and Goose Inn, the Star of Freedom Lodge of United Brothers enjoyed a substantial well cooked dinner provided by Mr & Mrs Abell. There was afterwards a firework display, around 1,000 people were present, and there was also dancing to the music of Wedgbury's military band. The Crown Inn in Redditch, Mr John Davis, had a concert and ball. At the Crown Inn, Wetherbed Green, near the canal bridge, a game and poultry dinner was prepared by the proprietor, Mr B. Briscoe.

Description of the line

The *Worcester Herald* of 6th August, 1859 devoted considerable space to a thorough description of the line. Insofar as this represents a unique view of the line, at that time, the article is reproduced here:

THE REDDITCH BRANCH RAILWAY

From the Barnt-green [*sic*] station the new line springs out towards Redditch in a curve which in about a quarter of a mile completes a semi-circle, passing on an embankment and a bridge over the Birmingham and Bromsgrove road. Then we arrive at a sand stone rock, called the Sandhills, which occasioned the engineers the principal difficulty in the cutting line (40 ft deep) they experienced on the whole route, and here a good deal of gunpowder has been used in blasting. This line then passes on a bridge over the lane from Alvechurch to Barnt-green; next a short embankment, then a cutting, and soon we pass under a bridge which conveys Aqueduct-lane, leading to the Birmingham turnpike road. A small wrought iron bridge takes the line over the Alvechurch-lane for the second time, and the railway continues on a slight elevation above the adjoining lands, being crossed by an occupation road at Mr Hodgett's farm, till it passes over the canal by means of an embankment and iron bridge, spanning it with one girder 80 ft. long. Planks, 9 in. thick, form the roadway of this bridge. The embankment continues at a height varying to a maximum of 35 ft, over a 10 ft culvert, to which the Alvechurch and Withybed-green road, over which it passes on a bridge, and next over a cattle arch for Mr Hodgett's farm. Soon after the embankment terminates, and in a shallow cutting the line runs under an arched brick bridge, on which the road from Bromsgrove to Alvechurch passes. Here we arrive at Alvechurch station, which is rather below the level of the adjoining land. But little progress has yet been made in this station; the platform walls are in the course of erection, but the plan for the buildings was not prepared at the time of our visit ... Two or three slight cuttings, and then an occupation road of Mr Walford's crosses the line on the level, as also a flat girder bridge, with corrugated iron sides. This bridge conveys the Grange-lane ... At Butler's Wood (about two miles from Redditch) is to be a short siding for the accommodation of conveying timber from the Hewell estate. Next we pass over a cattle arch on Mr Reeves's farm ... and on a plain brick arched bridge over the lane from Alvechurch and Redditch-road to Brockhill-lane.. An open water course, a few feet below the lines, takes you to Sufford's brook, where there is a viaduct, consisting of three skew arches, one of which serves for the road from Bates' Hill and Brockhill-lane into the great road from Redditch to Birmingham, another for the brook, and the third for an occupation path. An occupation road, for the accommodation of occupying tenants, next crosses the line on a level, and then we come to the Redditch terminus, about a gunshot from the town. Here is an engine-house, a turntable; a permanent tank, supplied from the well hard by, sunk for the purpose; a goods' shed, and the station house. The latter is not yet constructed for the residence of the superintendent, but has a booking-office, one room for the superintendent, a public waiting-room, and two ditto for ladies and gentlemen respectively. The building is of brick, faced with stone from the Sandhills-quarry, and has a square headed porch entrance from the town. There are also a carriage landing and cattle-pens, with a platform 300 ft long. At this terminus a new road has been made by the company on land generously given by the Baroness Windsor, which connects the Birmingham-road with Brockhill-lane there having been previously no carriage road connecting these two points except by passing a long way through the town) and thus two entrances from the station to the town have been provided.

The entire branch is five miles in length, all but a few chains; it is a single line at present, although land has been purchased for a double one ... The Midland Company have engaged to work the branch at 50 per cent of the produce; and the same company, we hear, intend to make a new station for use of the branch at the Barnt-green terminus, close to their own station.

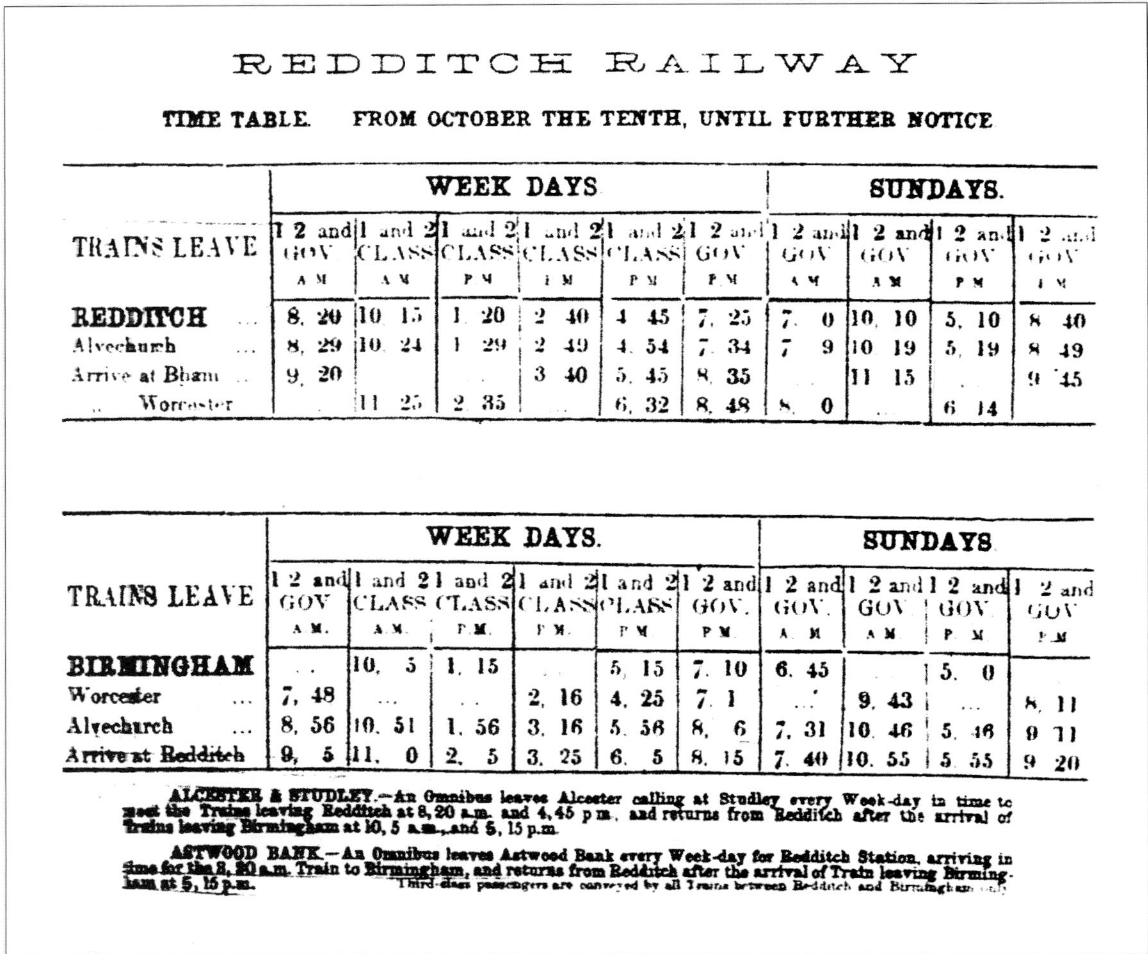

REDDITCH RAILWAY

TIME TABLE. FROM OCTOBER THE TENTH, UNTIL FURTHER NOTICE

TRAINS LEAVE	WEEK DAYS						SUNDAYS.			
	1 2 and GOV A M	1 and 2 CLASS A M	1 and 2 CLASS P M	1 and 2 CLASS P M	1 and 2 CLASS P M	1 2 and GOV P M	1 2 and GOV A M	1 2 and GOV A M	1 2 and GOV P M	1 2 and GOV P M
REDDITCH ...	8, 20	10 15	1 20	2 40	4 45	7, 25	7. 0	10, 10	5, 10	8 40
Alvechurch ...	8, 29	10 24	1 29	2 49	4. 54	7 34	7 9	10 19	5, 19	8 49
Arrive at Bham ..	9, 20		.	3 40	5, 45	8 35		11 15	.	9 45
.. Worcester	.	11 25	2 35	...	6, 32	8, 48	8, 0	...	6 14	

TRAINS LEAVE	WEEK DAYS.						SUNDAYS.			
	1 2 and GOV A. M.	1 and 2 CLASS A. M.	1 and 2 CLASS P. M.	1 and 2 CLASS P. M.	1 and 2 CLASS P M	1 2 and GOV. P M	1 2 and GOV. A. M	1 2 and GOV A M	1 2 and GOV P. M	1 2 and GOV P M
BIRMINGHAM	. .	10, 5	1, 15	..	5, 15	7. 10	6. 45		5. 0	
Worcester ...	7, 48	...	...	2, 16	4, 25	7. 1	...	9, 43	...	8, 11
Alvechurch ...	8, 56	10. 51	1. 56	3. 16	5. 56	8, 6	7, 31	10. 46	5. 46	9 11
Arrive at Redditch	9, 5	11. 0	2, 5	3. 25	6. 5	8. 15	7. 40	10. 55	5 55	9 20

ALCESTER & STUDLEY.—An Omnibus leaves Alcester calling at Studley every Week-day in time to meet the Trains leaving Redditch at 8, 20 a.m. and 4, 45 p.m., and returns from Redditch after the arrival of Trains leaving Birmingham at 10, 5 a.m., and 5, 15 p.m.

ASTWOOD BANK.—An Omnibus leaves Astwood Bank every Week-day for Redditch Station, arriving in time for the 8, 20 a.m. Train to Birmingham, and returns from Redditch after the arrival of Train leaving Birmingham at 5, 15 p.m.

Third-class passengers are conveyed by all Trains between Redditch and Birmingham only.

Public timetable for the Redditch Railway as printed in the *Redditch Indicator*, 15th October, 1859.

Working the line

As we have seen from the press reports, the initial services comprised three weekday trains between Redditch and Birmingham in each direction, and two on Sundays. Goods services were stated to have commenced on the same day as passenger services, but no details are known of these. The initial service did not last for long, as a revised timetable was issued to be effective from 10th October, 1859 which was also the opening date of Alvechurch station. The above press report mentioned that this station was not complete on the opening day. It was possibly still incomplete on this date, but at least it was open, as the timetable issued along with the *Redditch Indicator* of 15th October confirms. This new timetable is illustrated opposite and shows four weekday trains each way between Redditch and Birmingham, leaving at revised times, and two on Sundays. In addition, there were two trains each way on every day between Redditch and Barnt Green, mainly for connections to southbound trains.

From February 1860 the service was expanded to six trains each way on weekdays, but running only between Redditch and Barnt Green, and of these five were shown in the Working Timetable as being mixed trains. Four trains then ran on Sundays, again only for the short run to/from Barnt Green. However, by July of that year the timetable showed signs of considerable economy, there being only four each way on weekdays and two on Sundays. By the following February, the service had improved to five each way on weekdays and two on Sundays, but they still only ran as far as Barnt Green. In July of that year, whilst the number of trains remained the same, one service in each direction ran to/from Birmingham. More changes occurred by December 1861, as there were now five up weekday services (four through to Birmingham), six down services (four from Birmingham), with four each way on Sundays (two Birmingham and two Barnt Green only). The services seemed to have stabilized by mid-1864, as the timetables for June, July and August of that year show six trains each way on weekdays, of which five up and four down ran from Birmingham, one each way not stopping at Kings Norton and Moseley. The four each way Sunday trains were two for Barnt Green and two for Birmingham. However, the Winter service reverted to five up and four down trains, with two on Sundays. In the final year of its early life as a terminus, the services from Redditch during April 1867 reverted to the same pattern as in the summer of 1864. Five of the six trains in each direction ran as mixed trains. These changing patterns of services are entirely consistent with the agreement with the MR, under which the number of daily trains was 'to be settled from time to time according to the requirements of the traffic'.

At the Directors' meeting of 4th July, 1860, it was agreed that a mail train would be run from Redditch to Barnt Green every day except Sundays. The offer to do so had come from James Allport, General Manager of the Midland Railway, at the request of the Postmaster General, and was to cost the princely sum of £10 per annum!

Barnt Green station did not open with the Birmingham and Gloucester Railway, but was opened by the MR on 1st May, 1844, and renamed 'Barnt Green for Redditch' on 1st June, 1857. It was subsequently renamed 'Barnt Green for Lickey' on 1st January, 1868, but this did not last long, and it reverted to its original name of 'Barnt Green' on the following 1st July.

Fares were at first fixed on the basis of *3d.* per mile for first class passengers, *2d.* for second class and third class at *1d.*, whilst the free luggage entitlements were 120 lbs, 100 lb. and 60 lb. respectively. First and second class passengers were carried on

SECOND EDITION, CORRECTED.

Presented with the "REDDITCH INDICATOR," December 7th., 1861.

REDDITCH  RAILWAY.

TIME TABLE FROM DECEMBER THE FIRST, UNTIL FURTHER NOTICE.

Trains leave	WEEK DAYS.					SUNDAYS.			
	1 2 and GOV.	1 and 2 CLASS	1 and 2 CLASS	1 and 2 CLASS	1 2 and GOV.	1 2 and GOV.	1 2 and GOV.	1 2 and GOV.	1 2 and GOV.
	A.M.	A.M.	P.M.	P.M.	P.M.	A.M.	A.M.	P.M.	P.M.
REDDITCH	8, 20	*10, 0	2, 5	4, 55	*7, 40	7, 0	10,10	5, 10	8, 50
Alvechurch	8, 29	10, 9	2, 14	5, 4	7, 49	7, 9	10,19	5, 19	8, 59
Barnt Green	8, 42	10,18	2, 25	5, 31	8, 29	7, 15	10,37	5, 25	9, 15
Arrive at Bham	9, 20	10,55	3, 0	6, 10	9, 45	...	11,15	...	9, 45
" Worcester	...	11,28	3, 12	6, 15	8, 53	8, 15	...	6, 25	...

Trains leave	WEEK DAYS.						SUNDAYS.			
	1 2 and GOV.	1 and 2 CLASS	1 and 2 CLASS	1 and 2 CLASS	1 and 2 CLASS	1 2 and GOV.	1 2 and GOV.	1 2 and GOV.	1 2 and GOV.	1 2 end GOV.
	A.M.	A.M.	P.M.	P.M.	P.M.	P.M.	A.M.	A.M.	P.M.	P.M.
Birmingham	7, 5	10, 5	1, 0	2, 0	4, 45	7, 30	6, 45	...	5, 0	...
Worcester	7, 44	9, 32	...	2, 7	4, 43	7, 35	...	9, 50	...	8, 20
Barnt Green	8, 45	10,40	1, 40	2, 55	5, 35	8, 30	7, 35	10,40	5, 40	9, 10
Alvechurch	8, 51	10,46	1, 46	3, 1	5, 41	8, 36	7, 31	10,46	5, 46	9, 26
Arrive at Redditch	9, 0	10,55	1, 55	‖3, 10	5, 50	8, 45	7, 40	10,55	5, 55	9, 35

ALCESTER & STUDLEY.—An Omnibus leaves Alcester, calling at Studley every Week-day in time to meet the Trains leaving Redditch at 10,0, a.m., and 4,55, p.m., and returns from Redditch after the arrival of Trains leaving Birmingham at 10.5, a.m., and 4,45, p.m.

Third Class with all trains between Redditch and Birmingham.

* These two take Mails out. ‖ This Train brings a Mail in.

CHRISTMAS DAY.—Sunday Trains only will run on this day.

Public timetable for the Redditch Railway as printed in the *Redditch Indicator*, 7th December, 1861.

all trains, with 'Government' or 'Parliamentary' class passengers being conveyed on selected services, mostly the early and late services of the day.

Initial reports suggested that the trains were well patronized and kept well to their times. However, the *Redditch Indicator* of 4th January, 1862 was not so pleased with the services, as in its editorial column it was somewhat confusingly stated: 'True, one train, the 5.55 pm is promised as to arrive at 5.45, but, as that particular train has a knack of coming in "all hours", almost with a "latch key" why it may as well wait until next month for us'.

From 1860 there were two goods services each way between Redditch and Barnt Green, leaving Redditch at 11.30 am and 6.20 pm, returning at 12.10 pm and 6.45 pm respectively. From 1st December 1865 these were retimed to depart from Redditch at 11.10 am and 6.45 pm, and from Barnt Green at 11.50 am and 7.10 pm. These continued into the final year of the short branch, as reflected in the Working timetable for 1st February, 1867.

Returning to 1859, there was a further excursion run for the benefit of the inhabitants of Redditch on 1st October, 1859 to the Onion Fair in Birmingham, where presumably there were additional attractions other than onions. The return fare was a bargain at one shilling, and the report in the *Worcester Herald* of 8th October is interesting, although the final sentence is somewhat incomplete :

> RAILWAY TRIP - Notwithstanding the unfavourable nature of the weather on the morning of Saturday last, about 700 persons left this town for the railway trip to Birmingham. They arrived home in detachments, the last of which came in about half past ten at night - (Complaints are made to us against a porter for his incivility; the proper quarter to lodge these is in the manager's office. A book is in an accessible place at all the railway stations in which the public might enter complaints would check civility.)

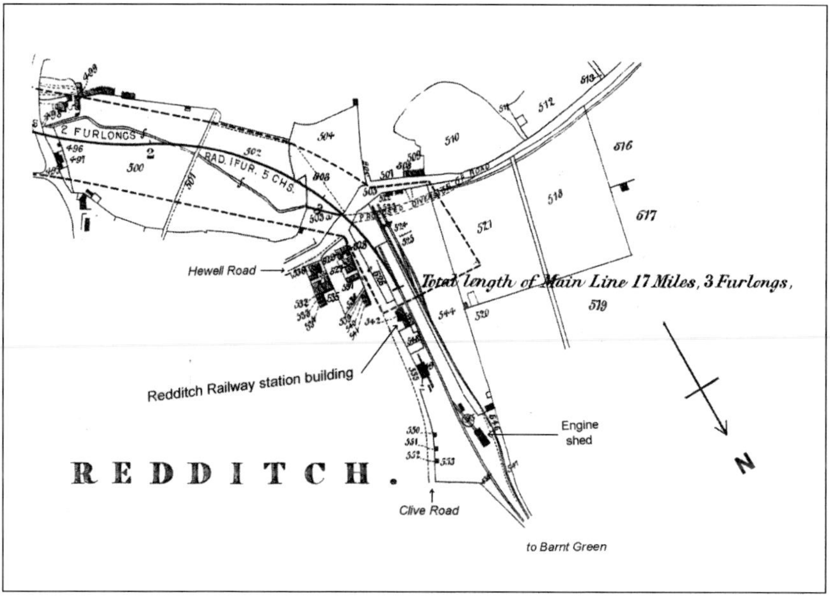

Detail from 1862 deposited plans for the proposed Evesham & Redditch Railway, showing the proposed alignment (*in the upper dotted line boundary*) and existing lines of the Redditch Railway. *Worcestershire County Archives*

The original station at Redditch was built in Clive Road in 1858. This rare view is believed to have been taken at some time late in the 19th century. Although of poor quality, it is included here as few photographs are otherwise available. An MR passenger train for Birmingham is passing in the background, and because it is barely visible, the locomotive type cannot be ascertained. *Redditch Library*

An interesting aerial photograph of the branch as it curves away from Barnt Green station, clearly illustrating the severity of the curve. A southbound freight is just pulling out of the down main loop, north of the station. However, the date of this view is not known, although it is subsequent to the repositioning of the up main platform. *Author's Collection*

During 1864, special concessions were advertised for persons wishing to take advantage of through tickets to Droitwich, which included a voucher for 'admission' to the brine baths. The return fares were 4*s*. 4*d*. (first class), 3*s*. 2*d*. (second class), and 1*s*. 10*d*. (third class). Hot baths were available at an extra cost of 6*d*. However, this largesse was not without its limitations, as it was stated that the tickets would not be available for the return journey unless they had been stamped at the Baths.

Crime on railway premises was a relatively new phenomenon, but there were always people who would be prepared to take advantage of a situation. In some instances, the sheer stupidity of the people is astounding, as the following report from the *Redditch Indicator* of 11th April, 1863 reveals:.

BREAKING OPEN AND STEALING FROM THE RAILWAY STATION

Yesterday morning, at half-past seven, when one of the porters, George Tilley, arrived on the premises to prepare for the duties of the day, he found that some person or persons had broken in during the night, and broken open several drawers. Mr Brooks and his assistants were promptly on the spot, and on examination it was found that two drawers in the Booking Office had been forced open, and from them had been stolen somewhere around 46*s*. One drawer in the private office had also been forced, but, there no money was deposited, only papers; and these had been lifted out and laid on the table. In addition to the money, one parcel was taken - articles of a lady's clothing, belonging to Miss Wakefield, a friend of Mrs Cartwright, of Headless Cross, who left it the previous evening in the cloak room.

The mode of entrance was by breaking a pane in the window of the waiting room looking on to the platform - pressing some clay against the glass - then, putting a hand through, and turning the fastening. The window is what is called a 'French sash', opening on a hinge. Clay, and other marks, are there to show this.

An active look-out is, of course, originated, to get on the track of the thieves; and any clue which might possibly lead to discovery, it will be well not to publish. Since the alarm was in type a man has been taken into custody – doubtless, the thief – on him were found all the money lost, some postage stamps, in peculiar quantities, a tie, or comforter, of Mr Brooks, and a small rule out of the drawer in the private office, but the parcel was not in his possession although evidence is abundant that he had it. He is at Bromsgrove lock-up, and the examination will not take place we believe until Wednesday next.

The proceedings of the fellow, and the way in which he was taken, show him to be fully as much fool as rogue. When Fox, the driver of the Redditch engine, was at Barnt Green, waiting to bring down the 10.55 train, the man went to him and asked when the next train was due to Birmingham. Fox told him; and he said, 'Why, they told me down there, there was one a little after 11'. 'Who told you?' 'The platelayers down the line; I've walked up the line'. He was also talking to Mr Moore, the station master at Barnt Green, who recommended him to go down to Alvechurch station, and book there for the 2 o'clock train to Birmingham, by 3rd. class, to save something. When Fox got down to Redditch he told Mr Brooks of this man, and said he really thought that was the thief; and Mr Brooks proposed to run up the engine specially, to look at him; the policeman thought it quite impossible (who would not think so?) but, they went, and he walked right into their hands at Alvechurch Station. There, they found the things in his possession described above; and, further, a lad who drives a cart for William Tolley, of Breedon, declared it was the same man to whom he had offered a lift in his cart early in the morning. The prisoner accepted the ride, and said he wanted to catch a train earlier than the one which left Redditch Station. He then had with him the parcel; and, so he had on several occasions when seen afterwards, but not when taken.He was dressed in black cloth cap and coat, and corduroy trousers, all, with shoes, ragged and dirty. He gave his name as Smith, Oldbury, and said he had been to visit an aunt at Redditch. It was generally believed (and reported even from the railway station), that the parcel missed contained silk to the value of £32. This, happily, proved to be an error. The silk parcel arrived safely by the delivery cart at Mrs Cartwright's.

On Thursday 24th March, 1864 a minor incident occurred when according to the *Redditch Indicator*, 'our engine strayed from its proper path and got into Mr Clift's siding, when it got off the rails; no injury sustained'. This siding had been put in at the expense of Mr Clift to serve the gasworks, which within eight years were to grow substantially. Evidently this incident related to nothing more serious than a minor derailment, but perhaps there was little else to report that week.

A more serious accident was reported in the *Redditch Indicator* of 9th January, 1864:

ACCIDENT AT BARNT GREEN

Yesterday, about midday, as Robert Hodgson, a porter, was what is called 'tail roping' some wagons out of a siding, hooking them on to the engine for that purpose, he called out to Fox, the engineer, to 'slack', and when he did so, the rope falling to the ground, caught to one of the points, and this not being observed by either when the engine was ordered on to draw the wagons, instead of taking its proper straight direction, the rope drew Hodgson up against the truck and crushed him badly. Mr Fletcher, who attended him, reports that no bones are broken, and that the man is going on well, but it will several weeks ere he can resume his duties.

Earlier it had been noted that at least some of the trains ran as mixed passenger and goods services. This is confirmed in the following report of the only known accident to a service train during the period of the Redditch Railway. It was reported in the *Redditch Indicator* of 30th May, 1863:

ACCIDENT ON THE REDDITCH RAILWAY

On Monday morning last an accident, which happily was unattended with serious results, occurred on the Redditch Railway, to the train leaving Birmingham at 10.5 a.m. The train was an exceedingly full one, and was a larger one than usually went upon the branch line. It consisted of what are termed 'mixed' carriages, but immediately following the engine and tender were four heavily laden coal waggons. With the exception of a little delay at starting the train ran smoothly and safely until it reached about a mile beyond Alvechurch, when the passengers were alarmed by a continuous 'jolting' and bumping of the carriages on the rails and 'sleepers', and were almost immediately terrified on finding that the train had fairly run off the rails, and that the carriages were in imminent danger of being precipitated down the embankment. The shaking they sustained was somewhat severe, so abrupt had been the stoppage, but the majority, we are glad to state, were 'more frightened than hurt'. The position, however, was a painful one. Women, of whom there were many, were crying out for help in a frantic manner, and when the carriages came to a standstill, were of course the first care of the male passengers. They were, with the exercise of a good deal of care, safely got out, and then the cause of the casualty was enquired into. It was found that one of the wheels of the third coal truck had flown off, in consequence of a fracture of the axle, and this was missing, and was picked up at a considerable distance down the line, there could be little doubt that the waggon had run along, until the circumstance just described occurred, without it. The engine and tender and the first two coal waggons, however, remained on the metals, and the driver, after the first alarm excited by the casualty had subsided, volunteered to take those whose business engagements were pressing on to Redditch. Several availed themselves of the means of reaching their destination, but others remained behind and walked to Redditch. The ballast and sleepers were torn up for a considerable distance by the dragging of the carriages when off the rails, and as the railway has only a single laying of metals, it was feared the traffic would be impeded. However, assistance was soon procured,

> and arrangements were made by which, with change of trains at the point of obstruction, passengers were conveyed to Birmingham.
> The Goods and Coal Trucks which caused this accident will, in future, not be allowed to be taken with passenger trains.This accident, though alarming, seems to form a piece with the good fortune in absence of serious accident, which has all along attended the line, and, by operating as a warning will, we hope, aid in continued safety.

It would appear fairly unusual to marshal coal wagons in a mixed train, but the expectation that mixed trains would soon be banned proved to be wishful thinking. Indeed, the Working Timetable for October 1876 reveals that the 1.55 pm goods train from Redditch to Evesham 'conveys passengers between Redditch and intermediate stations to Evesham' on Mondays only , and on Tuesdays and Saturdays it 'conveys passengers from Redditch and Studley to Alcester'. In the reverse direction, the 1.00 pm goods from Evesham was due to convey passengers 'between Evesham and Alcester' on Tuesdays only. In addition, the 7.09 pm and 9.07 pm passenger departures from Barnt Green for Redditch 'must take cattle when required'. However, although the practice was soon discontinued on this line, it survived as such on many other branch lines throughout the country, right up to the 1960s (but with the goods vehicles always *behind* the passenger coaches).

At Barnt Green, the main line platforms were staggered, with the down platform in its present position, south of the junction with the Redditch line, and the up platform north of this junction. The branch platforms were originally rather short and located on the sharp curve. The up branch platform was linked to the down main platform at the fork of the junction, and in between was sited a turntable, for the turning of those tender locomotives running on trains from Redditch to Barnt Green and back again. We learn from the company minutes that at a Directors' meeting on 18th October, 1859, and therefore shortly after the opening of the line, that some problem had occurred with it, as it was ordered that this turntable was to be repaired immediately.

Locomotives were also turned at the Redditch end, on the 42 ft turntable located immediately in front of the engine shed, as can be seen on the 1862 plan on page 29. The track layout in the station area is worthy of comment, as it does not seem possible for engines to have been released from their trains, without reversing out of the platform and into the goods yard, unless an additional engine was used to draw out the carriages, or wait for the next departure. All of these operations could have been eased by the simple expedient of an engine release loop, next to the platform. The only other possibility is that the drawing is not complete, but its detail in all other respects make this unlikely. This may have some bearing on a suggestion from the MR to build a new station further south, which was noted at a shareholders' meeting on 20th October, 1860. However, nothing further was done, as the likelihood of further railway developments were also being considered at this time. The engine shed was evidently extended from the rear at a later date, as from this extremely accurate and well drawn plan, it can be measured to be possibly 90 feet compared to the later shed of 118 feet. This is borne out by discussions held during 1869 between the Evesham & Redditch Railway and Stephen Ballard, contractor, for the 'exchange of land for an engine shed at Redditch', and a later estimate in 1872 of £3,800 for an engine shed. This amount would have built a three-road shed at this time, so it is evident that such plans were dropped in favour of extending the present building. The additional rear portion could be seen even in later years. The Directors' meeting of 18th October, 1859 also ordered that a coal stage and sand oven were to be erected immediately at the station, so the facilities for locomotive servicing must have been basic in the extreme up to this time.

Locomotives in use on the line were almost certainly all tender engines, as MR tank engines at this time were limited to shunting duties, and minor goods trips. For passenger services the Kirtley outside-framed 2-4-0s of the '150' class would have been used, whilst for goods workings his outside-framed 0-6-0s, known as by the MR as 'Standard Goods' (although actually comprising three similar, but not identical types built mostly by outside firms such as Kitson, W. Fairbairn and Robert Stephenson) were in common use throughout the MR system. These locomotives were based at Saltley in Birmingham, as the shed at Bournville was not opened until 1895.

The single line was controlled by electric telegraph from the outset, as this had been installed by the Electric Telegraph Co. in September 1859. Signals and points were operated by station staff at Barnt Green, Alvechurch and Redditch, and it is worthy of note that as late as 5th February, 1862 the Directors approved the erection of a 'sentry box' in the station yard at Redditch for the signalman to stand in.

The company had been in negotiation with the MR for them to run services and maintain the line even prior to its incorporation. At an extraordinary shareholders' meeting on 16th May, 1859, the Directors reported that an outline agreement had been reached with Mr Allport, General Manager of the MR, for them to work the line for 10 years, subject to review of the frequency of services and other safeguards relating to the satisfactory completion of the works. The terms were that the MR would pay interest on the loan of £11,500 out of receipts and then distribute 50 per cent of the remainder to the company. This agreement was finally ratified on 17th November, 1860.

With the impending new line from Evesham firmly fixed for the future, the MR agreed in September 1864 to lease the line in perpetuity, guaranteeing to pay dividends to shareholders at the rate of 4 per cent per annum. These terms were finally incorporated into an agreement dated 17th October, 1864, in which the MR also agreed to take up the loans, also referred to as Bond Debt, of £11,500 and to pay the debts of the company, which totalled less than £12,000. This agreement came into effect as from 1st January, 1865. Earlier, the terms of the Midland Railway (New Lines and Additional Powers) Act of 21st July, 1863, Acts Vict. 26 and 27, cap. 183 (Section 54) had empowered the MR to transfer the Redditch Railway Company to the MR Company, and for the dissolution of the Redditch Railway Company (Section 64). This was eventually carried out by the MR Board Minute No. 6842 (4th October, 1865) which ordered that solicitors should be instructed to complete the purchase and transfer of the undertaking to the MR. Their minute No. 7074 (14th August, 1866) ordered that the seal of the MR be affixed to the formal transfer. Thus the Redditch Railway continued as a separate legal entity, wholly owned by the MR, and as such continued to hold its half-yearly meetings until 1874, when under the terms of the Midland Railway (Additional Powers) Act, Vict. 37 and 38, cap. 160 of 30th July, 1874 the stocks of the Redditch Railway were to be consolidated into the MR. This absorption was approved by the final meeting of the company on 11th February, 1875. The MR eventually became part of the London Midland and Scottish Railway (LMS) under the North Western, Midland and West Scottish Group Amalgamation Scheme 1922, dated 30th December, 1922.

Chapter Three

The Evesham & Ashchurch Railway

Competition and planning the line

During 1860, the MR was presented with competition in this area by two proposed lines. The first was 'The Alcester Railway', which had absolutely nothing to do with the later, and better known, Alcester Railway, which ran from Alcester to Bearley. This line was intended to run for 16 miles 3 furlongs from the West Midland Railway at Honeybourne, northwards via Bidford, Wixford, Alcester, Studley and Ipsley to Redditch. Here it was intended to join the Redditch Railway at Pigeon Bridge, near to Windsor Road and the site of the later gas works. In this way, the line would have passed to the east of the town and thus bypassed the first Redditch station. The plans were deposited at Warwick County Court on 29th November, 1860 'at 7½ o'clock in the afternoon', but did not include the location of any proposed stations at that time, and it is unclear whether it was intended to make a north-facing junction to give access to Barnt Green. However, the topography is such that this appears likely, and so this railway would have at least required running powers over the Redditch Railway to Barnt Green. A separate station for Redditch would have been required, presumably on the eastern side of the town, and had this been built would undoubtedly have altered the shape of the town's development. The Engineer was given as Edward Wilson, and although the line was nominally independent, he was at that time the locomotive superintendent of the West Midland Railway, so that it is presumed the line had its backing. At this time, the Midland Railway had not given any assurances to the Redditch Railway as to its intentions to create a line southwards from Redditch, and so the Directors of the Redditch Railway were flattered by the attentions of this new enterprise, and supported it.

The second proposed line to trouble the MR was 'The Ashchurch, Evesham, Winchcomb and Honeybourne Railway', which would have fed into the MR trunk route at Ashchurch and taken traffic to the OWWR at Evesham.The plans for this proposed line were deposited at Worcester on the following day, 30th November, 1860 at 3.00 pm. The signature of the Engineer is not very legible, but appears to be P. Hampton. The line was backed by the OWWR and was to run from a south-facing junction, just north of Ashchurch station via Beckford, Sedgeberrow, Hinton, and Bengeworth for 11½ miles to Evesham, where it would make a connection with the OWWR near to its station. At Beckford, a triangular junction was to be formed for a single-track branch line running for just over 5½ miles to Winchcomb. However, the Bill for the proposed OWWR line was successfully opposed by the MR.

It is evident that the MR had already been planning its route northwards from Ashchurch to Evesham and eventually to Redditch, because on the same day as the OWWR plans had been deposited, the MR deposited its own plans for the line from Ashchurch to Evesham, some four hours earlier at 11.00 am. The route of the line followed closely that surveyed by Robert Stephenson on 30th November, 1845 for a line from Ashchurch to Hampton-in-Arden, as part of 'The Warwickshire and London Railway', which never received its enabling Act and so was never built. This line started at a south-facing junction, just north of Ashchurch MR station, running east through Beckford, Sedgeberrow, Hinton, Bengeworth, then south of Evesham to cross the proposed OWWR at Bretforton, and continuing via Pebworth, Welford, Long Marston and Weston-on-Avon to Stratford-on-Avon, Alveston, Hampton Lucy, and Warwick. Here a triangular junction was to be made with the proposed Birmingham & Oxford Junction Railway, then continuing through Hatton, and Honiley to Hampton-in-Arden, where it would join the London & Birmingham Railway at a north-facing junction, south of the station. The length of the line was given as being 42 miles 51 chains.

Thus the MR had been spurred into action to protect its position, and so without further ado included powers to build the line from Ashchurch to Evesham in Section Five of the Midland Railway (New Lines) Act (Vict. 24 & 25, cap. 57) which received Royal Assent on 7th June, 1861. Four years were permitted for the construction of the line.The need for this to proceed quickly was evidenced in that the line was authorized by the enabling Act to be built by the MR, as a branch of its main line from Birmingham to Bristol, instead of the normal procedure of establishing a separate company, as was done later for the Evesham to Redditch section. Thus time was saved in not having to include powers for the incorporation of this line as a separate company. The plans for the line were submitted by Charles Liddell and a Mr Gordon, as engineers. This latter person is believed to have been Alexander Thomas Gordon, an Irishman, who was the contractor for the first part of the nearby Tewkesbury and Malvern Railway (another MR venture) in 1861. The Act specified that the line was to be built within four years, and included a line linking the MR main line to the Tewkesbury and Malvern line at Ashchurch. Another interesting section of the Act specified that the receipts for any traffic between Evesham and Malvern were to be paid over to the West Midland Railway (which by this time incorporated the OWWR), less 30 per cent to cover working expenses. This was presumably a palliative to the WMR, as the MR would have a through route from Evesham to Malvern via Ashchurch.

Meanwhile, the MR had presumably influenced the Directors of the Redditch Railway to abandon their support for 'The Alcester Railway', as the minutes of its Board Meeting for 2nd March, 1861 record that this support had been withdrawn. Furthermore, to a certain extent 'The Alcester Railway' also duplicated the recently opened Honeybourne to Stratford line of the WMR. The Bill for the 'Alcester Railway' was also opposed by the MR, and it will come as no surprise that this proposal did not get beyond the Committee stage in the House of Commons.

To oversee the construction of the line, the MR set up an 'Evesham and Ashchurch Construction Committee', which held its first meeting at the Victoria Hotel, London on 2nd April, 1861, although most of the subsequent meetings of this committee were held at the MR headquarters in Derby. The first meeting was to establish the strategy for the route and the members of the committee, who were initially:

John Ellis - chairman
M.P. Price
J. Kenrick
E. H. Barwell
J. Lewis
J. Mercer
E.S. Ellis

The meeting agreed to appoint Charles Liddell as Engineer, to be paid at the rate of £400 per quarter, with Edward Richards as 'Engineer-in-Charge'. Subsequently, the committee appointed Messrs Hall and Bird as Resident Engineers.

Tenders for construction were solicited after the Act had been passed, and were examined at the committee meeting on 28th August, 1862, as follows:

	£	s.	d.
S. Ballard, Great Malvern	55,151	12	6
J. Firbank, Newport, Monmouthshire	56,512	17	7
Rennie & Co., Newport, Monmouthshire	59,099	16	4
G. Thompson & Co., Cheltenham	61,490	18	11
John Knowles, Matlock	69,989	13	10

Although on the list of bidders, Jackson, Bean & Co., of Blackheath did not submit a tender. The lowest bid, from Stephen Ballard was accepted. Prior to commencement of the work, Ballard formed a partnership with the renowned Thomas Brassey for this construction, which was a wise move in using Brassey's undoubted expertise in this field.

Permanent way materials were not included in these tenders, but were sourced separately and directly by the MR. At this same meeting, tenders for the supply of these materials were approved, as follows:

Rails			
Bagnall & Sons, West Bromwich	2,766 tons	£7 1*s*. 3*d*. ton	E, G, W
Chairs			
J. Swingler, Lambeth	1,177 tons	£3 19*s*. 0*d*. ton	A
Sleepers			
T.B. & S. Batchelor, Newport, Mon	38,120	3*s*. 8½*d*. each	G, E
Twisted spikes			
Simpson, Baylis & Co., Darlaston	154,880	£8 18*s*. 6*d*. ton	E
		£9 0*s*. 0*d*. ton	A
Wood keys			
Roe & Son, Derby	77,440	£2 11*s*. 9*d*. ton	A, E
Bolts, nuts, washers			
Horton & Sons, Darlaston	22 tons	£11 15*s*. 0*d*. ton	A, E
Fishplates			
R. Coad, Jnr, London	160 tons	£ 6 15*s*. 0*d*. ton	Masbro'
Timber			
Nicks & Co.	8,281 cu. ft	1s. 7d. cu. ft	Not given

Key – Delivered to A = Ashchurch, E = Evesham, G = Gloucester, W = Worcester

Construction

The route of the line authorized by the deposited plans, and by the enabling Act, differed from that as built in two places. Firstly, at Evesham, the MR line was shown as leading directly into the WMR station by a junction just west of the station. Secondly, at Ashchurch, the line was shown as joining the MR main line about ¼ mile north of Ashchurch station at a south-facing junction (as in the Robert Stephenson plans of 1845). About ⅛ mile south of this junction a further line diverged westwards at a north-facing junction to join the Ashchurch to Tewkesbury line, thus creating a triangle on the western side of Ashchurch. It was evidently realised at a later stage that this could cause operational difficulties in that Evesham

Above: Former MR Deeley class '3P' 4-4-0 No. 734 (with non-standard LMS tender) crosses the Evesham to Tewkesbury chord line on the level as it leaves Ashchurch station with an up main line stopping train on 29th April, 1948.

G. Parker/ Kidderminster Railway Museum

Right: Fowler '4F' class 0-6-0 No. 44108 approaches the railway crossing at Ashchurch with a main line southbound partly fitted freight on 30th July, 1954.

B. Moore/ Kidderminster Railway Museum

branch trains could not occupy the station at the same time as main line trains travelling in the same direction. Consequently, the plans were changed, and the line as built was included in Section Five of the Midland Railway (New Lines & Additional Powers) Act of 21st July, 1863 where it now joined the main line directly opposite the Tewkesbury line. This Act also specified an additional spur leaving the Evesham line just north of the junction to form the well known level crossing of the main line through to the Tewkesbury line. In practice, there seems to have been little in the way of through running, and this connecting line was primarily used for engine turning purposes. The Act did not extend the time for completion of construction.

Preliminary work had begun in September 1862 and progress was regularly reported upon to the committee by the Engineer, Charles Liddell. The surviving minutes of the committee record that by March 1863 two of the three cylinders used as the piers for the heavy bridge over the Avon at Evesham had been sunk, and that 1½ miles of double track had been ballasted. The bridge was expected to be completed by the end of May, and at a meeting on 30th May this was confirmed, along with all brickwork and earthworks.

An interesting report on 31st August, 1863 was that 'The contractor now has three locomotives working on the line, two of which are engaged in ballasting, so that the heaviest part of the work is not likely to be behindhand'. It is generally accepted that Brassey & Ballard had at least one locomotive working here, believed to be Manning, Wardle 0-6-0ST *Colwall* (Works No. 83 of 1863), which was an 'Old I' class locomotive with 11 in. x 17 in. inside cylinders, dispatched new by the makers on 3rd August, 1863 to Brassey & Ballard. However, the identities of the other two Brassey & Ballard locomotives can only be speculated on as another two Manning, Wardle 0-6-0STs, *Rutland* (4 of 1859) and *Malvern* (18 of 1860), both of which were also 'Old I' class locomotives with identical dimensions. These were delivered new to Brassey & Ballard at Colwall, Herefordshire on 16th September, 1859 and 17th December, 1860 respectively, where they worked nearby on the construction of the Worcester & Hereford Railway which opened on 25th July, 1860. Their next confirmed use by Brassey & Ballard was on the Enniskillen to Bundoran line in Ireland for the North Western Railway from 1864 to 1866, which required their conversion to 5 ft 3 in. gauge, and after which they were taken over by that railway as its Nos. 30 and 31 respectively. So their period of probable use here fits the dates nicely. One other locomotive used on the Worcester & Hereford Railway contract was Haydock Foundries 2-4-0 *Gipsy Lass* (42 of 1840), which is not thought to have been used here, as by 1862 it was in use on the Tenbury & Bewdley Railway contract. Bearing in mind that Brassey & Ballard were also working on the Tewkesbury & Malvern Railway from Ashchurch to Tewkesbury and Malvern Wells from 1862 to 1864, it is possible that these three locomotives were moved from one contract to another as circumstances required. Meanwhile, *Colwall* almost certainly passed on to the next section for construction, from Evesham to Alcester, as we shall see.

Liddell reported on 31st October, 1863 that 'the central part of the line is nearly complete, but contractor has not yet been able to commence work at the terminus'. This would seem to indicate that some of the land in the vicinity of the Evesham station area had not been acquired by this date, but the committee was reassured at the next monthly meeting, on 30th November, 1863, that the 'contractor has now been put in possession of the required land at both ends of the line'. Further progress was indicated on 6th January, 1864, when the committee resolved that a cheap temporary wooden building was to be erected at Evesham for the present.

This brings us to question of the stations, which were approved at a meeting of 30th September, 1862 to be erected for Hinton, Ashton and Beckford, and for 'a ticket station at Hampton'. However, the cost of the stations was not included in the original tenders, and the minutes of this meeting only refer to requesting Brassey & Ballard to give prices for these stations, which they evidently did. As we shall see, Brassey & Ballard sub-contracted the building of the stations to at least one local firm, although there are no further details regarding cost, which would have been included as an 'extra' in their final bill to the MR.

The spring of 1864 was a particularly busy time, and by 6th April of that year it was reported that the 'Permanent way is complete with the exception of about ½ mile in all at the two ends – the points and crossings are mostly laid in and the signals in a forward state. The station buildings (except Ashchurch) are so far finished that they may be prepared for opening of the line at any time within a fortnight'. However, there had been some slippages on the embankment at Evesham, but these were being worked upon.

On 11th May, 1864, the committee agreed to instruct the Electric International Telegraph Co. to instal telegraph equipment along the length of the line. The next meeting on 6th July reported that 'the line has been opened this day for goods traffic'. This was further commented upon in the *Alcester Chronicle* and the *Worcester Herald* issues of 9th July, in which they both reported: 'This line was opened for goods traffic on Friday last [1st July] and until further notice trains will leave Ashchurch daily at 8.5 a.m. and 1.20 p.m.; and Evesham at 9.25 a.m. and 3.30 p.m. The Government Inspector will within a few days inspect the line, after which it will be opened for passenger traffic.' Therefore, there seems to be some discrepancy concerning the actual date of commencement of goods traffic – either the 1st or the 6th of July.

The Government Inspector, Captain Tyler inspected the line on 8th July, 1864 but was unable to approve the line for the commencement of passenger traffic. In his report to the Board of Trade dated 11th July, he cited five issues requiring improvement:

> The junction at Ashchurch is temporary and the accommodation of a very inferior character.
>
> The line to Evesham starts from a very short platform with a single line for the arrival and departure at the back of the east platform; and if the incoming train from Evesham was to overrun the platforms by a few yards it would foul the main line.
>
> Some of the fishbolts are missing and many do not come through the nuts, and many keys are missing.
>
> The fencing is post and rail and is rather low in some places.
>
> The principal work is the viaduct over the River Avon, comprising two openings of 123 ft 7 in. each on skew and constructed with iron girders upon masonry abutments and a pier comprised of three cylinders in the river. These girders yielded deflections of about ¾ in under rolling loads of rather more than one ton to the linear foot, including a permanent set of about 1⁄16 in. I have recommended a few extra cover plates should be added to this and one other new bridge.

Unfortunately, on the day of his inspection, an accident occurred at Ashchurch, although it is not clear whether he witnessed it, or was even aware of it occurring. This was reported in the *Berrow's Worcester Journal* of 16th July, 1864:

PERSHORE RAILWAY ACCIDENT

An accident occurred on Friday morning [8th July], on the branch line of the Ashchurch and Evesham Railway. A navvy, named Wood, of Eckington, aged 45, was employed ballasting near the new station, and was getting from between two trucks when he slipped, and the truck moved and went over both his legs. One of his legs was nearly cut through, and the other slightly injured. The poor fellow was at once conveyed to Cheltenham Hospital, where it was found necessary to amputate one of his legs.

Subsequently, Liddell reported to the committee that the first four items had been attended to or were on order, but that he considered the strengthening plates for the Avon bridge to be unnecessary, and anyway they would cost an additional £500. Correspondence was entered into by the MR committee with the Board of Trade, and on 22nd August they agreed that this work would not be required. On 16th September, Captain Tyler made a further inspection and approved the line for passenger traffic.

Opening of the line

The line was double track throughout, and formally opened for passenger traffic on Saturday 1st October, 1864 and was widely reported in all of the local newspapers. *Berrow's Worcester Journal* of 8th October particularly commented on the inaugural train, as the following excerpts reveal:

On Saturday, the Ashchurch and Evesham Branch of the Midland Line was opened for passenger traffic. The first train left Evesham at 8.45, when a great concourse of people assembled to see 'the start'. In fact the inhabitants of that fine old town appear to have taken the matter up with great spirit. The Abbey bells were ringing, and a handsome flag surmounted the tower, while many other flags and banners floated from the principal dwellings. The mayor (Thos. White, Esq.), attended by the Corporation, and duly supported by the mace bearer, beadle, and other officials, preceded by the Rifle Brass Band, under the able superintendence of Bandmaster Wheatley, started in procession from the Town Hall, and took their places in the carriages to inaugurate the 'new line', and enjoy a 'free ride'.

Arriving at Ashchurch at 9.20 am, an interval was allowed for the arrival of trains from Malvern, Bristol, and Birmingham, showing that the station at that place has become of much importance, although the accommodation is as yet incomplete; however a new station will shortly be erected. Leaving Ashchurch again at 9.45, the view on the return journey is of the most charming character.

The description follows of many of the fine buildings and scenic views to be seen. Notable were Beckford station,

... an exceedingly pretty and commodious one, now richly decorated with flags and banners ... Ashton-under-Hill Station is also nicely decorated with garlands, &c., and here the Alveston band discoursed some excellent music. In a field adjoining was erected a booth, decked out with gay flags, and calculated to afford room to dine 300 people. 'Success to Hinton' is the motto hung out at the next station, where the flower wreaths entwined round the portico and pillars showed great taste. Here also a tent was placed for a general parish feast ... Six minutes' ride takes us to Bengeworth, where we pull up nearly opposite Hampton Church, and here the bells were merrily ringing, while flags and garlands were the order of the day ... We glide along a bold curve leading to

An undated view of the chord at Ashchurch leading from the Tewkesbury line (behind the camera) straight ahead to the Evesham line. As this line was singled in 1927, the view must be prior to that date. It closed completely in 1957. The route into Ashchurch station from Tewkesbury curves away to the right, where a Kirtley '690' class 0-4-4T with curved double frames is just departing the station. The signal box in the foreground is Ashchurch West.
Roy Burrows Collection

the bridge spanning the River Avon, whose 'softly flowing' stream has appeared at intervals during our journey. The contrast between this light and elegant bridge and the ugly, heavy, timber structure used by the Great Western Railway, and placed a few yards above stream, is striking ... We now arrive at the temporary station [at Evesham], which is trimmed off with pretty arches formed of evergreens and flowers, and surmounted by a crown, flags, &c. The decorations were profuse and done in capital style. A new Midland station is in course of erection within a few yards of the one used by the Great Western Company.

Alighting here, the procession returned to the Town Hall at Evesham and, on its arrival, three cheers each were given for the new railway, the contractors, the Mayor, and the Corporation. The distance from Evesham to Ashchurch is 10¾ miles, and combined with the further run of 14 miles to Great Malvern, forms one of the most delightful trips the inland counties can afford.

The Ashchurch, Tewkesbury, and Malvern line was opened in the glorious month of May, when the fruit trees were unusually full of rich blossoms, while the Ashchurch and Evesham Railway sprung into existence in brown October, when the said trees were exhibiting their extra abundance and overflowing stores of apples and pears. May the railway blossoms bear fruit in like manner, and benefit the proprietors and the country generally.

A lengthy report in the *Evesham Journal* of this date gives a much more detailed description of the festivities enjoyed at each of the stations en route, and although interesting enough provides little more detail for the student of railway history, with one exception. There is a reference to the fact that the station at Beckford was constructed by George Hunt of Evesham, as a sub-contractor to Brassey & Ballard. However, there is no reference to the builders of the other stations. The comment concerning the incomplete status of Evesham station is noteworthy, as we learn from the committee minutes of 2nd January, 1865 that 'Frost and Christmas have caused a suspension of work at Evesham station; there is no further unfinished work'. However, there is no further comment as to when the works at Evesham were finally completed.

The final minutes of the committee record on 6th December, 1865 that the Engineer, Charles Liddell was paid for his engineering work at the rate of £220 per mile for the 11 miles, a total of £2,420 overall, and that his account was finally settled on that date.

Services

As we have seen, there were two goods trains operating each way between Evesham and Ashchurch on weekdays from either the 1st or 6th July, 1864, and these continued to run during the time that the line was open only between these two points. Departures were at 8.05 am and 1.35 pm from Ashchurch, returning from Evesham at 9.25 am and 3.30 pm. The first three trips called at all stations en route and took either 55 minutes or an hour for the trip, although the final working of the day only called at Ashton and Beckford, so took only 40 minutes.

The initial passenger services comprised four trains each way on weekdays, leaving Evesham at 8.45, 11.20 am, 3.00 and 6.45 pm, returning from Ashchurch at 9.45 am, 1.30, 4.15 and 7.35 pm. There were two Sunday services at 8.20 am and 6.20 pm from Evesham, and at 9.10 am and 7.40 pm from Ashchurch, which were classed as 'Parliamentary', as were the first and last trains on weekdays. Each trip took 35 minutes in each direction, and stopped at all stations. It will be observed that the locomotive and stock were therefore stabled at Evesham. A copy of this timetable is illustrated below.

From 1st February, 1865 an additional service was run from Evesham at 5.10 pm (which omitted stops at Bengeworth and Hinton, so taking only 25 minutes for the trip); the return was at 5.40 pm from Ashchurch being described as 'Engine and Carriage', which presumably refers to an empty stock working as it ran non-stop.

Day trips were advertised from Evesham to Cheltenham (3*s*. return) and Bristol (5*s*. return), with half prices for 'covered carriages', which were carriages with roofs but not enclosed on the sides.

Later, the November 1865 timetable discontinued the 5.10 pm Evesham and 5.40 pm Ashchurch trains. these were replaced by a later service, departing from Ashchurch at 6.00 pm and Evesham at 7.40 pm. Furthermore, the 11.20 am departure from Evesham was retimed to 11.00 am and ran through to Gloucester, arriving at 12.00 noon. The return balancing working left Gloucester at 1.00 pm, maintaining an Ashchurch departure time of 1.30 pm.

In June 1866 this 11.00 am Evesham departure was again retimed to 10.40 am (arriving at Gloucester at 11.40 am), the 3.00 pm departure retimed to leave five minutes later, and the 6.45 pm departure to leave half an hour earlier.

ASHCHURCH TO EVESHAM.

TRAINS LEAVE			WEEK DAYS.				SUNDAYS.	
			a.m.	p.m.	p.m.	p.m.	a.m.	p.m.
ASHCHURCH ...	...	...	9 45	1 30	4 15	7 35	9 10	7 40
Beckford	...	...	9 57	1 42	4 27	7 47	9 22	7 52
Ashton-und'r-Hill	...	...	10 3	1 48	4 33	7 53	9 28	7 58
Hinton	...	...	10 9	1 54	4 39	7 59	9 34	8 4
Bengeworth	...	...	10 15	2 0	4 45	8 5	9 40	8 10
EVESHAM ...ar.	...	...	10 20	2 5	4 50	8 10	9 45	8 15

The 9.45 a.m., 7.35 p.m., and the Sunday Trains, are Parl.

EVESHAM TO ASHCHURCH.

TRAINS LEAVE			WEEK DAYS.				SUNDAYS.	
			a.m.	a.m.	p.m.	p.m.	a.m.	p.m.
EVESHAM	...	...	8 45	11 20	3 0	6 45	8 20	6 20
Bengeworth	...	...	8 48	11 23	3 3	6 48	8 23	6 23
Hinton	...	...	8 55	11 30	3 10	6 55	8 30	6 30
Ashton-und'r-Hill	...	...	9 0	11 35	3 15	7 0	8 35	6 35
Beckford	...	...	9 6	11 41	3 21	7 6	8 41	6 41
ASHCHURCH ar.	...	...	9 20	11 55	3 35	7 20	8 55	6 55

The 8.45 a.m., 6.45 p.m., and the Sunday Trains, are Parl.

Public timetable for Ashchurch to Evesham line, as printed in *Berrow's Worcester Journal* on 1st October, 1864.

Chapter Four

The Evesham & Redditch Railway

This railway built the line from Evesham in two sections; firstly from Evesham to Alcester, opening in 1866, then onwards to Redditch, opening in 1868. Therefore, we shall deal with the formation of the company, then construction and opening of this first section of the line, including the services from Ashchurch to Alcester. Next, we shall look at the construction and opening of the final section of the route, but the operation of services over this latter section will be dealt with in Chapter Seven, as these then relate to the complete route.

Formation of the company

As we have already seen, the line northwards formed part of the strategy of the MR to provide an alternative route to its established Birmingham to Gloucester line. Plans were deposited at Worcester County Court on 29th November, 1862 at 3.00 pm. The company was authorized on 13th July, 1863 by the Evesham and Redditch Railway Act, 1863 (Vict. 26 & 27, cap. 114). Share capital was authorized to £149,000 in £10 shares, and mortgage facilities of up to £49,600. Although this Act had the backing of the MR, there was opposition from the West Midland Railway, who had plans of their own to reach Redditch, and who were also concerned at competition for traffic at Evesham. These objections caused some minor changes to the original Bill presented to Parliament, one of which related to control over a junction between the two railways at the western end of Evesham. As events transpired, the junction here was rarely used, until remodelled by British Railways (BR) after nationalization. These objections caused only a minor delay in the passage of the Bill through the Houses of Parliament.

The authorized route per the enabling Act and the deposited plans differed from the route as built in that a spur of about ¼ mile was to connect the WMR east of Evesham station, joining the Redditch line about ¼ mile after it had passed over this line. Perhaps the intransigence of the WMR made it unlikely that it would ever be used, so that it was never built.

Subscribers to the enabling Act were given as Edward Holland, Benjamin Bomford, William Smith, Thomas White, and James Smith. The Directors of the company named by the Act were the first three subscribers mentioned above, plus John Edward Clift and Alan Lambert.

The first meeting of the company was held on 14th October, 1863 at 3 Princes Street, Westminster at which the provisional committee was formed. However, it was nearly a year later before the line had been marked out, according to the *Alcester Chronicle* of 1st October, 1864. Therefore, it would appear that the original promoters of the line were not very successful in their attempts to proceed with its construction, despite their backing from the MR, as there was a further unexplained delay before any further progress was reported. For we learn from the *Alcester Chronicle* of 11th February, 1865 that Brassey & Ballard had taken the scheme out of their hands. This confirms the events of the next meeting, held on 10th March, 1865. The company minutes of this meeting do not give details of any tenders submitted for the construction of the line, but simply refer to the contract awarded to Messrs Brassey

& Ballard 'with MR agreement' which totalled £198,000 and was to be paid in cash (£2,530), shares (£146,470) and debentures (£49,000). As these amounts correspond to the capital authorized by the enabling Act, it is reasonable to assume that financing of the line had been agreed with Brassey & Ballard. The small amount of shares, equalling the amount to be paid in cash, represents the shares held by the other Directors of the railway. At this meeting, the Directors were elected as follows:

William Wagstaff, 4 Great George Street, Westminster (Chairman)
Edward Holland, MP
Benjamin Bomford
Thomas Brassey
William Philip Price, Tibberton Court, Gloucestershire
Thomas Bluck, Beckford, Gloucestershire

This meeting also established the Contracting Committee to oversee the construction, and this consisted of Messrs Brassey, Price and Wagstaff. The Engineer was confirmed as Edward Richards.

Construction of the line to Alcester

The minutes of the Directors' meetings for this company are not particularly expansive, so we learn very little regarding the progress of construction. Nonetheless, there seems to have been little difficulty in the work, once it had been begun in earnest, and at a meeting only a year later, on 21st March, 1866 it was stated that the 10 mile line would be open by May of that year. This was very nearly achieved, as the First Notice of intention to open the line was submitted by the Secretary of the Evesham & Redditch Railway, Mr C. Hall, to the Board of Trade on 29th May, 1866, and the Second Notice on 16th July. Between these two, the Secretary confirmed to the Board of Trade in a letter dated 9th June, 1866 that the working of this single line railway would be by the Board of Trade's approved method of pilot guard. In this system, a pilot guard became the sole authority for a train to be worked on the line. Whilst this method had the virtues of simplicity and was easy for anyone to understand, it was rather too rigid in practice, and was soon replaced.

Although work seemed to have proceed well, quite a number of accidents befell workers on the line, each reported in the *Alcester Chronicle*.

Salford, 17th June 1865
On Tuesday evening last [13th June], while a navvie, known as 'Devonshire Jack', was at work on the line of the Evesham & Redditch Railway, near to Harvington Mill, a mass of earth about two tons in weight fell on him; he was extricated as soon as possible, and conveyed to his lodgings at Salford, but so serious were the injuries that he had received that he died about five o'clock the following morning. On Thursday afternoon, H.O. Hunt, Esq., Coroner for this division of the county, held an inquest upon the body at the Bell Inn, Salford, when the jury returned a verdict of 'Accidental Death'. The man's name is unknown; his only designation among his fellow workmen being 'Devonshire Jack'.

A report on 24th June about the funeral of the above, refers to him as being one Thomas Davis.

Evesham, 29th July 1865
On Wednesday [26th July] afternoon, about four o'clock, an accident attended with fatal consequences, occurred upon the line of the Evesham and Redditch Railway. The scene of the accident was not far from Evesham Station, where Mr. Bannister, jun., (son of the sub-contractor for that portion of the line), was assisting in shunting some ballast trucks, and while stooping down for that purpose, he called out 'back', when he should have called out 'forward', the result was that when the engine was put into motion, a collision took place, and his head was so severely crushed that he died about nine o' clock the same evening. An inquest has since been held, but the verdict was not known here at the time of going to press. He leaves a wife and two children, with a speedy prospect of a further increase of family.

Evesham, 9th June, 1866
On Wednesday week [30th May], as the workmen were engaged in blasting rocks on the works of the Evesham and Redditch Railway, a boy, named Moore, a son of one of the navvies, was struck on the head by one of the falling fragments and most seriously injured.

Alcester, 23rd June, 1866
On Thursday evening last [21st June], as John Smith, jun., of Bleachfield Street, who has for some time worked upon the line, was about to return home from Wixford, after his day's work; he attempted to jump upon one of the trucks attached to the locomotive engine, which was just on the point of moving on, but missed his hold, the wheels of several trucks passed over his right foot, crushing several of his toes, and ripping the calf of the leg for several inches in length, apparently from coming into contact with a spike. He was immediately conveyed home, and T.L. Smith, Esq. was speedily in attendance and bound up the injured part, but the extent of the injuries sustained cannot for the present be ascertained.

It is believed that Brassey & Ballard moved the Manning, Wardle locomotive *Colwall*, mentioned in the previous chapter, from the Ashchurch to Evesham contract to work on this section (and on the further extension towards Redditch). This was supplemented by a further locomotive, which is mentioned shortly in the press report on the special excursion of 14th July, 1866. This was one of the comparatively rare products of the Worcester Engine Co., and was actually their first locomotive, being their Works No. 1 of 1865, probably delivered new to Brassey & Ballard on this contract. It was an 0-6-0ST with inside cylinders, and named *Salford* after the village of Salford Priors on the line. Its subsequent history is not known.

Colonel Yolland performed the inspection of the line on 24th July, 1866. His report of 26th July to the Board of Trade described the line as being 9 miles 56 chains in length, and of single track, although sufficient land had been purchased, and overbridges built, so that it could be doubled at a future date. The rails were of 21 feet lengths, of 70 lb. per yard, and fixed to the sleepers by twisted spikes. The gravel ballast had a depth of 10 inches below the sleepers. There were six underbridges, eight overbridges and two viaducts over the River Arrow. The largest underbridge was where the line crossed the West Midland Railway at Evesham on the skew, and had a span of 56 feet, with brick abutments supporting wrought-iron girders. The viaducts each had three openings, the wrought-iron girders being supported on stone abutments, and the central piers being of stone on one viaduct, and cast-iron piers on the other. Turntables had been installed at Alcester and Evesham. It was noted that the station at Wixford was incomplete at this time. The *Alcester Chronicle* of 28th July, 1866 reported that the government inspector was accompanied by

Messrs S. Ballard, E. Richards, W. Richards, C. Hall and three unnamed MR officials. Two 'large engines' of the MR with a total estimated weight of 90 tons, were placed chimney to chimney in order to test the deflection of the underbridges on the line. The results of this test were satisfactory, but in his report Colonel Yolland requested the following improvements:

> The sidings at Harvington, Salford Priors and Wixford needed low signals to control access, interlocking with the points and signals on the station platforms, from where they are worked. These sidings were not to be used until this work was accomplished.
>
> The pillars supporting the girders over the River Arrow at Wixford should be braced together.

This work was completed, and Board of Trade approval was granted for the line to open for passenger traffic as from 17th September, 1866. It was noted that the platform at Wixford was to be extended to the north, reduced at the south end, and ramps were to be installed at each end.

Working the line to Alcester

All workings were performed by MR locomotives, stock and staff from the outset. Goods traffic had actually commenced from Evesham to Alcester on 16th June, 1866. The 8.05 am goods from Ashchurch continued as before, terminating at Evesham, with the return working also as before, leaving at 9.25 am. However, the afternoon goods working from Ashchurch was retimed to leave at 12 noon, arriving in Alcester at 2.20 pm. This returned at 2.55 pm, arriving at Ashchurch at 4.49 pm.

Prior to the start of regular passenger trains, a notable excursion was provided for the benefit of the workers on the line. This is most aptly recorded in the *Alcester Chronicle* of 14th July, 1866:

> *FIRST EXCURSION TRAIN*
>
> On Wednesday morning last, the usually quiet town of Alcester was thrown into a state of unusual excitement, in consequence of it having become known that a private Excursion Train for the purpose of conveying the personal friends of Stephen Ballard, Esq., of the firm of Brassey and Ballard, the eminent contractors for the Evesham and Redditch Railway, would leave the Alcester Station on a trip to Evesham and back, prior to it being publicly opened.
>
> Duly to celebrate the event of the day, the navvies, under the direction of Mr Wall, took upon themselves the task of giving a holiday appearance to the various bridges and stations along the line, by decking them with flags, and decorations of a verdant and floral character. Across the line, at the head of the platform at Alcester Station, in the form of a festoon formed of flowers, evergreens, &c., and suspended between lofty poles, was the motto, 'Success to B.B. Good health to them and theirs'; the 'B.B.' of course being the initials of their respected employers, Messrs Brassey and Ballard. Flags and other decorations likewise formed conspicuous objects at different points around the station. There was a similar motto at the little station of Wixford, but those at the other stations along the line, we are unable to particularize.
>
> Shortly after nine o'clock, the 'Salford', a small but comparatively powerful engine, together with two carriages arrived at Alcester Station , where a very large number of spectators were assembled ... at about half past nine the train was put into motion, and in due course arrived at Evesham, where two more carriages were attached, and the number of passengers was considerably increased; and it also received various other

> accessions to its numbers at other stations on the line, prior to the train again arriving at Alcester Station, when the passengers amounted to nearly 60 persons....The greater proportion of whom on their arrival at Alcester, proceeded on foot to the Swan Hotel, where a very *recherche* champagne luncheon awaited them, consisting of all the delicacies of the season, embracing ducks, lobsters, roast lamb, &c., together with various joints of a still more solid description, that *cetera desiderantur* would have been an almost inadmissable quotation; and the getting up of the whole affair did the highest possible credit to the landlord, Mr. W. Terrill.
>
> The repast being at an end, a number of the appropriate toasts and speeches were made by the gentlemen present...an omnibus and other vehicles provided for the occasion then drew up to the door, and the major part of the party proceeded to Ragley Hall, the magnificent mansion of the Marquis of Hertford, and after having surveyed its beautiful architectural proportions, and duly inspected the many objects of art and *virtu*, which are there collected, likewise taking a view of some of the pleasing and varied landscapes, and other sylvan beauties which are to be found within its extensive and noble park, they again returned to the Swan Hotel, and after a short stay there, the party separated for their different homes. At a quarter to six o'clock, the train was again in readiness for those of the party who were not resident in Alcester; steam was got up again, Alcester Station was soon left behind, and the excursionists, we believe we may say, reached their several homes in safety...

The official first day of public passenger services was Monday 17th September, 1866 with the intermediate stations at Wixford, Salford Priors and Harvington opening at the same time The first train from Alcester, departing at 8.15 am, was extended as a special excursion to Malvern, consisting of 12 carriages, presumably four-wheelers. The *Alcester Chronicle* of 22nd September reported at least 100 people taking the through excursion, with many others going only as far as Evesham. Although there were a considerable number of spectators at all vantage points along the line, there is no comment as to the usual celebrations and decorations associated with such inaugural services. The *Evesham Journal* of the same date commented upon the lack of a general enthusiasm, saying that that 'at Alcester everything was quiet - no general holiday - no public demonstration - nothing to denote anything of importance to the town had occurred'.

It transpired that on the previous Saturday, the Alcester town bailiff arranged a public meeting to discuss ways of celebrating the opening, but only five persons turned up. Another attempt to encourage some form of celebration was made by a group of 20 shopkeepers, calling themselves the 'principal shopkeepers', who stated that they would be closing their shops in support of general celebrations. However, this offended those shopkeepers not listed as being 'principal', and no general closing took place. *Berrow's Worcester Journal* of the same date described the lack of events as being the result of 'petty jealousy and divided interests'. Had the Midland Railway not arranged the excursion to Malvern, it seems likely that most people would not have been aware of the railway opening.

In the meantime, the temporary station at Evesham, which had opened with the line from Ashchurch on 1st July, 1864, had been replaced by a more permanent bulding.

The opening services were of four weekday trains each way, which closely replicated the original four train service on the opening of the section from Ashchurch to Evesham two years earlier. These departed from Alcester for Ashchurch at 8.15 , 10.55 am, 2.45 and 5.45 pm and from Ashchurch at 9.45 am, 1.30, 4.15 and 7.35 pm. They stopped at all stations, except the 1.30 pm from Ashchurch and the 2.45 pm from Alcester, which did not stop at Harvington and Wixford until November 1866. Even then, rather oddly the 2.45 pm Alcester departure stopped on Mondays only, and the 1.30 pm Ashchurch departure stopped only on Tuesdays. These conditional stops may have been related to the market days held at Alcester. All trains conveyed first and second class passengers, whilst the first and last trains each way were 'Government' trains, featuring open carriages. These took an extra three or four minutes longer than the remaining two trains, which managed to complete the journey between Alcester and Evesham in 25 minutes. On Sundays there were two trains each way, both being first, second and 'Government' classes, leaving Alcester at 7.50 am and 5.50 pm, and Ashchurch at 9.10 am and 7.40 pm. This frequency continued at least until April 1867. However, by March 1868 there were no Sunday services, and the 5.45 pm weekday train from Alcester was extended on to Gloucester. In the opposite direction by this time, the 9.45 am and 7.35 pm from Ashchurch both started from Gloucester.

At the time of opening, the fares between Evesham and Alcester were: first class - 1*s*. 9*d*. single, 2*s*. 8*d*. return; second class - 1*s*. 3*d*. single, 2*s*. 0*d*. return; third class ('Government') – single 9½*d*.

It was previously mentioned that the system of pilot guard working, approved by the Board of Trade was fairly short lived. This is supported by a letter from James Allport, General Manager of the MR to the Board of Trade on 14th January, 1867 in which he stated that the method of working was to be by Train Staff and Ticket as from 21st January. The Board of Trade had no objections to this change.

RAILWAY TIME TABLE.

ALCESTER TO EVESHAM.

WEEK-DAYS.—DOWN. SUNDAYS.

		Week-days 1&2 gov.	Week-days 1 & 2 class	Week-days 1& 2 clss.	Week-days 1&2 goy.	Sundays 1& 2 gov.	Sundays 1& 2 gov
		a m	a.m.	p.m	p.m	a m	p.m
	ALCESTER	8 15	10 0	2 45	5 45	7 50	5 50
2	Wixford......	8 21	10 5	...	5 51	7 56	5 56
4	Salford	8 27	10 10	2 53	5 57	8 2	6 8
6	Harvington	8 33	10 15	.	6 3	8 8	6
9½	EVESHAM	8 43	10 25	3 4	6 14	8 18	6 18

EVESHAM TO ALCESTER.

WEEK-DAYS.—UP. SUNDAYS.

		Week-days 1 & 2 gov.	Week-days 1& 2 clss.	Week-days 1& 2 clss.	Week-days 1& 2 gov	Sundays 1& 2 gov	Sundays 1& 2 gov
		a.m.	p.m	p.m	p.m	a.m	p.m
	EVESHAM	10 35	2 8	5 10	8 12	9 47	8 17
3½	Harvington	10 45	...	5 10	8 12	9 57	8 27
5½	Salford	10 51	2 20	5 23	8 28	10 3	8 33
7½	Wixford	10 57	...	5 28	8 31	10 9	8 39
9½	ALCESTER	11 5	2 30	5 35	8 40	1015	8 45

Public timetable for the Midland Railway Evesham to Alcester line, as printed in the *Evesham Journal* on 6th October, 1866.

Evesham station around 1900, with the crew, station staff and other onlookers taking a keen interest in the photographer, as a Johnson 'Standard Goods' 0-6-0 is standing at the up platform. The locomotive appears to be finished in the light green livery adopted by Samuel Johnson from 1883. Meanwhile, a Kirtley 0-6-0 with curved double frames is standing at the end of the down platform. *Almonery Heritage Centre Collection*

Construction of the line from Alcester to Redditch

Although the opening from Evesham to Alcester marked a further step in the completion of the through route, work had been continuing northwards on the 7¼ mile extension to Redditch. This work appears to have gone well, with only the boring of the tunnel at Redditch causing any problems. In fact, the *Alcester Chronicle* reported as early as 9th June, 1866 that some 60 men were already at work on removing soil preparatory to the commencement of work on the tunnel, which was expected to take about 18 months to complete, mainly due to potential drainage problems associated with expected underground water and the loose nature of the earth. The first shaft had been sunk at this time, but this had initially filled with some 20 ft of water. Work on the tunnel had commenced from the northern end, and at first a rather risky procedure was adopted. This involved boring a preliminary tunnel for about 80 yards, sufficient in size to enable wagons to be propelled inside. The loose earth roof of the tunnel was then dislodged directly into these wagons and removed. Needless to say, a collapse of the roof occurred, fortunately without loss of life or injury. This method of working changed shortly afterwards, ensuring adequate shoring of the tunnel bore. The tunnel was originally planned to be 370 yards long as shown on the deposited plans, but eventually worked out at 340 yards.

By 1st August, 1867 the Directors were able to inspect the completed bore of the tunnel, and in the following November a contractor's locomotive worked a train of trucks though it.

The principal change at Redditch was the construction of a new station, some ½ mile to the south of the original Redditch Railway station in Clive Road. This was to be sited adjacent to Bromsgrove Road, and at the junction with the later Plymouth Road. Stables for horses, a timber yard and a carpentry shop were to be erected nearby. However, it seems that the bridge over the line in Bromsgrove Road erected by Brassey & Ballard did not meet with the approval of the local Board, as to its construction and position. The *Worcester Herald* of 2nd May, 1868 reported that the Board were considering possible legal action against the contractor, who was unwilling to make the changes required by the Board. No further details have emerged about this dispute, and it seems likely that the Board quietly demurred.

Only two further stations were erected on this new section of line, at Coughton, and at Studley & Astwood Bank - the latter not being particularly close to either village.

Mr C. Hall, the Secretary of the Evesham & Redditch Railway issued a First Notice of intention to open to the Board of Trade on 27th January, 1868, and a Second Notice on the 12th March. Colonel Hutchinson agreed to inspect the line on the following day. His report, dated 20th March, confirmed the line as being single and 7 miles and 26 chains long. Once again, land had been purchased and overbridges constructed with a view to possible doubling of the line in future. However, the tunnel at Redditch was definitely of single line bore. The permanent way was of similar specification to the earlier line, except that the ballast was thicker, at 18 inches below the sleepers. The steepest gradient was stated as 1 in 100, and the tightest curve was of 15 chains radius. There were 10 overbridges, of which seven were entirely of brick, two had brick abutments and cast-iron girders, and one of wooden construction. Of the eight underbridges, seven were entirely of brick, one had brick abutments and cast-iron girders, and this had the longest span, of 20 ft.

Several items required attention before permission for passenger services could be granted:

At Coughton, the down distant signal arm needed to be more visible, and the goods signal arm required repositioning.

At Studley, some fencing required making good, the goods signal arm also required repositioning.

For Redditch tunnel, it was thought necessary to provide some form of telegraphic or other communication to prevent two trains being on the line at the same time.

In Redditch, further fencing needed to be made good, planking was required on the steps of the wooden footbridge, additional bolts were required on the wrought iron bridge [presumably over Hewell Road]. Two additional stop blocks were needed in the goods yard, and a shelter for passengers was to be erected on the up platform, and the station nameboard to be put up.

As a result, the Board of Trade wrote to the company on the following day, saying that the opening would have to be delayed for one month until the work was complete. However, a letter from Colonel Hutchinson to the Board of Trade on 28th March stated that the works were either completed or in hand, and that he had no objection to the opening of the line. As a result the Board of Trade issued its approval on 30th March for immediate opening.

Separately, Mr C. Hall had written to the Board of Trade on 25th March confirming that the method of working would be by Train Staff and Ticket, and giving full details of the method of working.

Opening of the through route

The line was formally opened to goods and passengers on Monday 4th May, 1868. An excursion train left Redditch for Evesham at 9.40 am, but this was not the first train, as the 7.15 am from Evesham had already arrived in Redditch at around 8.00 am, and then promptly departed southwards again. Starting at the southern end, the *Evesham Journal* of 9th May reported that no particular celebrations had been arranged there, but the Workman Pleasure Grounds had been specially opened, with a band provided for dancing. The excursionists were estimated at 900 on that train alone, plus many more on other trains which ran from Redditch, Alcester and Birmingham. The excursion train returned from Evesham at 7.00 pm.

At Alcester, there was similarly no public display of celebration, although *Berrow's Worcester Journal* reported on 9th May that the bells were rung as the first train approached, and that there were a fair number of spectators along the line. However, as if to make up for their previous lack of enthusiasm, a dinner had been arranged for 80 notable persons at the Corn Exchange. Although both Ballard and Brassey had been invited, Thomas Brassey was unable to attend. Stephen Ballard nonetheless took part in a sumptuous dinner, which started at 4.00 pm, and was described in the *Alcester Chronicle* also of 9th May in considerable detail. Suffice it to say that the dinner menu was vast, and truly international in both presentation and flavour. It was provided by a Mr Andrews of Leamington. A considerable number of toasts were proposed and drunk, and there were many speeches, most of which were also reported at some length. The proceedings continued until 10.00 pm, although Stephen Ballard had left earlier, as he had arranged a special train to take him to Evesham, in order that he could make a connection with a further train (probably on the West Midland Railway) to his home.

At Studley the situation was entirely different. The *Alcester Chronicle* reported:

A very crowded platform at Redditch station around 1900. Possibly this was a holiday weekend, or the train approaching from the Birmingham direction was an excursion. It is not possible to identify this type of locomotive, other than to comment that it has the polished brass safety valve surround typical of both Kirtley and Johnson locomotives. The passenger stock at the up platform is formed of close-coupled six-wheeled vehicles.

Author's Collection

> OPENING OF THE RAILWAY - On Monday last, great excitement prevailed at Studley upon the occasion of the opening of the railway. The day was almost a general holiday, many of the shops were closed, and the whole aspect of affairs showed that work was, for once, almost suspended; flags were waved from many of the windows, and at Mr George Edkins, maltster, two arches of evergreens were placed in front of the house with the mottos 'Health and Prosperity to Brassey and Ballard', and 'Success to the New Railway', with flags suspended from the windows of the house. From the factory of Messrs W. Hall and Co., to the house of Mr B. Stephens, opposite, were suspended several flags. Towards the time when the first train was due, numbers of people, of all sizes and ages, thronged the way leading to the station, and continued to do so until after the excursion train had departed; and in the evening all available space near the station was crowded with people waiting for the appearance of the excursion train, which arrived at the station about 8 pm. Besides those who went to Evesham, many treated themselves with a ride, either to Alcester, Redditch, or Birmingham, and we believe it to be the general opinion of all who tried it, that the line is all that can be desired.

At Redditch, there were only moderate celebrations, with the *Worcester Herald* reporting that a sheep was roasted at the Rifleman Inn, in Park Road, and nearby the station. This newspaper recorded the number of passengers on the excursion as 569, so presumably they had inside information! The *Redditch Indicator* of this date meanwhile confined itself to an account of the day out in Evesham for the excursionists, and included a rather pithy comment about the dinner enjoyed by 'the good folks' at Alcester. Perhaps their reporter had not been invited. All in all, everyone enjoyed themselves on this day, which was apparently blessed with fine weather.

Final events for the company

With the opening of the through route, and the new station at Redditch, the old station in Clive Road was closed. It is believed to have survived as both a store, and a house for a number of years, but it is not clear when it was finally demolished.

The Evesham & Redditch Railway continued as a separate and nominally independent company, providing dividends for its shareholders until its ultimate demise. The first dividend was declared at a Shareholders' Meeting held at the Raven Hotel in Shrewsbury on 28th September, 1869. This dividend amounted to 5 per cent, and was the largest to be declared by the company. In each subsequent year until 1882, interim and final dividends were declared in March and August or September of each year. Successively, these totalled 2½, 3, 3¼, 3⅛, 3⅜, 3¼, 3¾, 3⅝, 4½, 3¾ and 3¼ per cent. A final dividend of 1⅓ per cent was distributed upon absorption.

Under Section 29 of the Midland Railway (Additional Powers) Act of 12th July, 1882 (Vict. 45 & 46, cap. 130), the railway was absorbed by the MR with effect from 1st July, 1882. The final event was the dissolution of the company under Section 31 of the Midland Railway Act of 25th June, 1886 (Vict. 49 & 50, cap. 113).

Another view around 1900 of Redditch station, this time looking south from the footbridge. A down train of six wheelers has been brought to a stand, as a northbound train approaches, hauled almost certainly by a Johnson 0-6-0. The vaulted portion of the canopy over the down platform is noticeable on the left, and the narrow waiting room on the up platform on the right. *Author's Collection*

Chapter Five

Connections at Broom Junction

At Broom, a single line from Stratford-on-Avon swept in from the east to join the Evesham & Redditch Railway. Although this line was built by the Evesham, Redditch & Stratford-on-Avon Railway, it connected to, and had the backing of, the East & West Junction Railway. However, prior to the opening of this line in 1879, there had been several earlier attempts to construct similar lines in this area, most of which were intended to continue further westwards to Worcester. To help to understand the final outcome, we shall now look at each of these, in chronological order.

Warwickshire & London Railway

Predating the Redditch Railway and the Evesham & Redditch Railway, this railway consisted of two lines, one of which, from Ashchurch to Hampton-in-Arden was described in Chapter Three. Here we are concerned with the second line, which was proposed to run from Worcester to Weedon in Northamptonshire, with branches to Droitwich and Alcester. Both lines were engineered by Robert Stephenson, and plans were deposited at Worcester on 30th November, 1845. It may be remembered from Chapter Two, that the London, Warwick, Leamington & Kidderminster Railway also proposed a route from Weedon to Worcester in 1845. However, this latter was surveyed by John Addison and the route was quite different, not passing through Broom.

This line commenced near to Foregate Street in Worcester, at first proceeding northwards, then turning at right angles to the east near Rainbow Hill, to cross the OWWR. It continued eastwards via Warndon, Oddingley, Huddley, Huddington, Grafton Flyford, Dormston and Abbots Morton to Broom. Here a triangle was to have been formed, with a single track branch of 3 miles 1½ chains heading north to Alcester. The line continued eastwards through Binton, passing to the south of Stratford, then via Kineton to Fenny Compton, where it would have crossed the Birmingham & Oxford Junction Railway, to which it was also to be connected by way of a west to south spur. Continuing eastwards via Byfield and Charwelton the line joined the London & Birmingham Railway at Weedon at a south-facing junction. The length of the main line was given as 54 miles exactly. The single-track branch to Droitwich was to have left the main line at Huddington by an east-facing junction, and run for 4½ miles to a north-facing junction with the OWWR just south of Droitwich station.

This proposal was backed by the London & Birmingham Railway, which in the previous year, 1844, had also prepared plans for an alternative scheme from Weedon to Worcester, titled the London, Worcester & South Staffordshire Railway. This passed south of our area, and from Worcester was to continue to Kidderminster, Stourbridge and Wolverhampton. Both of these lines were withdrawn after the GWR-backed Birmingham & Oxford Junction Railway and the OWWR received Royal Assent in 1846. But the seeds for future schemes had been sown.

PROPOSED LINES BETWEEN BROOM AND WORCESTER

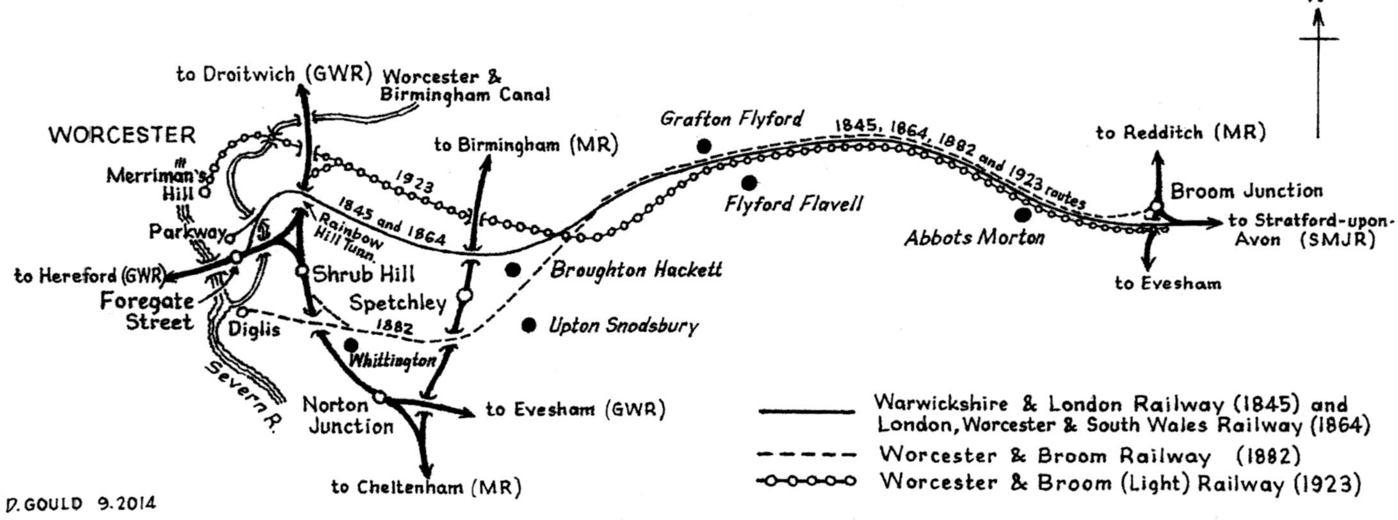

London, Worcester & South Wales Railway

On 23rd June, 1864 the East & West Junction Railway (EWJR) had been authorized to construct its line from Towcester to Stratford. Later in the same year, this scheme sought to connect with the proposed EWJR line at Stratford, and use running powers over that line to connect with the London & North Western Railway (LNWR) at Blisworth. Its own line then followed a similar route to Worcester as the Warwickshire & London Railway , where it was to provide its own terminus station at Parkway, near to Foregate Street. It was also to make a west-facing junction with the GWR near to Foregate Street station, so that it could then enjoy running powers over the latter's lines to South Wales, and thus to justify its title!

At Broom, the line was to connect to the proposed Evesham & Redditch Railway by an east to north spur, then to cross over this line before continuing to Worcester.

The company had been formed on 8th November, 1864 and the plans deposited at Worcester on 30th November, 1864 were engineered by James B. Burke, in which the line was given as 22 miles and 3 furlongs. The local press followed events with some interest, and the *Alcester Chronicle* reported that its enabling Act had passed 'standing orders' on 24th January 1865, and approved by the Select Committee on 16th June, 1865 despite opposition from the GWR. Slightly earlier, a rival branch line from Broom to Stratford, engineered by Edward Richards, on behalf of the Evesham & Redditch Railway, was dismissed by a Committee of the House of Commons in April 1865. The London, Worcester & South Wales Railway Act of 24th January, 1865 (Vict. 28 & 29, cap. 170) provided for share capital of some £320,000 with loan facilities of up to £106,000. A further Act in the following year (Vict. 28 & 29, cap. 164), authorized some minor diversions, but despite a promising start, the line lacked financial resources and was never built.

Alcester & Stratford-on-Avon Railway

This line of 8½ miles was virtually identical to the proposed 1865 branch of the Evesham & Redditch Railway from Broom to Stratford, although the engineers were given as James B. Burke and Joseph F. Burke. The plans were deposited at Warwick on 29th November, 1870 but once again nothing more was heard of this enterprise.

Evesham, Redditch & Stratford-on-Avon Junction Railway

This was a revival of the earlier branch of the Evesham & Redditch Railway from Broom to Stratford, and was more successful, in that Royal Assent was granted on 5th August, 1873 (Vict. 36 & 37, cap. 145) for the 7¾ mile single line railway. The Engineer was again James B. Burke. The Act also authorized incorporation of the company with a share capital of £90,000 and loans of up to £30,000. This company was much more substantial than the 1864 scheme in that the whole of the share capital was taken up by the promoters, who were the 'proprietors and other persons interested in the EWJR', even without the provision of any interest. The Act also provided for running powers over the Evesham & Redditch Railway, although this was never used except for the 5 chains between the junction and the station at Broom. The line was constructed without any known problems, although a cutting of about 25 ft deep and ½ mile in length was necessary at Summer Hill near Bidford.

The resident engineer was a Mr D.A. Stanley. The original plans included a triangular junction at Broom with both north- and south-facing junctions on to the Evesham & Redditch Railway, but the south-facing junction was dropped in a deviation to the plans, deposited at Warwick on 15th June, 1877. The line was completed by October 1878 and inspected by Major-General Hutchinson of the Board of Trade on the 10th of that month. A report in the *Alcester Chronicle* of 12th October, 1878 suggested that the coal requirements of Stratford would in future be met by the MR using this new line, as it had previously to send coal using the GWR route. It was expected that large new coal wharves would be erected at Stratford to cope with this traffic. The report concluded with the expectation that the line would open 'within the next few weeks'. It would seem that the reporter had gained the distinct impression that there was no particular urgency in the matter of earning revenue. He was correct, as the line did not open from Broom to both passengers and goods until 2nd June, 1879 and was worked by the EWJR from the outset.

As Broom Junction was only an exchange platform, it was not shown in public timetables until 1st November, 1880. So in the intervening period, passengers could not start or terminate their journeys at Broom, instead they could only transfer from Evesham or Redditch trains to Stratford trains, or vice versa. Binton was at first the only intermediate station, with Bidford not opening until 22nd February, 1885. Running powers were also given to the Easton Neston Mineral & Towcester, Roade & Olney Junction Railway (later to become the Stratford-upon-Avon, Towcester & Midland Junction Railway) in their Act of 15th August, 1879 from Towcester to Broom. Thus it can be seen that Broom was beginning to form the hub for several potentially useful routes.

The opening service on this line on 2nd June, 1879 was performed by outside-cylinder 2-4-0 No. 4A *Ceres*, which continued until August of that year when it was replaced by inside-cylinder Beyer, Peacock 0-6-0ST No. 1. *Ceres* is believed to have been purchased from the famous contractor Thomas Brassey, although it may have been only hired. Its origin is uncertain, but it is generally accepted to have come from France, possibly via Thomas Crampton, who had many interests in France and was the primary contractor for the EWJR in 1871. The Beyer, Peacock No. 1 (Works No. 1830 of 1879) was purchased new from the makers, but its limited water capacity proved to be a liability, so it was sold in 1890 to the Rother Vale Collieries Co., for use at their Treeton Colliery, near Sheffield. In 1929 it was unusually given the running number, 'No. 0', and survived nationalization until scrapped in 1959.

Services continued at the frequency of five trains each way, although one of the up trains only ran on Tuesdays and Fridays. In August 1866 the EWJR purchased a Yorkshire Engine Co. 2-4-0T No. 1 *Hope* (Works No. 185 of 1872) from the defunct Potteries, Shrewsbury & North Wales Railway, which was regularly seen on services between Broom and Stratford until 1895, as its water capacity was too small for it to work eastwards from Stratford. This engine had an eventful life, as it was later sold to the dealer B.P. Blockley of Bloxwich, Staffordshire who subsequently sold it on to the Cannock & Rugeley Collieries Co. Ltd in 1905. There it became their No. 8 *Harrison*, and in 1916 was rebuilt as an 0-6-0T, finally being scrapped in 1955.

Thereafter, passenger trains appearing at Broom were likely to have been in the charge of Beyer, Peacock 2-4-0T Nos. 5 and 6 (2466/7 of 1884), or Beyer, Peacock 2-4-0 No. 13 (4495 of 1903). As passenger trains were air braked only until about 1903, any of the three air-braked Beyer, Peacock 0-6-0s, Nos. 10, 11 and 12 (Works Nos. 3613 of 1895, 3812 of 1896 and 4126 of 1900) may also have deputized during times of shortage. Liveries of the EWJR locomotives were crimson lake lined in black, and edged in yellow on both sides of the linings. Metal number plates were fitted to the cab sides. However, after 1903 all new engines appeared in a dark blue.

The working of Broom station was of some interest, as although this consisted of a single island platform, it was initially treated as two separate single lines. The western face was used by the Stratford trains, and the eastern face by trains on the Redditch to Evesham route, and so the two single lines crossed at the south end of the station. This practice only lasted until October 1892, when, following a visit from the Board of Trade inspector, Major Marindin, new signalling arrangements that permitted the use of the island platform as a loop were approved.

Regrettably, the EWJR had never achieved its expectations, and had been in the hands of the Receiver since 1875. Matters did not improve, and this inevitably affected the Evesham, Redditch and Stratford-on-Avon Railway Company, which joined it in the Receiver's hands on 2nd June, 1886. In fact, all passenger traffic on the EWJR, except for that between Broom and Stratford, ceased during the years from 1877 to 1885. Operations on the whole line from Broom to Blisworth were controlled by a committee with the lengthy title of 'The East & West Junction, Stratford-on-Avon, Towcester & Midland Junction Railway Companies Joint Committee', which was empowered by an Act of 1883 to work the line. This committee was formed of representatives of all of the railway companies involved, but did not take over operation until 13th April, 1891.

It is interesting to note that at a Directors' Meeting of the Evesham & Redditch Railway on 22nd March, 1880 it was reported that the EWJR 'had failed to develop traffic and had not worked trains according to its agreement'. Evidently the MR were not satisfied with the efficiency of their partner at Broom, and in December, 1881 the MR agreed to the joint management of Broom Junction and to the sharing of costs.

The line survived due to its usefulness as a through route, with even the London & North Western Railway taking an interest. On 15th March, 1887 they began a trial goods service from Blisworth to Broom Junction. Unfortunately, it proved to yield little traffic, and was curtailed on 31st October, 1888.

The MR had a much more strategic interest in the line, as it afforded it a much shorter route from London to Bristol, than by using their main lines via Burton or Derby and Birmingham. From 13th April, 1891 it began a regular goods service from London (Somers Town) to Avonmouth, using its own engines. In the reverse direction, these trains notably conveyed bananas landed at Avonmouth Docks. However, the MR engines proved too heavy for the track, and so EWJR engines were used between Olney and Broom and in December 1891 the EWJR purchased three ex-LNWR Ramsbottom 'DX' 0-6-0s (LNWR Duplicate Nos. 1891, 1945 and 1966) which were used on these services.

The passenger service over the whole line to Blisworth had been reinstated in 1885, and by January 1903 consisted of departures from Broom at 8.17, 11.10 am, 2.37 and 6.17 pm.

An attempt to sell the Evesham, Redditch & Stratford-on-Avon Junction Railway, along with the EWJR was made in 1901, but was unsuccessful. The whole concern struggled on until the passing of the Stratford-on-Avon & Midland Junction Railway (Amalgamation) Act of 1st August, 1908 (8 Edw. 7, cap. 77) which enabled all of the companies to combine into one as from 1st January, 1909, which we shall look at shortly.

Broom East signal box and junction as seen from the Stratford direction in July 1960 just a few weeks after the official closing of the route eastwards. The more frequently used line towards Evesham curves away to the left, and that towards Broom Junction station and Alcester to the right.

N. Forrest/Transport Treasury

A view southwards from beneath the road overbridge at Broom, showing the 1934 Broom North signal box. This LMS-style gabled ended box was a replacement for both the Broom South signal box on the same site, and also for the original Broom North located at the north end of the station platform. The Stratford line curves away to the left beyond the box, and the date is around 1960.

J. Tarrant/Kidderminster Railway Museum

Worcester & Broom Railway

Plans for this 14 mile line were deposited at Worcester on 29th November, 1881, with the Engineer being given as Joseph F. Burke, who had engineered the 1870 scheme. However, it was not until 14th August, 1885 that it received its enabling Act (Vict. 48 & 49, cap. 200), and is believed to have been sponsored yet again by the backers of the EWJR. The interchange at Broom featured an additional spur, running from west to north, thereby creating a triangle as well as a crossing of the Evesham & Redditch Railway, then continued on the same route westwards until near Broughton Hackett, where it took a more southerly direction than the earlier schemes, crossing the MR main line south of Spetchley, and the GWR Oxford line near to Whittington. At this point a further spur was envisaged, running east to north to join that railway just south of Shrub Hill station. The line then continued west to terminate at a station at Diglis, close to the banks of the River Severn and the basin of the Worcester & Birmingham Canal.

Although construction started at Broom, and an embankment was begun on the western side of the Evesham & Redditch Railway, work was soon stopped. Once again financial difficulties were apparently to blame, and bearing in mind the circumstances of the EWJR at this time, it is not surprising. Despite extensions of time being granted to this scheme under the Worcester & Broom Railway Acts of 1888 (Vict. 51 & 52, cap. 15) and 1892 (Vict. 55 & 56, cap. 119) no further progress was made, and the Act of 1st July, 1894 (Vict. 57 & 58, cap. 11) formally abandoned the project.

Stratford & Midland Junction Railway

Continuing this chronological survey, the Stratford & Midland Junction Railway (SMJR) came into being on 1st January, 1909 at which time the first train of the day had been curtailed to run to Stratford only, with the remainder running largely as in 1903. Thus at Broom, the weekday arrivals were from Stratford at 8.00 am, and from Blisworth at 10.50 am, 2.20 and 6.00 pm. In the reverse direction trains departed for Stratford only at 8.17 am, and through services from Broom to Blisworth at 11.10 am, 2.41 and 6.20pm. There were no Sunday services.

By 1915, the arrivals continued as before, but the third one originated at Kineton, and the last from Stratford. The first departure was retimed to 8.15 am and ran through to Kineton, the next two departures were continued, but the last train now only ran to Byfield. By 1921, the first train had been discontinued, and only the 10.52 am arrival (with return at 11.15 am) ran to/ from Blisworth. The remaining two trains, arriving at 2.30 and 8.00 pm, and departing at 3.10 and 9.10 pm were for Stratford only. These services continued after absorption of the SMJR into the LMS in the Grouping of 1923.

Services had improved a little by April 1933, with four (Monday to Friday) and five (Saturdays) trains in each direction. Arrivals were at 7.43 am from Stratford, 10.47 am from Blisworth, then from Stratford at 2.36, 5.50 (Saturdays only), 8.00 (Saturdays excepted) and 8.36 pm (Saturdays only). Departures were at 8.12 am for Stratford, 11.15 am for Blisworth, then Stratford at 2.58, 6.30 (Saturdays only), and 8.55 pm. These services continued into 1937, although there were slight changes to the departure times of the first, third and last trains of the day.

The outbreak of war in 1939 brought about a reduction in services to two each way, curiously and perhaps somewhat inconveniently both running in the morning. The

Broom Junction station in the early 1930s as seen from the boarded crossing, which provided the only pedestrian access to the station. The original Midland Railway angled running-in boards are visible, one for each direction, and the grounded coach body on the platform was even then in use as a store, probably for parcels. Broom North signal box (removed in 1934) can be seen in the centre right distance. *Roy F. Burrows Collection/Kidderminster Railway Museum*

A view southwards from the road overbridge at Broom Junction on 18th May 1930, showing the line towards Stratford curving off to the left, and the Evesham line continuing straight ahead. The hipped roof of the second Broom Junction South signal box (replaced in 1934) is in the left foreground. On the right is the 40 ft 10 in. turntable, installed for the benefit of locomotives on through trains between Stratford and Evesham until the south chord was installed in 1942, shortly after which the turntable was removed. *C. Gilbert/Kidderminster Railway Museum*

first train ran between Broom and Stratford, and the second train was the through working to Blisworth. These services remained until the last train ran on 16th June 1947, although passenger services were not officially withdrawn until 23rd May, 1949.

Motive power for the passenger services continued mostly as prior to 1909, mainly because of the SMJR use of air-braked stock using the rather low pressure of 50-55 psi, compared to 70 psi when used by other railways, and its very slow conversion to vacuum-braked stock. However, it was not unknown for one of the two Stroudley 'Terrier' 0-6-0Ts owned by the Edge Hill Light Railway to be borrowed when the SMJR was short of motive power. SMJR locomotives retained their EWJR style number plates, but were painted black with a green and yellow lining, and featured the letters 'SMJ' painted in gold on their tenders. Any of the nine Beyer, Peacock 0-6-0s, which were allocated the LMS Nos. 2300-2 and 2304-9 were also likely to turn up on passenger workings as likely as goods workings, until their eventual replacement by LMS 'Standard' types of 0-6-0 from 1924 onwards.

Turning to the goods services, the MR through 'banana trains' from Avonmouth to London continued until 30th September, 1912 when they were rerouted via Wigston and Birmingham. These trains had also conveyed other goods from Bristol, notably hardware. Coal traffic was also seen passing along the route, this time arriving from the Warwickshire coalfields, via Redditch, and passing on to the Great Central Railway at Woodford en route to their destination at Neasden.

However, by the 1930s the LMS had reintroduced several through goods services to Bristol over the route. Daily express goods for St Pancras were due to pass Broom at 3.33 and 9.40 am, and for Bristol at 3.38 and 5.25 am. The 'banana specials' for Avonmouth had been reintroduced, and ran 'as required', passing through at 4.22, 6.10 and 8.05 pm. Of course, at this time only the east to north spur existed, so that all such trains had to reverse or change engines at Broom. For this purpose, a turntable of 40 ft 10 in. diameter had been provided at Broom, on the up side, opposite the junction. It is presumed to have been installed shortly after the opening of the line, as even tank engines were totally prohibited from running bunker first on the section to Stratford. After the LMS upgraded the line, these through workings taken on by MR Johnson 0-6-0s, although subsequently they were handled by the able Fowler '4F' 0-6-0s. Local goods workings were powered by these former MR designs of 0-6-0, although a number of former Lancashire & Yorkshire Railway Aspinall '11' class 0-6-0s are known to have been used until 1933, for example LMS Nos. 12103, 12105, 12107 and 12119. Johnson MR '2228' class 0-4-4Ts Nos. 1418, 1419, 1426 and 1427 are also known to have worked from Stratford shed, on both goods and passenger duties.

A new spur was installed during World War II, running east to south for some 35 chains (nearly ½ mile) to eliminate the necessity for reversal at Broom of heavy wartime traffic over the SMJR route to Bristol and to South Wales, opening on 17th May, 1942. A new LMS pattern gable-ended signal box was installed at Broom East Junction, to control the two connecting spurs, and came into operation on the same day. A further new signal box was added at Broom West Junction on the up side of the Redditch line, coming into use on 29th September of that year. This box was of the ARP design which incorporated a concrete floor and 14 in. thick walls, hopefully to survive the attention of the Luftwaffe! Not only did this new curve assist the war effort, but with peacetime the route was seen to have gained new potential. Eventually, from 4th June, 1951 the opportunity was taken to run through trains servicing the steel industry from the Great Central route at Woodford West Junction, and from Banbury through to South Wales. By 1956 there were five trains from South Wales to Woodford each way, two of which in each direction did not run on Monday mornings, but did on Sundays, with the effect

SMJR 0-6-0 No.11 was built by Beyer, Peacock (Works No. 3812) in May 1896. It subsequently ran firstly as LMSR No. 2305 and later as No. 2398, and was withdrawn in June 1930. Although principally a goods engine, it was more than likely used on passenger turns occasionally. *Real Photographs*

SMJR 2-4-0 No. 13 was the only engine of this type built for the SMJR, and was purchased for working the through coaches from the GCR at Woodford to Stratford-on-Avon, and so was fitted with both air and vacuum brakes. It was the only purely passenger engine on this railway, which really only had the need for mixed traffic engines. It would have made regular appearances at Broom Junction. Built by Beyer, Peacock (Works No. 4495) in July 1903, it was withdrawn in April 1924 without having carried its allotted LMS number, 290. *Real Photographs*

This view at Stratford-on-Avon SMJR shed shows 0-6-0 No. 17 (built by Beyer, Peacock for the EWJR in November, 1907, Works No. 5102). Larger than the earlier engines, it nonetheless retains the traditional outside frames and springs above the running plate. It was renumbered 2311 by the LMS and withdrawn in March 1925. Behind can be seen one of the former LBSCR Stroudley 'A1X' 0-6-0Ts that were to be seen on the SMJR line. One (SMJR No. 7) was purchased in November 1920 and condemned in November 1924. The other two (purchased in April 1919 and July 1920) actually belonged to the Edge Hill Light Railway (its Nos. 1 and 2), but were maintained by the SMJR at Stratford. *Real Photographs*

Typical SMJR passenger stock included the composite first/second four-wheeler No. 6, seen on the left as converted to a six-wheeler about 1910. This was originally built by the Birmingham Railway Carriage & Wagon Co. in 1885, as was the former third class four-wheeler No. 10 seen next to it. This coach was substantially rebuilt in 1909 to a six-wheel saloon with high grade furnishings for use as an inspection coach and by Directors. Nevertheless it was included in normal trains, as seen here. Both were painted in crimson lake all over at this time (although No. 10 has retained a white roof), thereby conforming to the Midland Railway style. *Real Photographs*

that the line closed only from 6.00 am Sunday to 6.00 am Monday. There were also four Gloucester to Stratford trains daily, and one Westerleigh (Bristol) to Clifford Sidings (Stratford) each way. Local traffic was catered for by three local workings between Broom and Stratford, mostly with exchange traffic from the Redditch line. All of this traffic meant that both spurs were in fairly constant use. The south curve had initially been subject to a 15 mph limit and the north curve to 12 mph, although both were later eased to 20 mph. The wartime Riddles 'WD' class 2-8-0s and BR Standard '9Fs' from Ebbw Junction shed (Newport) became synonymous with these workings for many years, although both LMS Stanier '8Fs' and Churchward/Collett GWR 2-8-0s were not unknown. The local goods workings were powered by Stratford's allocation of 0-6-0s, which in February 1953 comprised Johnson '3F' Nos. 43520 and 43568, and Fowler '4F' Nos. 43873, 44043, 44186, 44242, 44524, 44567 and 44587. Although no locomotives were officially allocated to Stratford after that date, they continued to be stabled there, until closure of the shed on 22nd July, 1957 - although the shed had actually been demolished the week before!

In 1960, a new east to south spur was installed at Stratford (Old Town) to connect the SMJR to the former GWR route from Birmingham and Stratford via Honeybourne to Cheltenham and Gloucester. At the same time a south to west spur was installed at Fenny Compton, to enable trains to run directly from Banbury to Stratford without reversal. Although the connection at Stratford was ready on 7th March, 1960 and the new signalling implemented by 24th April, through running over the new route (including trains from the Great Central line) did not begin until 12th June, 1960. The line from Stratford to Broom was therefore closed completely from the next day, including both curves at Broom.

The SMJR was not to be denied 'the last rites' by railway enthusiasts, and a number of special trains passed over the entire route, hauled by a variety of locomotive types, including an LMS Compound 4-4-0, a Fowler '2P' Clas 4-4-0, a GWR 'Dukedog' (No. 9015), and even Holden ex-GER 'B12' class 4-6-0 No. 61572 made it to Stratford. One dmu tour from Birmingham in 1960 managed to include both of the curves at Broom in its itinerary.

Worcester & Broom (Light) Railway

Never one to overlook a lost cause, the inimitable Colonel Holman F. Stephens promoted this scheme in 1923, by way of a Light Railway Order. The plans were deposited at Worcester on 30th November, 1923 at 11.00 am. At Broom there were no further spurs envisaged, and the line continued westwards on the same alignment as earlier schemes, until near to Grafton Flavell where it diverged firstly southwards, then after a mile or so, swung northwards to cross the original planned routes, and to pass beneath the MR main line north of Bredicot. In Worcester the line passed beneath the GWR Droitwich line at Blackpole, where it made connection by way of an east to south spur. Shortly after it crossed the Worcester & Birmingham Canal, and then kept fairly close to it until reaching a terminus 56 yards north of St. George's Lane North, near Hangman's Hill. The Act quite astonishingly gave running powers over the LMS line to Redditch and to Evesham, over the SMJR to Stratford, and over the GWR to Shrub Hill station in Worcester.

Despite Colonel Stephens determined efforts, which culminated in a public enquiry in Worcester on 21st March, 1924 the project lapsed in 1926 when it was removed from the list of applications before the Minister of Transport.

Chapter Six

Description of the line

As we have already seen, **Barnt Green** was situated on the Birmingham & Gloucester Railway and the station opened there on 1st May, 1844. The area had hitherto attracted little attention, but after the opening of the railway, the tourist appeal of the nearby Lickey Hills began to have a much more immediate impact than had previously been possible. Now even half-day trips from Birmingham to enjoy the fresh air and beauty of the district were possible. Inevitably, such benefits attracted the more wealthy families, who could afford to build houses there, away from the spreading industrialization of Birmingham and the Black Country, and so a new community was born.

The B&GR station was provided with two staggered platforms, the down platform being in the present position south of the junction, and the up platform being north of this junction. Access to the up platform was via a boarded crossing from the down platform, although a footbridge was later installed.

When the Redditch Railway was opened, the up branch platform was placed joining the down main line platform, with the down branch platform opposite. A turntable was installed in the angle between the branch and main line platforms, which can only have had a minimal amount of use, as after the opening of the through route in 1868 there were few trains terminating at Barnt Green, and there had been only a small number before that date.

Initially the station was named 'Barnt Green', but this changed to 'Barnt Green for Redditch' on 1st June, 1857 when a horse-drawn omnibus connection was available. This was changed again prior to 1st January, 1863 to 'Barnt Green for Bromsgrove Lickey', and then finally reverting to simply 'Barnt Green' from 1st July, 1868 shortly after the through route to Evesham and Ashchurch was opened. The station nameboards at this time were white letters on a blue background, which was the standard MR configuration at this time, and several similar examples of more minor notices along the line lasted until closure.

The junction signals were worked at first by watchmen and switchmen at the station under the supervision of the MR, and part of their costs were charged to the Redditch Railway until absorption. The first signal box, sited on the up main line platform and controlling the junction opened in 1869. A Single Line Junction signal box was erected on the up side of the branch line in 1883, at the start of the single line section. During a major reconstruction in 1894, the double track section of the branch line was extended by 350 yards southwards, including widening of the bridge over Hewell Road, and the Single Line box repositioned accordingly, still on the up side of the line. These changes came into operation as from 9th December of that year. The turntable was removed, and both of the branch platform faces were similarly extended. Unfortunately, the sharp curve of the branch could not be eliminated without considerable rerouting of the line, and this, combined with the falling gradient of 1 in 74, would prove to be an operating nuisance, particularly for northbound trains. A lattice iron footbridge connecting the two branch platforms and the down main platform to the up main platform was also installed at this time. The main line platforms otherwise remained unaltered until 1927, when the up main platform was moved further south so that it was opposite the down main platform, and on the site of what had been an up refuge siding.

Gradient Profile

For clarity minor gradient changes have been omitted

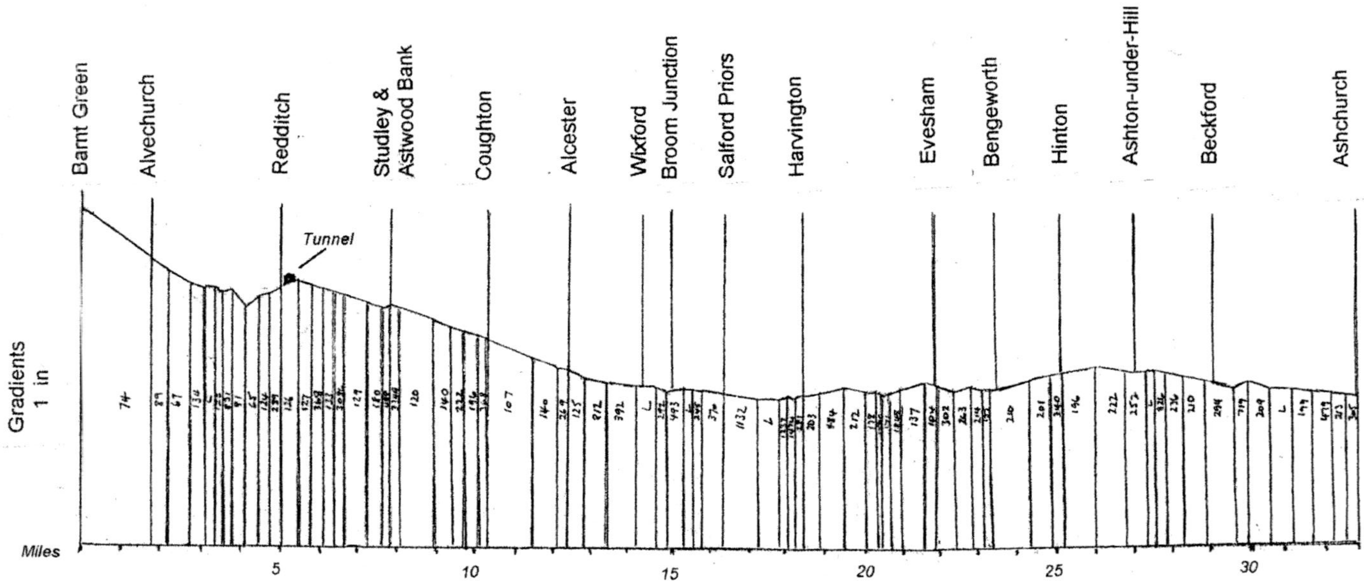

Barnt Green station around 1910, with the branch line platforms on the left and the down main platform in the centre. The original arrangement of staggered platforms for the main line is apparent, with the up main platform in the right foreground and continuing behind the photographer. A goods refuge siding occupies the site of the later up platform, on the right, beyond the footbridge. *Lens of Sutton/R. Carpenter*

The branch line platforms at Barnt Green, looking north towards the junction, probably around 1910. The original up main platform can be seen in the distance. The platform fencing is of spear and railing iron construction, but was later replaced by the more familiar MR diagonal wooden style. The chimney for the modest waiting room on the down branch line seems out of all proportion to the rest of the building. *G. Dow Collection/Kidderminster Railway Museum*

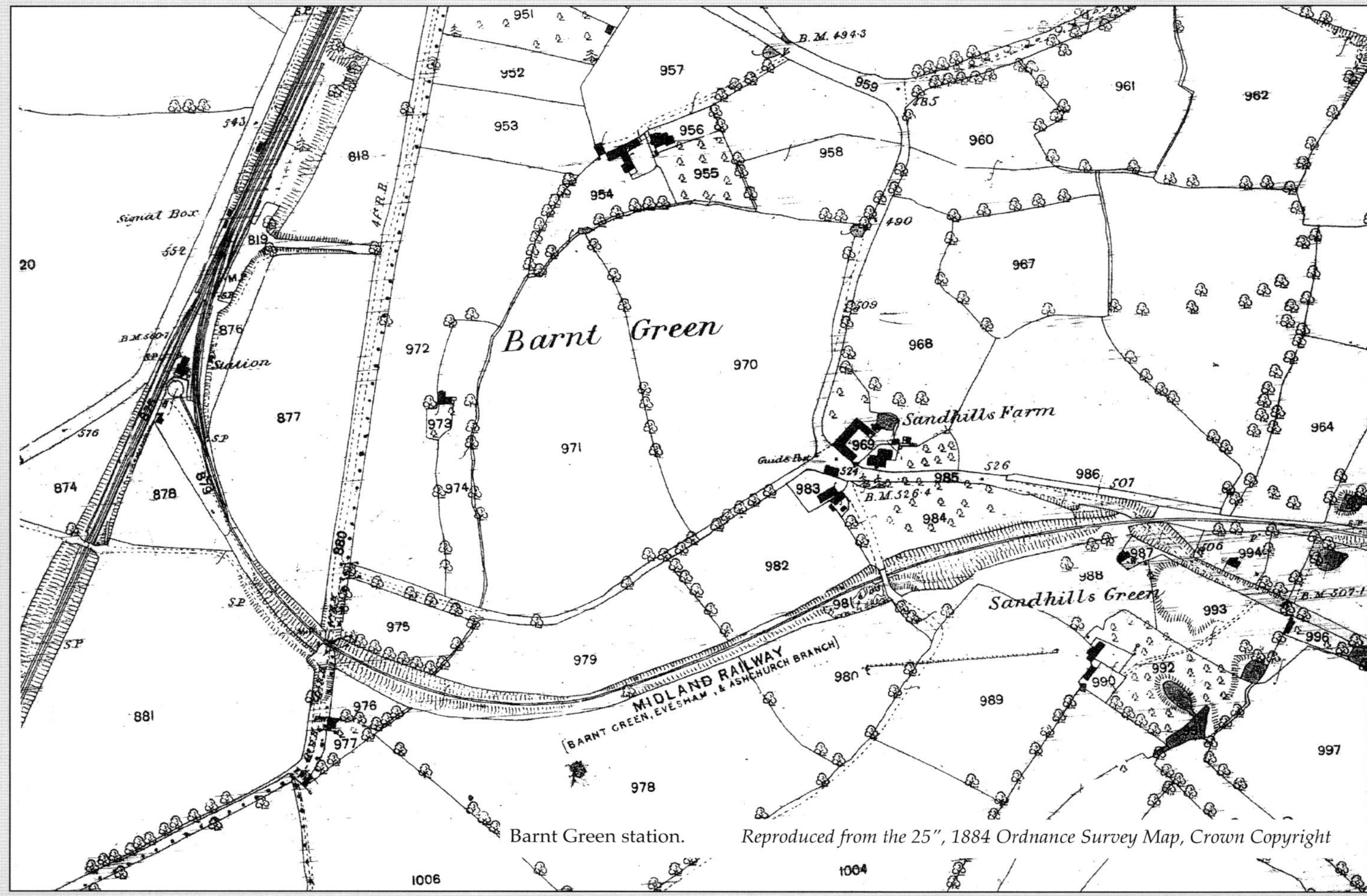

Barnt Green station. *Reproduced from the 25", 1884 Ordnance Survey Map, Crown Copyright*

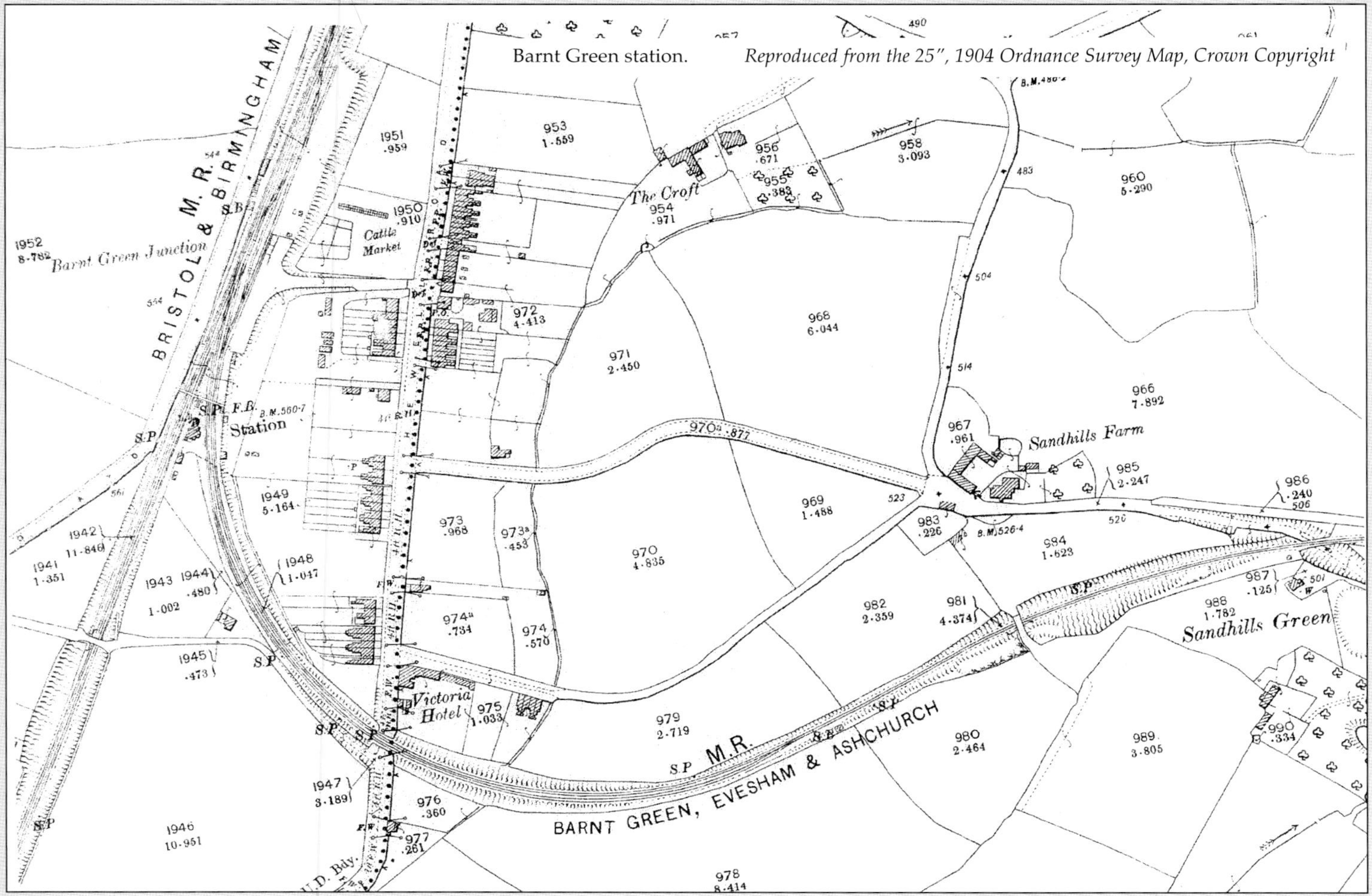

Barnt Green station. *Reproduced from the 25", 1904 Ordnance Survey Map, Crown Copyright*

One of the later batch of Fowler class '4' 2-6-4Ts fitted with side window cabs, No. 42416, pauses at Barnt Green en route for Birmingham New Street with a stopping train from Evesham in 1962.
Lens of Sutton/R. Carpenter

There are plenty of passengers at Barnt Green as 'Jubilee' class 4-6-0 No. 45576 *Bombay* arrives with an up main line local service on 22nd May, 1961. The convenience of this platform adjacent to Fiery Hill Road can be appreciated, as was the small bookstall (just behind the locomotive) which saw good business, not only from commuters, but from day trippers alighting here for a walk in the Lickey Hills.
Author

The station buildings from the opening of the Redditch Railway remained until the 1970s, consisting of a principal gable-ended red brick building of a vaguely triangular shape, in the fork of the platform faces, which combined as station master's house, booking hall, toilets and staff accommodation. The red brick construction was pleasingly offset by white ornamental stone and brick quoins around the doorways and windows. The fairly simple wooden passenger accommodation on the original up main platform was replaced by a more substantial gable-ended red brick waiting room on the new platform, which featured a cantilevered wooden awning. Simple red brick waiting shelters with gabled roofs and spacious glazing were provided on the branch platforms and a larger one on the down main platform, each one sporting a rather tall, centrally positioned chimney. Fencing along the rear of the branch platforms was originally of wrought-iron spear construction, later replaced by the familiar MR wooden sloping style. Access to the station had originally been via the roadway at the side of the up main platform, but after this was repositioned and the goods yard alongside the down main line was developed, the principal roadway was at the side of the down branch platform. Pedestrians then reached all other platforms by way of the footbridge, but a boarded crossing was provided across the northern ends of the platforms, for heavier loads to be transported. A separate pedestrian entrance was available at the south end of the down main platform.

A small goods yard was provided on the down side, north of the station, and included a goods shed and cattle dock. A water column may have been sited near to the early turntable, but otherwise no locomotive watering facilities were ever provided.

Leaving Barnt Green, the down starter signal was notable in being a survivor of the MR lower quadrant pattern signal until replaced by a British Railways upper quadrant signal in 1961. Passing 'Barnt Green Single Line' signal box (25 chains or ¼ mile), the driver accepted the token for the line to Redditch. This section of line was initially worked by the train staff and ticket method until replaced by electric train tablet working on 20th September, 1891.

Having turned through 90 degrees since leaving Barnt Green, the line now heads eastwards, but after passing through the sandstone cutting at Sandhills, it turns to head southwards and on to an embankment, leading shortly after to the crossing over the Worcester & Birmingham Canal on an 80 ft plate girder bridge, which was renewed by the MR in 1909. The line has been falling at a constant 1 in 74, and continues so, as half a mile later it passes beneath Station Road to enter **Alvechurch** station (1 mile 66 chains or 1¾ miles). This station was not quite ready for the opening of the line on 19th September, 1859, being finally opened some three weeks later on 10th October. The main two-storey gable-ended building was normally painted cream, featured a ground floor bay window on to the platform, and comprised the station master's accommodation. A single-storey red brick building was attached to the northern end, comprising the booking office and staff room. Next was a simple wooden hipped-roof waiting room, which may originally have been a goods shed, as the 1884 Ordnance Survey map shows a 'goods shed' in this position.

The goods yard contained one siding, with a capacity for 10 wagons, and accessible only in the down direction. A headshunt to the south could only be accessed by 'fly-shunting'. Indeed the Supplementary Regulations permitted the use of a tow rope by up trains. In earlier times, the use of horses to move wagons may have been a more practicable solution. In the yard, a weighbridge with attendant

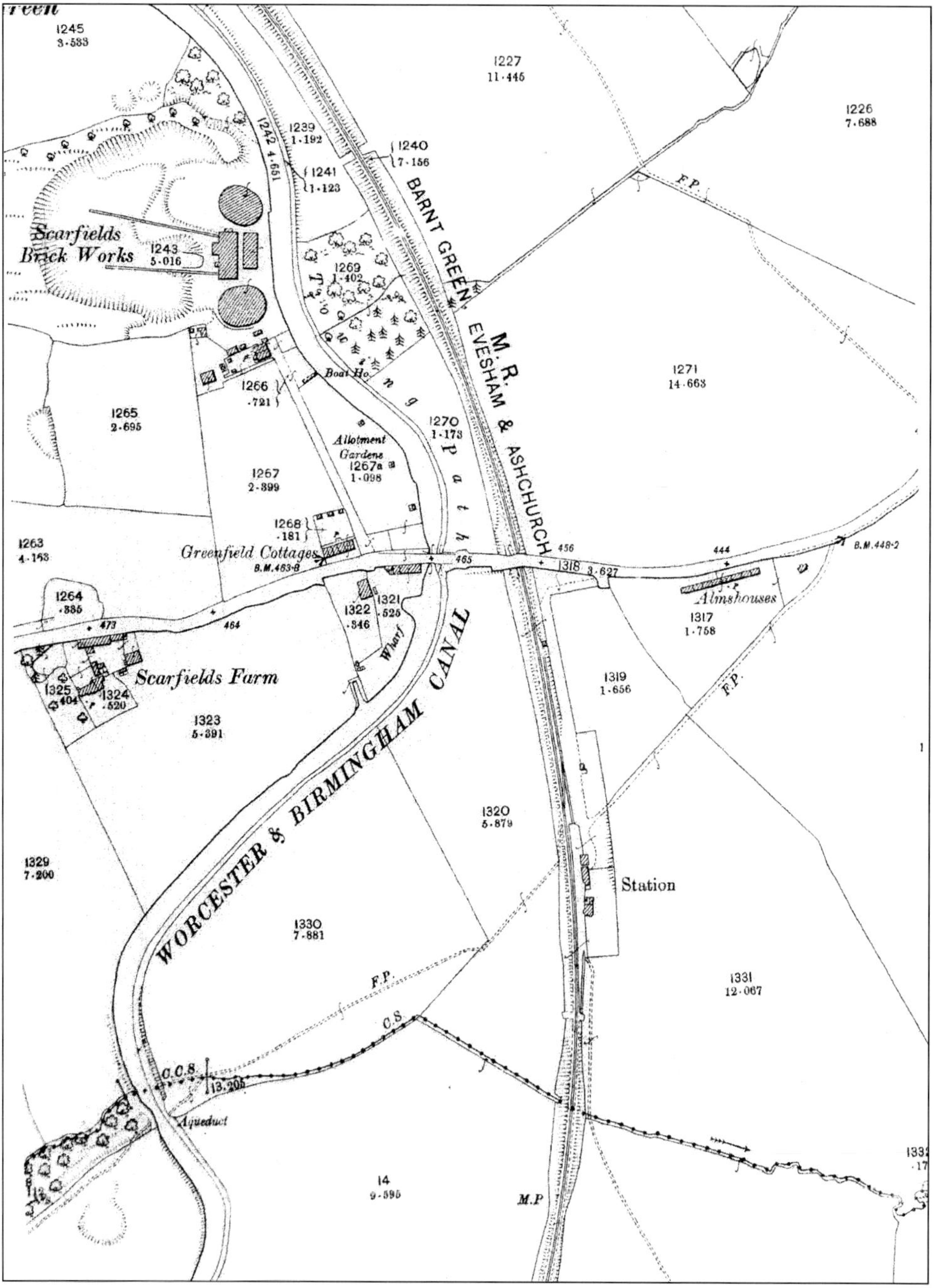

Alvechurch station. *Reproduced from the 25", 1904 Ordnance Survey Map, Crown Copyright*

Alvechurch station in the 1930s. At this time, the low hipped-roof building was still in use as a goods store. A family, complete with pram, await the next train. *Almonery Heritage Centre Collection*

Alvechurch station in 1962, revealing a well-tended platform, with roses tumbling over the fence. The substantial station master's accommodation is in the foreground, and in the background a number of coal wagons are standing in the single-road goods yard which was accessed from the running line by a single, south-facing point. Consequently, the siding extension nearest to the camera had to be 'fly-shunted', or perhaps in earlier days wagons were moved by the coal agent's horse. *Lens of Sutton/R. Carpenter*

Ivatt class '4' 2-6-0 No. 43036 rolls through the pastoral Worcestershire countryside from Alvechurch, and passes the Redditch down distant on 23rd July, 1962 with the 6.18 pm (Saturdays excepted) from Birmingham New Street to Evesham loaded to five coaches.
Author

Stanier class '5' 4-6-0 No. 44812 of Saltley shed accelerates a lightly loaded 7.10 pm (Saturdays excepted) Redditch to Lawley Street (Birmingham) class 'H' freight towards Butler's Hill on the northern outskirts of Redditch on 23rd July, 1962. *Author*

brick-built gable-ended office was the sole concession to goods traffic, although a coal merchant did later erect a small office. Certainly, in later years the only visible traffic appeared to be incoming coal.

Originally, a signal box had been provided (some time before 1st November, 1875), sited on the station platform, but this is believed to have been removed in 1885, as part of its necessity had already disappeared by that time, as we shall shortly see. Opposite the northern end of the platform ramp, a public footpath crossed the line on a boarded crossing, next to which was the ground frame for control of the points into the goods siding, unlocked by means of the train tablet. This was probably installed in 1885 with the removal of the signal box, and was contained in a corrugated iron hut. A further footpath from the south gave access to the station platform at the opposite end to the main driveway from Station Road.

Leaving Alvechurch, the line continues to descend, first at 1 in 89, then at 1 in 67, before easing and gradually levelling out, as it passes through pleasant, pastoral land, mixed with woods and copses on the slightly undulating countryside with fine uninterrupted views to the east. Amidst this landscape we arrive at the site of **Baroness Windsor's Model Farm Siding** (2¾ miles), which was at a rather isolated location near to Butler's Wood, and about ½ mile south of Shortwood Dingle. This comprised a single south-facing siding, accessible only to down trains, and for which the points were operated from a ground frame, unlocked by means of the key attached to the train staff or tablet. The site for this siding had been forecast as early as 7th August, 1859, when in a *Worcester Herald* of that date, it was stated that, 'At Butler's Wood is to be a short siding for the accommodation of conveying timber from the Hewell estate'. It was opened in July 1873, following an inspection by Colonel Yolland on behalf of the Board of Trade on the 14th of the month, but had been removed by 1884. As Baroness Windsor had been generous with her support for the original Redditch Railway, and in the sale of land for that purpose, the MR was presumably inclined to be reciprocal in its generosity in providing this facility, as well as mindful of the potential traffic to be derived. The removal of this siding would have been a primary factor in the decision to remove the signal box at Alvechurch, referred to above.

The line now starts to climb at various fairly easy grades, finally reaching a 30 ft embankment near Bordesley, on the outskirts of **Redditch,** and reaching a lofty steel plate girder bridge. This is supported on brick abutments at each end, and with two brick piers gives three openings under which pass Windsor Road, Sufford's Brook (also known as Batchley Brook) and an access road to the gas works site. Immediately afterwards on the west side was the looming presence of Redditch Gas Works, which although opening in 1843 was not rail served until 1864. In 1873 the works were expanded by the addition of three 40 ft gasholders, a meter house and a retort house, which were served by a single siding, adjacent to the Redditch Gas Siding hipped-roof signal box. At some time prior to 1903, two further sidings were put in, one parallel to the existing siding, and one curving round to the back of the works, where a shute was provided for the loading of coke directly into wagons. Access to this siding was prohibited to locomotives, and movements of wagons were made by capstan haulage. The siding next to the running line was designated as a reception road, from where wagons of incoming coal would be moved as required by locomotives to the inner siding on which was situated a rotary tippler. Here, incoming coal wagons were positioned so as to be inverted for discharge into a hopper for processing. Gas coal was sourced from collieries in South Yorkshire (mostly from Elsecar and Waleswood collieries), Nottinghamshire and Warwickshire and initially the wagons were stabled

Right: Ivatt class '4' Mogul No. 43012 passes Redditch gasworks on 7th January, 1961 with the 1.36 pm (Saturdays only) Barnt Green to Evesham, which originated from Kings Norton carriage sidings as an empty coaching stock working to Barnt Green. The loaded coal wagons in the foreground are waiting to be moved to the rotary wagon tippler for unloading, and the empty wagons on the left are waiting to be loaded with coke from the retort house. *Author*

Below: This 1962 view of Redditch station shows the rebuilt up platform waiting room with its extended cantilevered canopy with deep vertical edging, contrasting to the canopy on the down platform supported by cast-iron uprights, and edged with shallower and more decorative boarding. The footbridge, positioned against the side of the Bromsgrove Road overbridge shows up well. To the right and beneath the footbridge is the connecting 'tunnel' which lead to the original goods shed, in use as a parcels depot since around 1927. *Joe Moss/R. Carpenter*

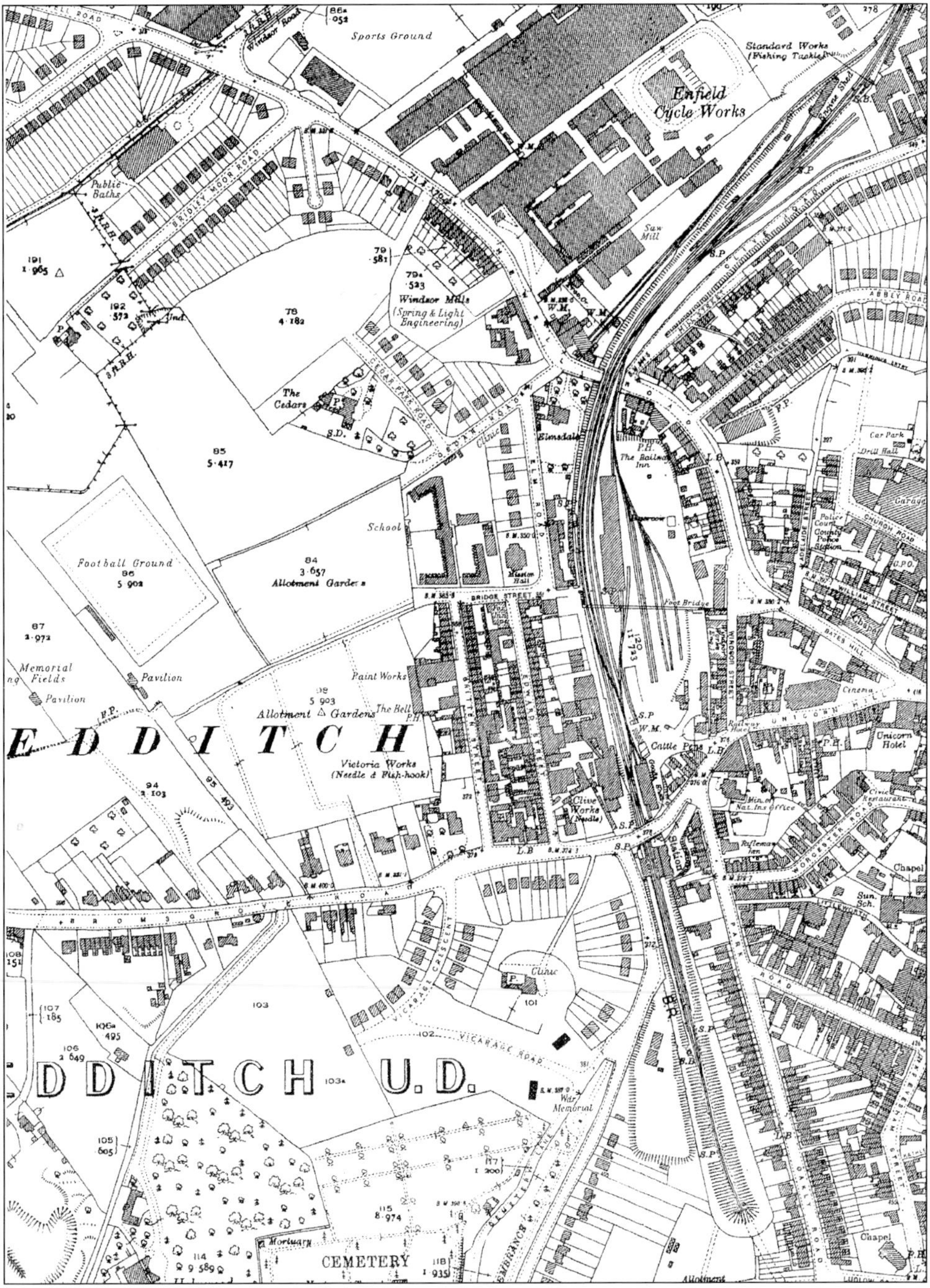

Redditch station. *Reproduced from the 25", 1948 Ordnance Survey Map, Crown Copyright*

Redditch station looking north around 1910. The original, narrow waiting room on the up platform can be seen on the left, and in the centre a tall inner home signal protrudes above the Bromsgrove Road overbridge. A shunting signal is sited beneath the road bridge on the down line, presumably for engines to use the crossover to the up line. This signal was later replaced by an upper quadrant on a short post sited to the right of the running line. An engine, possibly a Kirtley 0-6-0 is just visible in the goods yard through the overbridge. *Author's Collection*

The station approach at Redditch taken around 1905. Park Road veered off to the left, and the road crossing the bridge is Bromsgrove Road. The drive down to the station was quite steep, and in winter could be treacherous. The original station master's house is just visible to the left of the main station building. By the time the author was familiar with the station, the trees behind the central lamp post were about three times the height shown here ! *R.S. Carpenter Collection*

in the goods yard, and later in one of the sidings adjacent to Clive Road. They were called off from these positions, usually 10 at a time for the gas works. The works used around 18,000 tons of coal annually.

The line serving the gas works was originally part of the Redditch Railway goods line, which had been extended northwards. This continuation towards the gas works ran parallel to the main running line, beneath a double track railway underbridge carrying a minor lane, and was later often used for stabling of passenger stock during weekends. Southwards it continued on its original formation, behind and at a lower level than the engine shed, although the two goods sidings of the original goods yard were taken over by T. & M. Dixon's coal yard.

Before continuing with the description, it is necessary to explain the changes to the signalling and yards in Redditch after the opening of the through route in 1868. At that time the single line continued to a point just south of the crossing over Hewell Road, where lines first led from the north into the goods yard, and then the main line became double to run into the new (second) station. It is presumed that signalling and control of points to the goods sidings was effected from the station at that time. A signal box, named Redditch North was opened in 1885 on the up side south of the Hewell Road bridge, but before the footbridge from Bridge Street to Windsor Street was reached. This box replaced an earlier box (opened before 1875 and simply named 'Redditch'), and controlled entry into the goods yard, which comprised three long through sidings and one south-facing terminal road. The goods shed, with two roadside loading bays, was positioned on a site known as 'Pound Meadow' at the north side of the road overbridge carrying Bromsgrove Road, and nearby was a separate siding for a loading dock and cattle pens. Redditch South signal box was also opened in 1885, at the south end of the up platform where the line once more became single.

By 1904 the three goods loops had been reduced to two, and land purchased for a further four terminal sidings. The track was remodelled so that rail entry into the goods yard was reversed, being accessible from the south end only.

Around 1925/26 there was a further major remodelling of the trackwork at Redditch, requiring extensive additional construction. The double track was continued northwards adjacent to the engine shed, and the new Redditch North signal box (*see below*). An additional bridge over Hewell Road was constructed, carrying the new running line, plus two more leading into the goods yard, which was again remodelled to be accessible from the opposite direction, i.e. this time from the north. This then contained six sidings, and a headshunt was provided parallel to Clive Road, nearly reaching the original Redditch Railway station house, which was still extant at the time. All this work was completed when the following signal box changes came into effect on 17th January, 1926.

The MR Redditch Gas Siding signal box was closed and replaced by a new hipped-roof box of standard LMS design 125 yards further south, on 8th November, 1925 but not receiving the name Redditch North until 17th January, 1926. This box was situated at the rear of Allcock's fishing tackle works and directly opposite the engine shed, at the new point of the start of the double track working into Redditch. It also replaced the old, 1885 Redditch North box which closed at the same time. The old Redditch South signal box was also replaced by a new LMS hipped-roof box on the same site, coming into use on 25th August, 1925.

A new goods shed was subsequently erected in the goods yard around 1927, having a capacity for 18 wagons compared to four or five of the existing one, which was thereafter used as a parcels depot. A fortunate facility for this new use was the

Redditch station approach from the top of the driveway at the junction of Park Road and Bromsgrove Road around 1968. The parcels office is in the gabled section of the building to the right, whilst the passenger booking office along with the main waiting rooms occupied the remainder. The left-hand poster advertises a Dick Whittington pantomime at the Alexandra Theatre, Birmingham, featuring amongst others: Ted Rogers, the Dallas Boys and Cy Grant. Haig's Whisky is featured on the next poster. *Redditch Library*

A roadside view of the goods shed at Redditch dating from 1868, and taken just 100 years later. At this time, it has lost one of the loading bay covers. This goods shed was used from around 1927 as a parcels depot after the opening of the new larger goods depot further north. Although passenger traffic was at an all time low, the building still seems to have been used for some purpose at this time, judging from the lorry and the Hillman Imp parked nearby. *Redditch Library*

pedestrian tunnel beneath the Bromsgrove Road overbridge to give railway staff direct access to the station, where many of the smaller items were accepted for parcels delivery and collection or transferred to parcels vans attached to passenger workings. The road entrance to the goods yard was retained along with the nearby weighbridge and office, and the cattle pens and end loading dock. The new goods shed was positioned about half way along the goods yard, and contained one covered through line, with a substantial cantilevered canopy for road vehicles. It contained nine bays, and around 20 personnel were employed there as office workers, porters, checkers, plus a further eight or nine delivery drivers. A 10 ton crane was available, but many items were unloaded directly in the yard latterly using a mobile crane. For the unloading of the early LMS and BR containers, especially for the Dunlop depot at Hunt End, a 10 ton capacity electric crane was sent out from Birmingham. By 1932 the goods sidings had capacity for 188 wagons, which would contain such inward goods as aluminium ingots from Scotland, Canada and Australia for High Duty Alloys and Reynolds Tubes, fertilisers for local agriculture, and of course, coal. Outgoing goods included cycles, motorcycles and engines from the Enfield Cycle Co. Ltd, and BSA Components Ltd, needles and fishing tackle from Abel Morrall & Co. Ltd, Allcock's, Barnes Corporation, etc., springs from Herbert Terry & Son Co. Ltd, Lewis Spring Co. Ltd and the Heath Spring & Notion Co. Ltd, and other products from Alkaline Batteries Ltd, and the Hymatic Engineering Co. Ltd. It can be seen that a considerable number of manufacturing concerns had become established here, and this is reflected in the increase in the population from 3,314 in 1841 to 6,737 in 1871, to 13,493 in 1901, to 22,209 in 1933, finally reaching around 30,000 in 1964. By 1984 the population was in the order of 77,000.

Meanwhile, because the goods yard had expanded in width as well as changing direction, the footbridge from Bridge Street required lengthening, and was doubled around this time (1926). The closely spaced steel mesh enclosing its steel construction led to it becoming less than affectionately known as 'The Birdcage'. The eastern end of this footbridge terminated just short of Windsor Street, which was almost always known as 'Gas Street', as an original gas works had been sited here, although not for over a hundred years! Pedestrians were then faced with a narrow passageway to reach Windsor Street, which was a particularly unpleasant place on a dark night. John Wright's timber yard was sited nearby, at the eastern extremity of the goods yard, where newly harvested timber arrived for seasoning and cutting, often in loads as much as 200 tons.

Eventually, the old Redditch Railway station building was demolished, probably in the 1930s, and the opportunity was taken to extend the headshunt and instal two new sidings alongside Clive Road during 1942. These were exclusively for incoming coal, although when empty the headshunt was often used at weekends for the stabling of passenger stock.

Opposite, the shed had been extended to 118 ft at an early date, to provide an additional internal stores area at the rear of the shed. An estimate of £3,800 had prepared in January, 1872 for an engine shed, but this seems unlikely to have been accepted, as such a cost at that time would have built a three-road shed with a capacity for nine engines, as built at Coalville, Leicester and Skipton. As there was apparently a desire to improve the locomotive accommodation at that time, it seems much more likely that this is when the extension was carried out, at a much lower cost. When the 42 ft turntable and outside spur were removed, sometime before 1903, a headshunt to a wooden coaling stage was installed, which remained until the

This photograph was taken from the steeple of St Stephen's church, Redditch during repair work being undertaken in 1905. The intrepid photographer actually took four views, at each point of the compass from his vantage point. This view down William Street towards the goods yard is interesting because it shows the 1885 'Redditch' signal box just to the left of the tall factory chimney in the centre of the picture. Also, the footbridge leading from Bridge Street at this time did not extend all the way to Windsor Street (centre left of picture). *Chris Jackson Collection*

Fowler 'Jinty' 0-6-0T No. 47276 propels a parcels van into the parcels depot at Redditch on 14th June, 1962. It was a rare occasion to see any movements into this building. Abel Morris' needle works is on the other side of the running lines. *Author*

end of steam. This replaced a coaling stage previously sited next to the turntable. A replacement wooden office and enginemen's mess room was added directly in front of the water column and ash pit. Succumbing to the usual corrosive effects of soot and smoke, the shed roof was renewed during 1938/39 using the 'single pitch' style then fashionable on the LMS, whilst the shed doors had disappeared at an unknown date. A new concrete ash pit was added by October 1957 and the shed road relaid.

In 1911 Redditch shed was designated 3C by the MR, with Saltley being the parent depot and responsible for the allocation of locomotives to Redditch. However, in later MR years and through the LMS era into BR days, it became a sub-depot of Bournville for administrative purposes, although Saltley still continued to supply the locomotives, which sometimes included some of Bournville's official allocation. The situation seemed to have been clarified after Redditch was included in the Western Region (WR) administrative area from 1st February, 1958. However, in practice, Saltley still continued to provide the pilot engine until 1960 when Bromsgrove became the parent depot, and supplied the engine. Passenger engines stabling at the shed were invariably from Saltley shed, right up until closure of the shed on 1st June, 1964.

The station building at Redditch (4 miles 58 chains or 4¾ miles) remained largely unaltered until demolition. It was a single-storey red brick building with a deep tiled roof, situated in a cutting at the end of a short, steep approach road, which was somewhat inconveniently arranged to exit at an acute angle into the junction of Bromsgrove Road and Park Road. This was only relieved by the useful siting of a newsagent, tobacconist and sweet shop on the corner. The station building was of an 'H - plan' with the two gable ends facing the platform and entrances. It contained the booking office, parcels office, staff accommodation, ladies' and gentlemen's waiting rooms and toilets, but unusually no station master's house. The canopy contained a glass hipped central section, was cantilevered over the down platform, finished with decorative edging and supported by cast-iron columns. One oddity was a small brick and concrete building erected on the down platform around 1959. This was the station master's office, which was a replacement for part of the original building that had been destroyed in a recent fire. On the up side, a smaller waiting room of wooden construction on a dwarf brick base, with no platform awning, was sited opposite the main building. This was rebuilt at some time, possibly around the start of the 20th century, with a cantilevered awning, which had somewhat plainer edging than that on the down platform. Due to its situation in the cutting lower than the adjacent Plymouth Road, the up side waiting room was always very damp, which may explain the need to replace the earlier structure. A brick-built gentlemen's toilet alongside was a particularly unpleasant place, and only resorted to in cases of dire emergency ! A lattice steel footbridge was situated hard against the Bromsgrove Road overbridge, replacing the original wooden structure, but most passengers chose to use the adjacent boarded crossing, especially during inclement weather – it was much quicker! At one time a separate passenger entrance was available directly off the road overbridge on to the middle landing of the footbridge on the up side, but by 1960 it had been sealed off for many years. The platforms were of sufficient length for trains of six coaches, and water columns were sited at the ends of each of them. After the change in administration to the WR in February 1958 the platform nameboards, which were rather small and entirely of wood, were simply repainted brown, with white letters.

Leaving Redditch, the line climbed past Redditch South signal box and past the interesting MR down advanced starter and up inner home signals that were

The single-road shed at Redditch on a Sunday in March 1960 with Ivatt class '4' 2-6-0 No. 43046 standing over the ash pit. At this time, four engines would be stabled at the shed from Saturday night to Monday morning. *Author*

Looking down from the top of Redditch tunnel towards the station on 21st January, 1962. The up inner home and down starter are both positioned on the same post, and are both of MR lower quadrant style. These were replaced by a bracket post containing upper quadrant signals shortly after this photo was taken. Redditch South signal box is visible at the start of the double line section at the end of the platforms. *Author*

A view from inside the engine shed at Redditch, showing the engine inspection pit, which ran the length of the single-road shed. Stores were kept alongside the internal wall on the left, but the wooden hut next to the water column, ash pit and where 'Jinty' No. 47276 is standing acted as the office and mess room. The date is 3rd November, 1962. *Author*

mounted on either side of the same post. These lower quadrant signals were replaced by standard BR upper quadrants, mounted on a new cantilever bracket gantry during 1961. After 1880 the section southwards was controlled by block telegraph system, but on 11th October, 1891 electric train tablet working was introduced. As the line continued at 1 in 126 through the blue brick-lined 340 yds-long tunnel beneath the Ridgeway, engine crews on down trains faced an unpleasant few minutes, as the tunnel had not been built with a generous clearance. So for them it would have been a considerable relief to emerge into the fresh open countryside, where shortly afterwards the summit of this gradient was reached, and the line crossed into Warwickshire. The next two miles were an easy downhill run, with no gradient steeper than 1 in 127 until the next station.

At **Studley and Astwood Bank** (7 miles 64 chains or 7¾ miles) there was a block post and so tablets were exchanged here when the signal box was open. Although there was no passing loop in the station platform, goods trains could be put into one of the two loops in the goods yard in order for other trains to pass or overtake. Such manoeuvres are thought to have occurred only rarely, although this location generated a significant amount of goods traffic. The two loops were sited on the up side and gave sufficient flexibility that both up and down goods services could deposit or pick up wagons and shunt them to or from the goods shed, and the separate siding alongside. The capacity of the sidings was given as 55 wagons. The substantial goods shed was of red brick construction with a steeply pitched tiled roof, a cantilevered wooden awning for road vehicles and contained a 1 ½ ton hand crane. The line through the goods shed continued for a short distance to an end-loading dock. The spacious goods yard also contained cattle pens, a weighbridge, and for many years the local concern of T. & M. Dixon also had a small depot here for coal, and John Wright another for timber. Redditch supplied a lorry and driver for local deliveries.

A hipped-roof MR pattern signal box had opened on 25th May, 1891 replacing an earlier structure dating from November 1875, and was situated at the north end of the platform on the up side. This box was switched out when not required for the daily goods service, and from 14th June, 1954 was open only from 7.00 am to 3.00 pm on weekdays. The goods shed also abutted the north end of the platform, which in common with most of the stations on the route, was renowned for its well tended flower beds and some imposing lilac trees on the bank opposite. The station buildings consisted of a range of gable-ended red brick buildings of a fairly plain style but with patterned tiled roofs. The main building comprised the station master's house. An extension on the north side contained the booking office, waiting rooms and toilets, whilst a further separate store was positioned a little further on. The LMS nameboards gave way to large enamelled WR chocolate and cream nameboards after the administration was changed in March 1958. Steps from the road overbridge at the south end of the station gave a separate pedestrian entrance to the main driveway that served both the station and goods yard.

This station was rather inconveniently situated for its namesakes. Both Studley and Astwood Bank were rather sprawling towns or villages, in fact they would be better described as districts, and were over a mile each from the station. Because of its location, the station also served the nearby villages of Sambourne (even though this village had more than once petitioned for a station of its own), Spernal Ash and the Crabbs Cross district of south Redditch.

Leaving Studley, the line made several turns as it continued its steady descent through open farming land dotted with small woods and copses until reaching

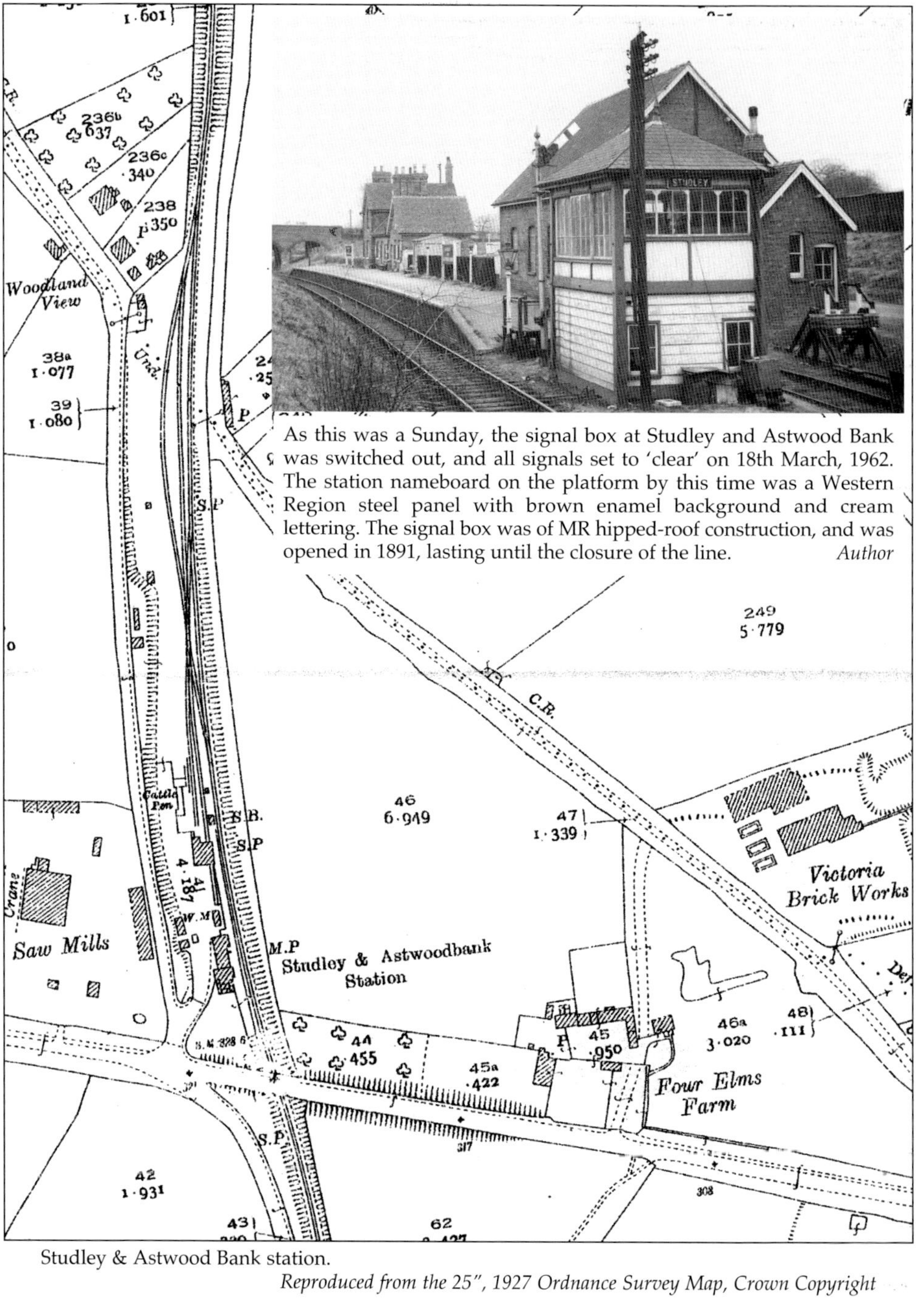

As this was a Sunday, the signal box at Studley and Astwood Bank was switched out, and all signals set to 'clear' on 18th March, 1962. The station nameboard on the platform by this time was a Western Region steel panel with brown enamel background and cream lettering. The signal box was of MR hipped-roof construction, and was opened in 1891, lasting until the closure of the line. *Author*

Studley & Astwood Bank station.

Reproduced from the 25", 1927 Ordnance Survey Map, Crown Copyright

Ivatt class '4' 2-6-0 No. 43013, long a resident at Saltley, calls at Coughton station with a northbound passenger service on the last day that this station remained open, 21st June, 1952. Two passenger are about to board the train, and the flower beds still appear to be well kept despite the impending closure. *J. Moss Collection/R.S. Carpenter*

Coughton (10 miles). The layout here consisted of a single loop for up goods trains to shunt into the single siding whose only facility was an open loading bank behind the platform, although surprisingly a weighbridge was originally situated in the goods yard. The loop and siding had a total capacity for 26 wagons. A signal box was originally provided here, prior to 16th August, 1877 but this was closed on 11th October, 1891. Thereafter access to the loop was via ground frames situated at each end of the loop, controlled by the usual keys attached to the train staff or tablet. The small station building was simply constructed of red brick, with plain gable ends. A lengthy footpath led from the road overbridge some 50 yards south to the platform. Although reasonably convenient for the small village of Coughton, there was in reality little passenger traffic and the station closed on 30th June, 1952 to all traffic. The loop and siding were used for the storage of redundant carriages for some time afterwards.

Dependent on the time of year, it was just possible, as the train passed through Coughton, to get a glimpse to the east of the well known Coughton Court, with its fine Tudor gatehouse and later 18th century Gothic wings. This had been the home of the Throckmorton family, who were involved in the Throckmorton plot of 1583 in which Elizabeth I was to have been overthrown in favour of Mary, Queen of Scots. However, despite its popular reputation, the family were not involved in the Gunpowder Plot of 1605. They had actually lent the house to Sir Everard Digby, who was one of the conspirators, and it was his involvement that provides the link to this event. The house is now a National Trust property.

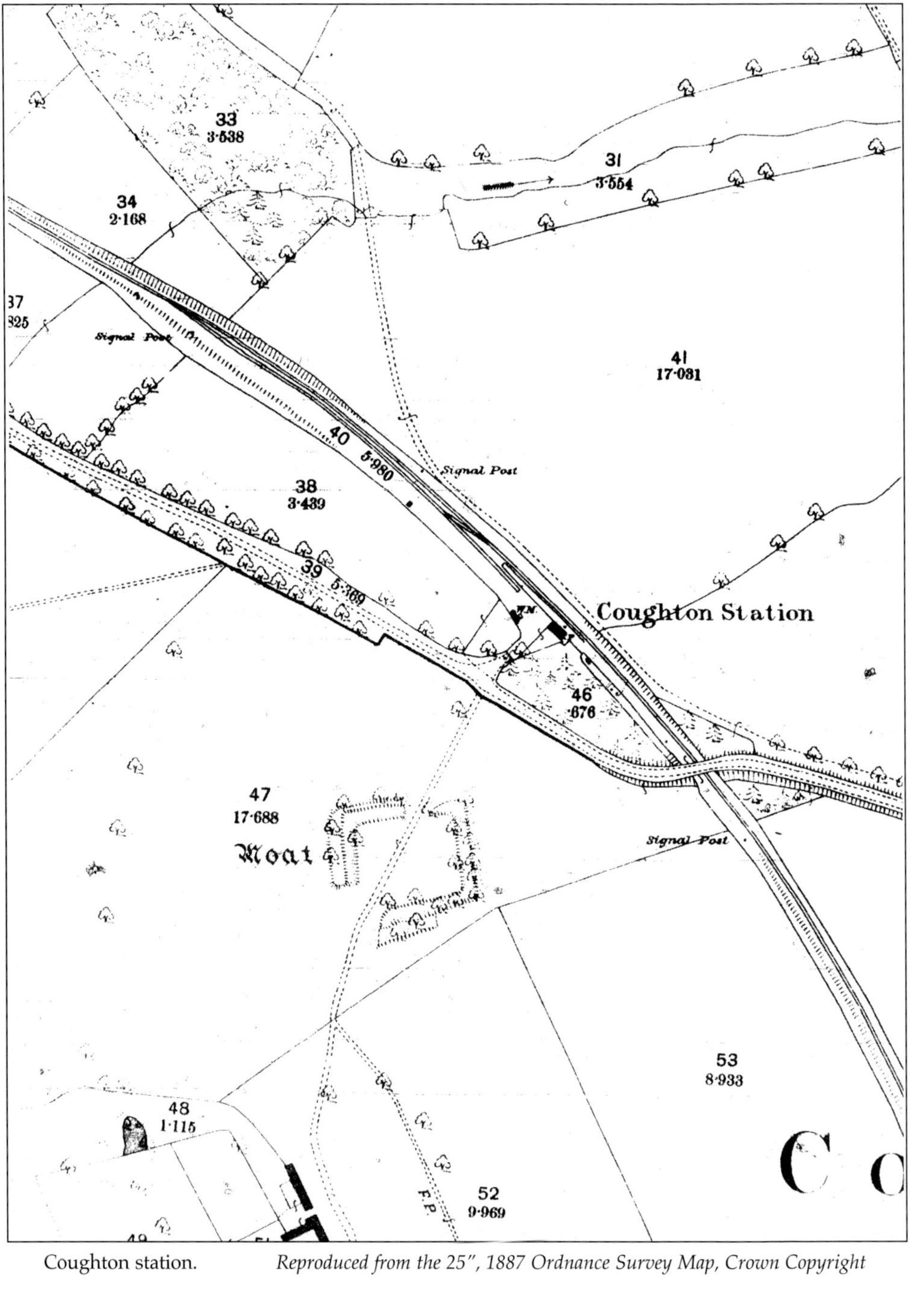

Coughton station. *Reproduced from the 25", 1887 Ordnance Survey Map, Crown Copyright*

Coughton station had been closed for some 10 years by the time this photograph was taken, on 18th March, 1962. This accounts for its derelict state as seen here. The station was only ever a basic design of booking hall cum waiting room, and without the usual staff accommodation or goods storage facilities. *Author*

Continuing its descent, but now on a straighter course southwards the line reached **Alcester** (12 miles 12 chains or 12⅛ miles). This town (pronounced 'Olster') owed its prosperity to being at the confluence of the Rivers Alne and Arrow, as well as the junction of a Roman road from Worcester (now the A422) and Ryknild Street, at which time it enjoyed the Roman name of 'Alunacastra'.

Entering the double track section here, the first item of note was the single line from Bearley running in from the east, which will be briefly described below. The lengthy loop here provided sufficient space for two trains to be held in each direction, thus permitting the overtaking of slow goods trains, as well as passing. The goods yard (capacity 40 wagons) was situated on the down side before reaching the station, and contained a further loop, and three short sidings, one terminating beyond the red brick, gable-ended goods shed, one at a loading dock and one at a cattle dock. A 1½ ton crane was provided at the goods shed. There was considerable traffic in livestock, both for the weekly cattle and sheep market, and also to the abattoir of the Alcester & District Cooperative Society located adjacent to the goods yard. The station building consisted of a two-storey brick station master's house, which featured gable ends facing east, west and south. A range of red brick buildings was attached, which contained the booking hall, waiting rooms, toilets and staff rooms, with an attractive patterned tiled roof. Following the transfer to the WR, the LMS station nameboards were replaced by brown enamelled boards, with cream lettering. A further siding was provided on the up side, south of the station with a capacity for 12 wagons.

The station was originally only provided with a single platform, on the down side, but to coincide with the opening of the line from Bearley, a loop was installed on 4th September, 1876, and the up side platform was constructed. This included a small brick-built waiting shelter with gable ends, windows at each end and an open entrance. Behind this platform was an orchard, which apart from its delightful blossoms during Spring and early Summer, also gave a clue that the line was

A deserted station at Alcester on 18th March, 1962. The down platform on the right displays the main station buildings, comprising a two-storey station master's house, and toilets (nearest), stores, booking hall, waiting room and staff offices. The goods shed can be seen beyond this range of buildings. On the left, the up platform featured only a small brick waiting shelter, and in the distance can be seen the signal box. *Author*

Viewed southwards on 18th March, 1962 from the down platform, the first part (as far as the second chimney) in this range of station buildings at Alcester, was in fact an addition, built by the Alcester Railway for the branch to Bearley. It contained the booking office and staff accommodation used by the GWR, who operated that line. The MR lower quadrant signals here remained until closure. *Author*

Alcester station. *Reproduced from the 25", 1938 Ordnance Survey Map, Crown Copyright*

At Alcester, the divergence of the GWR branch to Bearley was at almost the same point as the line northwards towards Redditch once again became single. In this view taken on 18th March, 1962 the former GWR line (*on the right*) is abandoned, and the sleepers placed across the track indicated that the track had been removed from just beyond that point. *Author*

The former GWR locomotive shed at Alcester was actually built by the Alcester Railway, and opened in 1876, closed in 1915, reopened in 1923 and was finally closed in 1939. By the time of this photograph, believed to be from around 1950, the years of neglect had taken their toll, but it was not finally demolished until around 1960. *Author's Collection*

heading into the fruit growing area of the Vale of Evesham. Alcester became a major point for such traffic, in addition to other outgoing goods from the needle industry for which Alcester became famous. In fact, by 1790 Alcester was the chief seat of needle making in the country, before the gradual move to Redditch mentioned earlier. Coal was, as usual, a staple inbound traffic.

The 6½ mile line from Bearley was authorized on 6th August, 1872 and was constructed by the independent Alcester Railway. It was opened on 4th September, 1876 and worked from the outset by the GWR, which eventually absorbed the Alcester Railway with effect from 1st July, 1883. Passenger accommodation at Alcester was provided in an extension on the northern end of the existing range of single-storey buildings on the down side. This provided a separate booking office and waiting room for GWR passengers, and the line at Alcester was represented by its own station master and porters. Initially, there were six weekday trains each way, all stopping at the only intermediate station at Great Alne. There were never any trains on Sundays. By 1889, the last round trip of the day had been dropped, and by 1902 the first two trains of the day were mixed goods and passenger trains. In 1910 one round trip goods working was introduced, but this was only to run as required, and in 1914 one further passenger service was added on Saturdays only. However, the effects of World War I were soon felt when the locomotive shed at Alcester was closed as from 1st November, 1915. All services were suspended as from 1st January, 1917 and the entire track was removed by the following 25th March, for use in France.

The local population often criticized the GWR for their poor connections at Alcester. Bearing in mind that they made every effort to give good connections at Bearley on to GWR services, it was extremely difficult to also connect with MR services at Alcester, over which they had absolutely no control, and after a journey of only 7½ miles.

Services were not resumed until 18th December, 1922 on which date a further halt was opened, at Aston Cantlow, but at first trains only ran from Bearley to Great Alne. The complete track was restored by 29th July, 1923, and full service through to Alcester commenced two days later with the usual five trains each way. However, this state of affairs was interrupted by World War II, and as from 25th September, 1939 all services were once again suspended. The transfer of the Maudslay factory from Coventry to a site at Great Alne during the War, resulted in unadvertised workmen's trains being run from Coventry and Leamington from July 1941, but all services once again ceased as from 3rd July, 1944. The line was closed officially, and entirely as from 1st March, 1951, although for many years it was used to store redundant wagons. During July 1960 the track was removed, at which time the attractive but derelict red brick locomotive shed at Alcester and the timber-built halt at Aston Cantlow were also demolished. The station building at Great Alne became a shop and post office, but has since been converted into an attractive dwelling.

Goods facilities at Alcester were shared with the MR (and later LMS), and the costs apportioned according to use. However, there was not a great deal of goods traffic originating on the GWR line, and most traffic involved the transfer of goods from the MR to the GWR. The station was also used as a sub-Post Office, being first recognized in 1896, when postal regulations required that letters posted here should have 'R.S.O. Warwickshire' added. The franks for mail posted at the station were in the care of the station master.

The first signal box at Alcester was erected before the loop was added in 1876, and was sited on the south end of what was to become the down platform. This was

Right: Another example of the MR practice of mounting two signal arms for opposing directions on a single post was to be found at the south end of Alcester station. Here the down advanced starter and up inner home are treated in this manner. On the right, a short up siding is seen terminating just by the road overbridge.

D. Ibbotson

Below: The brick-based LMS gabled-ended signal box dating from 1932 at Alcester which replaced two earlier MR boxes. The goods yard is behind the box, and the usual pile of domestic coal is just visible in this July 1960 view. The frame at the foot of the steps and next to the running line protected the signalman when exchanging tokens, although the single line section was in the distance as the line curves to the left.

N. Forrest/Transport Treasury

supplemented at the opening of the Bearley line on 4th September, 1876 by a new Junction signal box on the up side, opposite the junction. The Station box was replaced by a new MR hipped-roof box on the same site on 17th December, 1905 and the Junction box was replaced on 28th May, 1922. However, both of these boxes were closed on 24th April, 1932 and replaced by a new gable-ended standard LMS box on that date, sited on the down side midway between the junction and the station.

Leaving the station, there was another example of the MR lower quadrant down advanced starter and up inner home signals being mounted on the same post, which again lasted until 1960 when it was replaced by BR standard upper quadrant signals mounted on a cantilever bracket. The line continued its descent, firstly at 1 in 125, but then easing after half a mile. Shortly after, at MR bridge No. 45 the line made its first crossing of the River Arrow on a plate girder bridge, so that the river now ran on the up side of the line. Although the line had been running in the broad valley of the River Arrow (which is an Anglo-Saxon name for 'the swift one'), it was only from this point that it started to run close to it. The river had been well named, for this stretch was to see the next bridge washed away more than once during the line's history. Notwithstanding its propensity for flash floods, the river was at other times one of the most idyllic, meandering through the rural countryside and typifying that sense of tranquility for which the English countryside has become so well known. Its banks were lined with weeping willows and were the homes of kingfishers and otters, whilst herons enjoyed their hunting in the usually quiet flowing waters, which teemed with fish. On the same side could be seen the magnificent parklands surrounding Ragley Hall, the ancestral home of the Earl of Yarmouth, who had been instrumental in the formation of the Alcester Railway. However, the house itself could not be glimpsed from the railway.

About a mile further on, the line recrossed the River Arrow at MR bridge No. 48, which had been reconstructed as a plate girder bridge following serious flooding in 1915. The river now ran on the down side of the line, as it entered **Wixford** (14¼ miles). The village, with its famous hostelry 'The Fish Inn', adjoined the station, and was set in a particularly pleasant and relaxing elbow of the River Arrow. There was no passing loop at the station, which boasted a single platform, with only the minimum of passenger facilities, in the form of a small wooden waiting room, and a separate gentlemen's toilet. Steps ran from the road overbridge at the south end to the platform, and beyond this bridge lay a single loop which sufficed as the goods yard, with a capacity of 20 wagons. Rail access was controlled by a ground frame at each end of the loop, unlocked by the customary train staff or tablet keys. A dusty track ran from the lane to this area, where a temporary ramp was used whenever livestock was loaded to or from wagons, as an auction was held periodically in an adjacent field. Such was the somnolent atmosphere that little passenger traffic was seen, other than anglers at weekends, and the station and goods facilities were closed as from 2nd January, 1950. The siding was lifted shortly afterwards, but the station was left to become gradually overgrown.

A little over half a mile further on, we arrive at **Broom Junction** (14 miles 67 chains or 14¾ miles). The history of this station and junction has already been dealt with, so it is sufficient to describe the station and running lines. The station comprised a single island platform, which became a true passing place from October 1892, and comprised a rather narrow wooden booking office and waiting room mounted on dwarf brick walls, which oddly had brick ends. There was also a collection of small buildings including a corrugated iron stores and an old coach body of indeterminate vintage, used as a parcels store/mess room and painted cream. The LMS-style

Right: The station at Wixford in 1949 facing towards Alcester. The rudimentary wooden booking office and waiting shelter had recently been supplemented by a brick-built toilet on the neatly kept platform.
Joe Moss/R. Carpenter

Left: Wixford station looking north in 1960. As passenger services had been withdrawn from here in 1950, the wooden station building had been removed, although the brick-built toilet building remained on the platform.
J. Tarrant/ Kidderminster Railway Museum

Right: The goods siding at Wixford viewed from the road overbridge and looking south in 1949. No goods facilities were ever supplied here, although a temporary loading ramp for livestock can be seen in the centre of the picture. The wagons appear to contain sections of pipework, probably in connection with some work proceeding in the district at that time.
Joe Moss/R. Carpenter

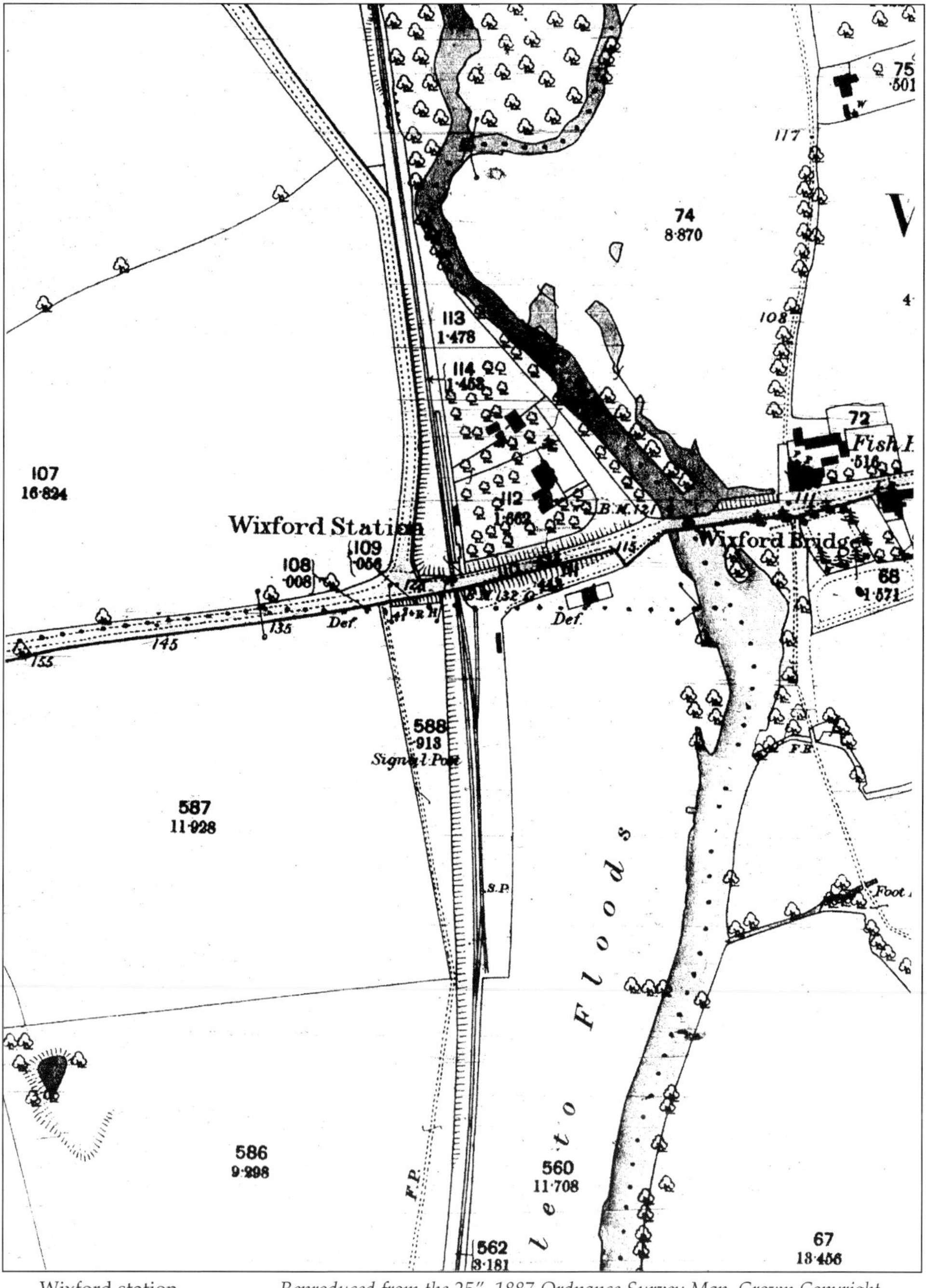

Wixford station. *Reproduced from the 25", 1887 Ordnance Survey Map, Crown Copyright*

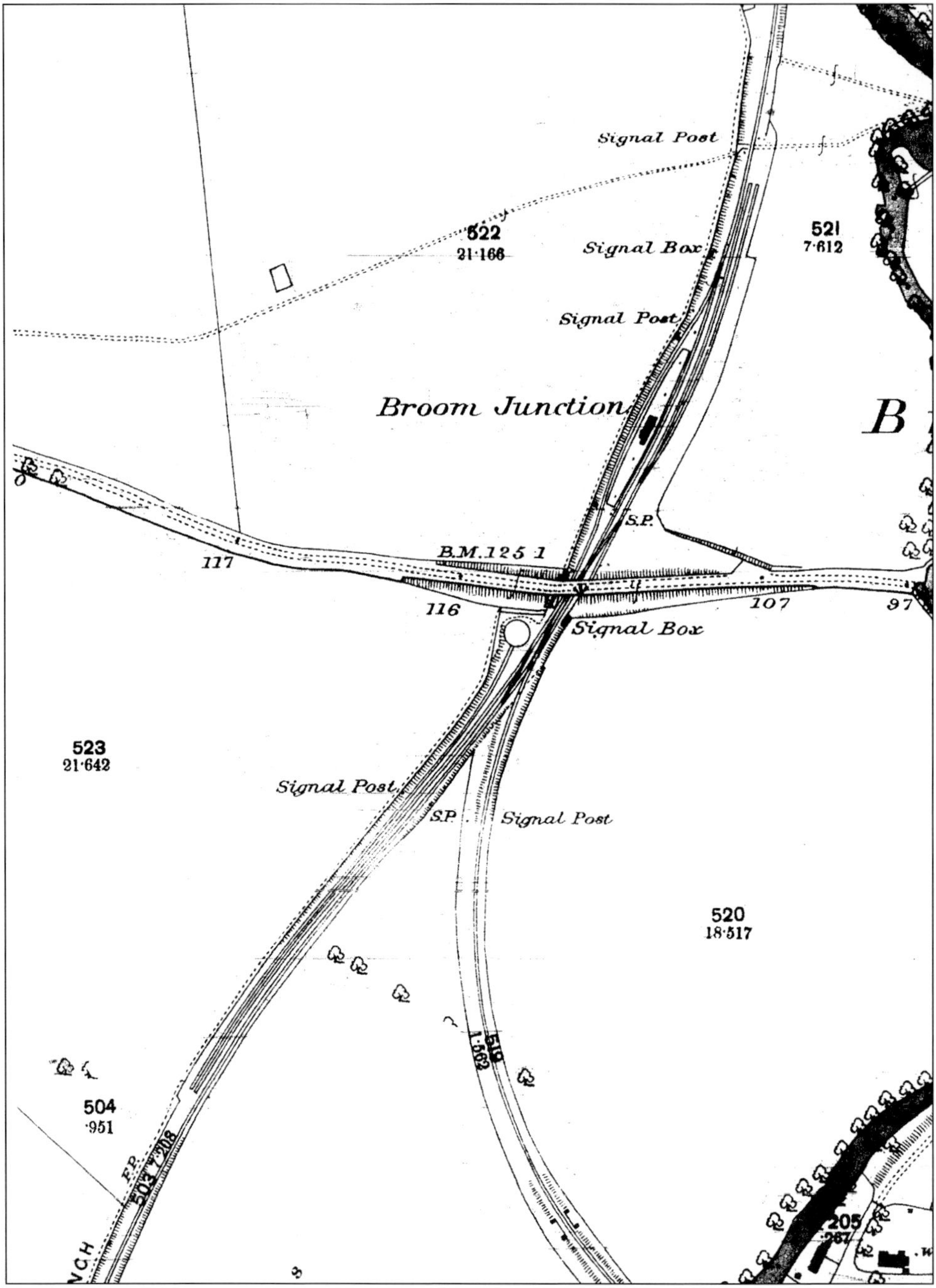

Broom Junction station. *Reproduced from the 25″, 1887 Ordnance Survey Map, Crown Copyright*

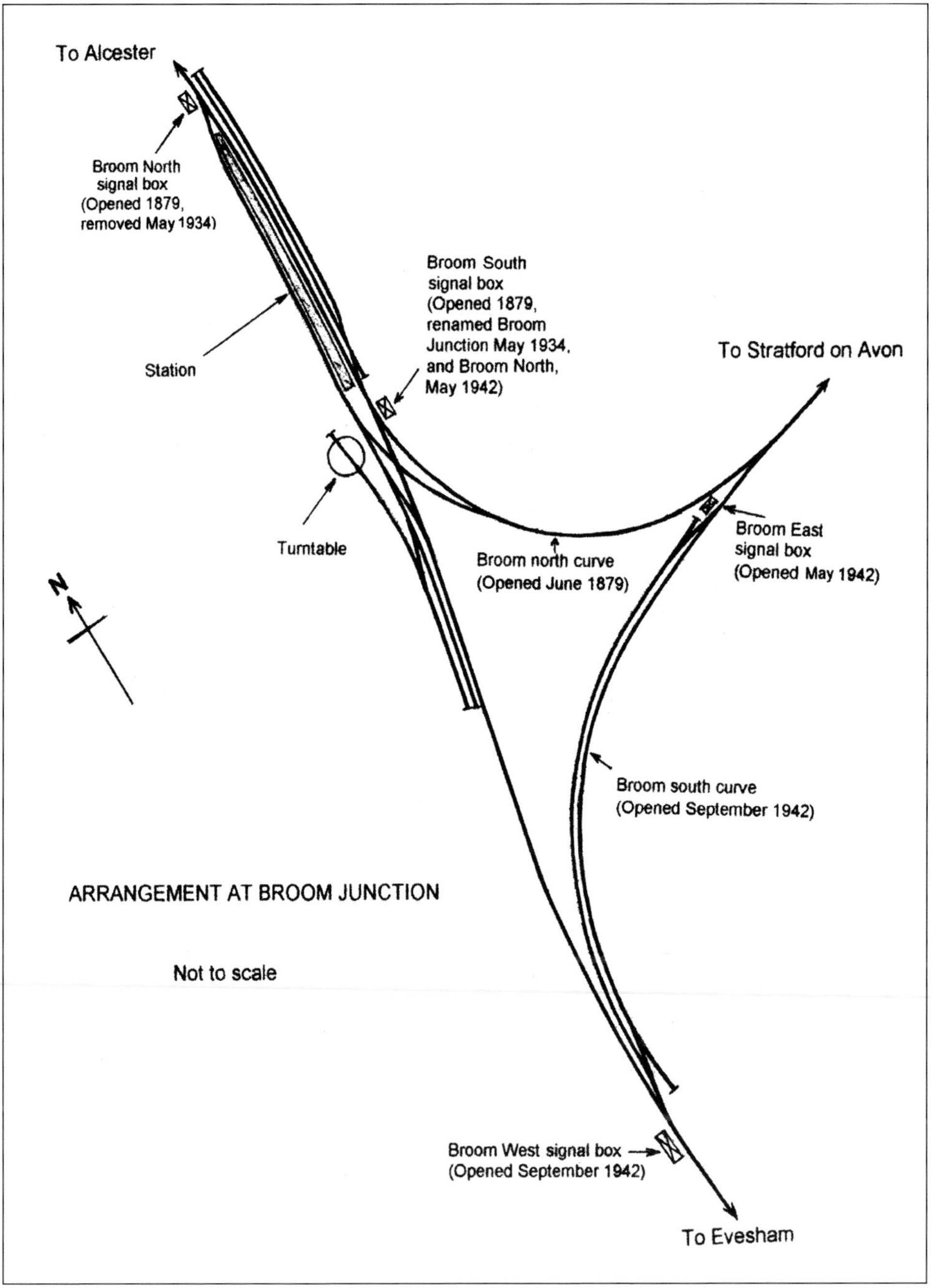

Arrangement at Broom Junction - not to scale.

Broom Junction station looking north in July 1960. The neat appearance of the station is enhanced by its lack of traffic at the platforms, with the sidings in the background also being almost empty. *N. Forrest/Transport Treasury*

The island platform station building at Broom Junction *circa* 1955, looking south. *A.T. Locke/Kidderminster Railway Museum*

wooden nameboards on the platform remained until closure. Passenger access was by way of a boarded crossing from the goods yard to the south end of the platform. There were two sidings on the down side, opposite the platform, with a total capacity of some 46 wagons. For most of its life, the goods yard would have been the scene of transfer traffic with the SMJR, as the amount of goods for this rather sparse district was limited to agricultural goods and the odd wagon load of coal. In fact, goods traffic was not dealt with here until February 1882.

The original North signal box was opened on 2nd June, 1879 and was located on the up side, north of the platform, and was matched by Broom South signal box opening at the same time, and located just south of the road overbridge, at the junction of the SMJR line. The South box was replaced by a standard MR hipped-roof box on 9th October, 1892 on the same site, at which time block working was commenced; the North box was replaced on 3rd September, 1913. Both of these boxes were subsequently closed and replaced by a new LMS pattern gable-ended box on the South box site on 6th May, 1934 which was then renamed Broom Junction box. When the new east to south curve was laid in 1942, a new LMS pattern gable-ended box was erected on the SMJR route at Broom East, the existing Broom Junction box was renamed Broom North, and a further box as already described, was erected at the south end of the new curve alongside the Redditch line, and named Broom West. The two boxes at Broom West and East officially closed on 1st July, 1962, and Broom North on 5th July, although by that time the SMJR route had been unused for two years.

Leaving the station, and after passing beneath the road overbridge, there were two sidings on the up side, with capacity for 60 wagons, that were primarily for the use of exchange traffic with the SMJR line. Just before these stood the turntable, which was removed some time after the south curve was put in, the triangle thus created making it no longer necessary.

On a reasonably straight course, the line continued almost level in the valley bottom, closely following the River Arrow until reaching **Salford Priors** (16 miles 18 chains or 16¼ miles). The station here closely resembled that at Studley and Astwood Bank, being of red brick construction, with a two-storey gable-ended station master's house with attached single-storey booking office and waiting room. Remarkably, the station managed to retain its LMS 'hawkseye' nameboard, latterly painted brown with cream lettering, until closure. The substantial red brick single-road goods shed with a 1½ ton crane, was placed alongside the single platform, and reached by a siding coming off a goods loop. This loop also gave access to a south-facing siding alongside which were the cattle pens and loading dock, with a further loading dock for general traffic being placed at the end of an opposing north-facing siding. Thirty-five wagons could be accommodated in the loop and sidings. A weighbridge and brick office was positioned in the goods yard, whose driveway also gave road access to the station. Pedestrians also had a separate entrance via steps from the overbridge at the south end of the station, which carried the Stratford to Evesham road (A439) over the line. The station not only served the people of Salford Priors, but especially during the 1930s the people of Dunnington (1½ miles to the north) also used it, as the Redditch to Evesham bus service only operated on Saturdays at that time.

Opposite the platform were the works of Bomford & Evershed, agricultural engineers, and for many years it was notable for a fine display of agricultural equipment, which was for sale or hire. Much of this was of considerable vintage, including steam ploughs, traction engines and road rollers, as late as 1960. The successors to this firm, still occupy the site, and also the former station buildings.

The northern end of Salford Priors station looking towards Alcester in 1949, with the LMS 'hawkseye' style running-in board still extant. The goods yard can be seen behind that, and on the right, the works of Bomford & Evershed are served by a single siding leading from the main running line in the distance. This was accessed by a ground frame at that point.

Joe Moss/R. Carpenter

Salford Priors station looking north on a bright winter day in 1960. The size and style of this station and goods shed are almost identical to those at Harvington and Studley.

Almonery Heritage Centre Collection

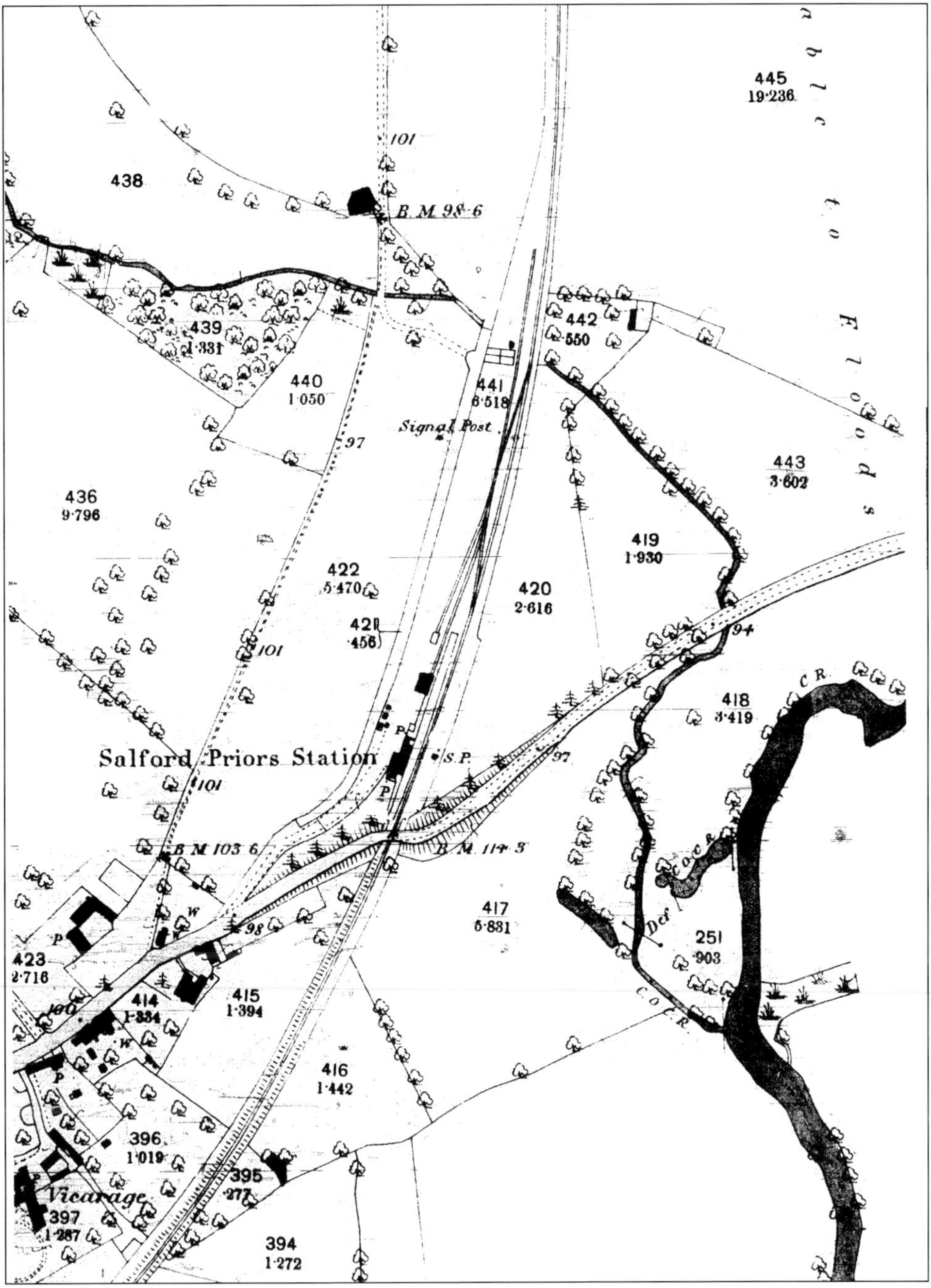

Salford Priors station. *Reproduced from the 25", 1887 Ordnance Survey Map, Crown Copyright*

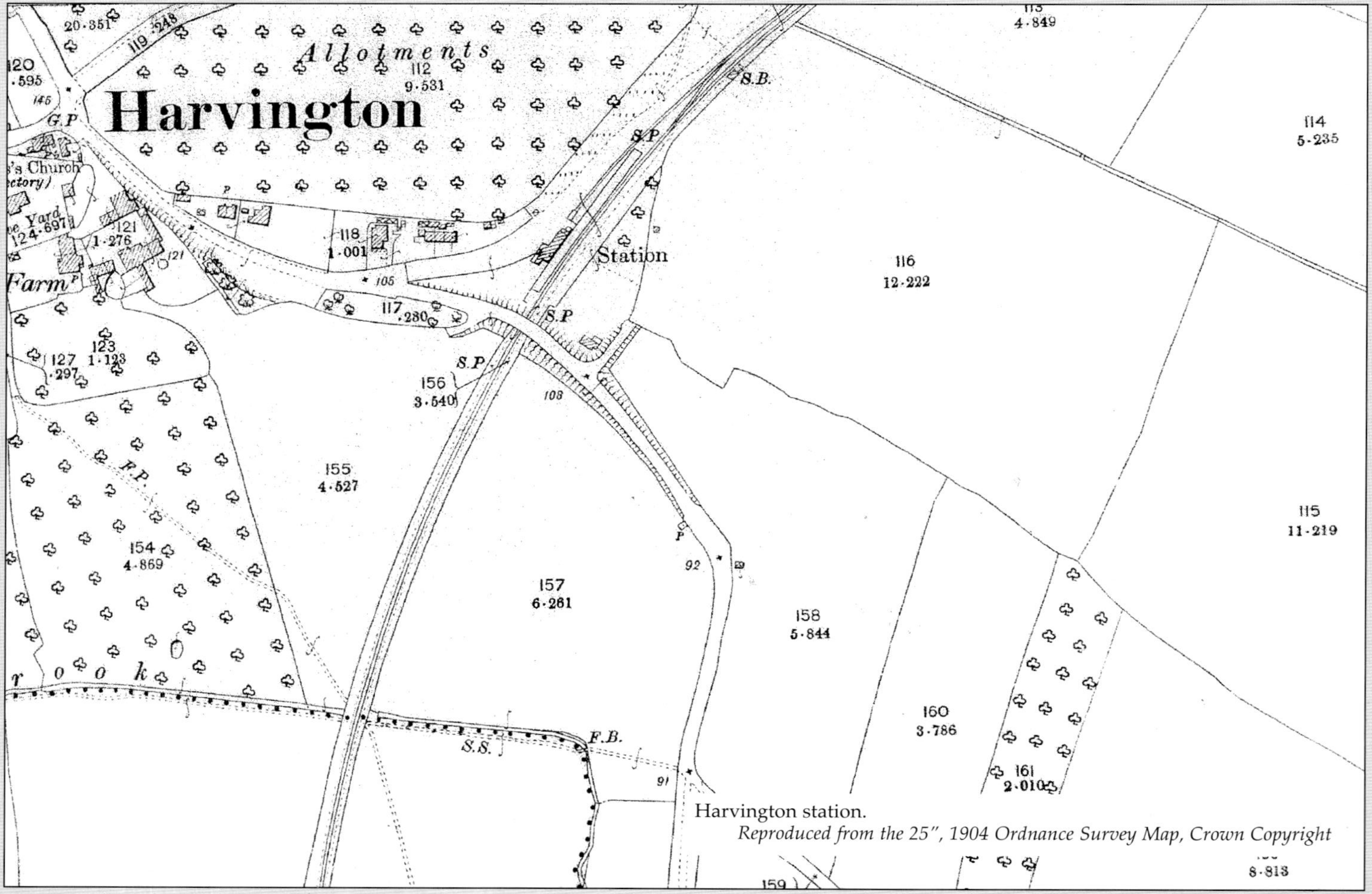

Harvington station.
Reproduced from the 25", 1904 Ordnance Survey Map, Crown Copyright

Rail access was provided into these premises, directly off the running line, between the two points giving access to the goods loop. This was controlled by a ground frame at the points, and was opened in July 1910. A further ground frame controlled movements onto the goods loop and was sited on the down side opposite the end of the station platform. As the station was not a block post, no signal box was provided.

The line shortly passed into Worcestershire, then after no more than a couple of hundred yards back into Warwickshire, whilst nearby the Arrow joined the River Avon. It continued fairly level through an area now containing more orchards and thus becoming more closely identifiable as being in the Vale of Evesham. After a mile, the line started to climb slightly, passing over a number of small brooks feeding into the Avon, passed finally back into Worcestershire and entered **Harvington** (18 miles 19 chains or 18¼ miles). The station building was an exact replica of that Salford Priors, including the tastefully patterned tiled roof, and here too, the LMS 'hawkseye' station nameboard lasted until closure. The track layout was also similar, but the goods loop only led to one siding, facing north and terminating behind the platform. The capacity of the sidings was 25 wagons. However, no goods shed was provided, although as if to make up for this, a signal box was necessary as this was the site of a block post. This was opened on 2nd June, 1891 and was a standard MR hipped-roof box, lasting until closure on 1st March, 1964. One further feature was an attractive allotment garden beside the railway, directly opposite the platform, supplementing the flower beds on the platform. Passenger and goods access was by a driveway leading from a lane that passed over the line at the south end of the station and led to the village of Harvington.

A charming scene at Harvington station in the summer of 1914, with passengers, mostly comprising children, waiting for the next train to Evesham, for which the signal has already been lowered. *R. Carpenter Collection*

Looking southwards towards Harvington station in 1962, with the MR hipped-roof signal box on the left. Although the goods yard on the right comprised but a single siding, the box was necessary as Harvington was a block post. *Joe Moss/R. Carpenter*

Harvington station during 1960 and looking particularly well cared for, with a Stanier '8F' class 2-8-0 approaching hauling a southbound freight. The LMS 'hawkseye' running-in board remained until closure. *Almonery Heritage Centre Collection*

The line then ran quite close to the western bank of the River Avon, undulating slightly and giving more fine views to the east. The pretty village of Offenham was clearly visible on the far bank of the river, only reached by means of a ferry, but trains made no connection for it. As the line reached the outskirts of Evesham it made a sudden 90 degree turn to the west, and crossed the GWR Oxford to Worcester line on a tall plate girder viaduct supported on brick pillars about ¼ mile before the station. Originally, the line became double immediately prior to entering the station, and as it passed beneath the Birmingham to Cheltenham road (A435), but this section was extended some 180 yards northwards in 1905. **Evesham** (21 miles 59 chains or 21¾ miles) comprised two platforms linked by an open lattice iron footbridge erected in 1905. The main station buildings were on the up side, reached by a driveway shared with the neighbouring GWR station, which also gave access to the GWR goods shed and the MR loading docks. The MR station buildings were single storey, comprising the original booking office, waiting rooms, toilets and staff offices. The style was reminiscent of that at Barnt Green, being of a light red brick, with cream surrounds to the windows and doorways. A glass canopy of three bays, supported on iron columns, was later extended by two additional bays at each end, so as to run the entire length of this building. Beneath the canopy a green bookstall, belonging to W.H. Smith, was opened during the 1930s. From 1931 both the GWR and LMS stations came under the control of the LMS station master, and were worked as one station until closure of the former LMS station. During this period, the LMS booking office was closed, and tickets were issued at the GWR booking office. The effect of the combined station was reinforced with the numbering of the platforms as numbers 1 and 2 for the Redditch line, and numbers 3 and 4 for the GWR line.

No passenger accommodation at all was provided on the down side, being perhaps indicative that few passengers were expected to join southbound trains at Evesham. A small stores and mess room was located towards the south end of the down platform. Behind this platform, edged at the rear by wrought-iron spear

Evesham station around 1900 with a group of passengers awaiting the next up arrival. The station running-in boards are the typical MR angled style, and would have contained white letters on a blue background. The lengthy steel bridge carrying Briar Close can just be seen in the background. *Almonery Heritage Centre Collection*

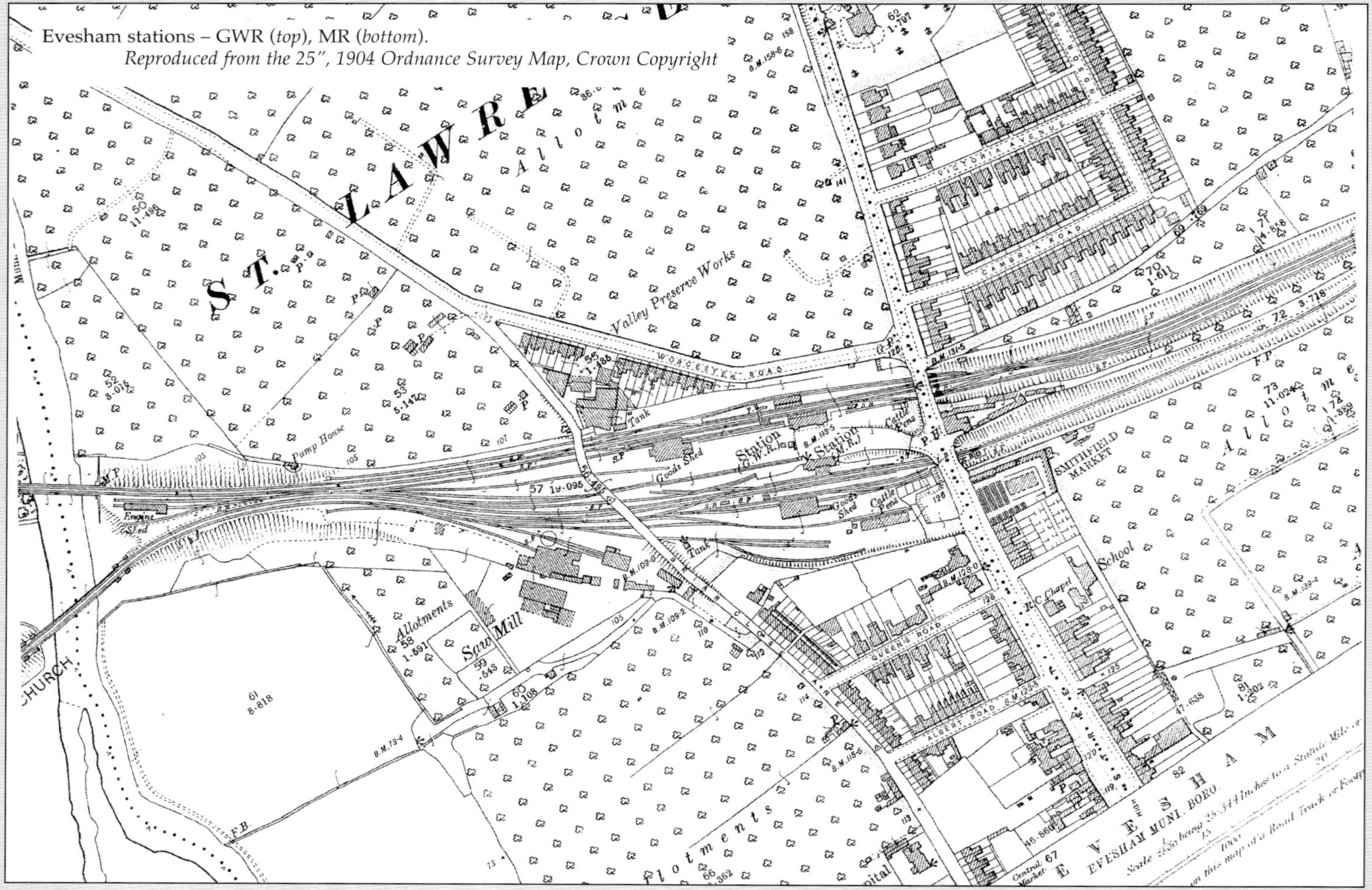

Evesham stations – GWR (*top*), MR (*bottom*).
Reproduced from the 25", 1904 Ordnance Survey Map, Crown Copyright

The station staff at Evesham pose for their photograph around 1900, beneath the splendid glass canopy on the up platform, initially of three bays only. This was prior to the installation of a bookstall on the platform. The rails seem to be ballasted with ash. *Almonery Heritage Centre Collection*

Looking north from the up platform at Evesham station, shortly before services were withdrawn. A Collett '57XX' 0-6-0PT stands in the down platform with the shuttle service to Ashchurch. The station buildings and all equipment are still in good order *Kidderminster Railway Museum*

Evesham station up platform in July 1960 as viewed from the down platform. The platform canopy here created a pleasant atmosphere for waiting passengers, of which there seem to be a number. *N. Forrest/Transport Treasury*

The glass canopy over the up platform at Evesham was a feature that was replicated at many MR stations throughout the country, and contributed to making such stations feel grander and more opulent than their status implied. Compared to the earlier views it is evident that the glass canopy had been extended by a further two bays in each direction along the station buildings. The W.H. Smith bookstall seems also to be doing some brisk business on this July day in 1960, and the NSU 'Quickly' moped adds a period touch. *N. Forrest/Transport Treasury*

fencing, originally ran a goods loop, opened in 1905 by extending an existing south-facing siding and installing a crossover to the up line, but reverted to the original arrangement in 1935. This 1905 work had been possible following the extension of the double line section northwards from the station for a distance of 180 yards, which came into operation the previous year, on 3rd July, 1904. The LMS station nameboards were renewed in the WR style of brown enamelled steel, with cream lettering, from 1958. Water cranes were sited at the end of each platform.

The sole original signal box, sited on the up platform and dating from before 1875 was replaced on 23rd September, 1890 by two new standard MR hipped-roof pattern boxes being positioned at the south end of the down platform ('Evesham South'), and at the start of the single line section ('Evesham North'). However, the North box was replaced on 25th June, 1905 when the double line section was extended and the new box was accordingly positioned seven chains further north. The South box was replaced by a standard LMS pattern gable-ended box on 14th October, 1934 on the same site. On the following 20th January, the South box took over the functions of the North box, and as it was then the sole LMS box, it was renamed at that time simply as 'Evesham': the North box being closed.

The large brick-built single-road goods shed with a slate roof was positioned south of the station, and was furnished with a 5 ton crane. It was originally a two-road affair, one road being bricked up prior to 1900. Access to this goods shed was from a separate driveway leaving the main road further south than the station access road, and also led to the even larger iron-framed corrugated iron shed believed to have been erected around World War I, and intended mainly as a fruit store. This building was notable for being painted black, and before World War II bore the name of the occupiers, 'The British Basket & Besto Co. Ltd' also proudly proclaiming it to be their 'Chip Basket Store'. This had nothing to do with fried potatoes, but referred to the types of fruit baskets stored there. Along the sides it clearly bore the legend 'LMS Railway' until its final demolition in the 1960s. The sidings hereabout terminated at a cattle dock and end-loading bay. The total capacity of the goods sidings here was given as 110 wagons in 1934. It will come as no surprise to learn that Evesham became the chief railhead for the shipment of fruit and market garden produce from the area, including of course, the famous asparagus crop, still so popular. The goods depot was renamed Evesham South Goods Depot on 4th September, 1951, to distinguish it from the WR goods depot.

Apart from this produce, Evesham is still remembered as the site of the terrible Battle of Evesham, which took place on 4th August, 1265 during the Baron's War. This battle was fought in the middle of a ferocious thunderstorm, and lasted for around three hours, during which some 4,000 men-at-arms, 160 knights and 18 barons were slain. Henry III's son, Edward, using a cunning strategy defeated the Earl of Leicester (Simon de Montfort), who was one of those slain. The banks of the River Avon have been popular with tourists for many generations, and the nearby area was enhanced by the opening of leisure gardens by the local Workman brothers in the latter half of the 19th century. The attractive town also features the picturesque ruined Evesham Abbey, founded in 714 by Ecgwine, bishop of the Hwicce people. The town had enjoyed quite good transport links even before the coming of railways to the area, with daily coach services to London, Bath, Bristol and Worcester by 1841, while at this time Redditch had only a service to Birmingham, and this only three times a week.

South of the station, a lengthy road bridge of iron girder construction on brick abutments ran over both the MR and GWR routes, and beyond which was

The turntable outside the MR shed at Evesham continued in use long after the shed was closed and demolished. As all the lines at Evesham eventually came under Western Region control, locomotives from the WR shed also used it, and here we see 'Manor' class 4-6-0 No. 7818 *Granville Manor* being turned on 14th November, 1963. This engine's overall wheelbase was 52 ft 1¾ in., providing evidence that the original 42 ft turntable had been replaced, some time after 1930 when the original was last recorded by the LMS. *Almonery Heritage Centre Collection*

Stanier 'Black Five' 4-6-0 No. 44660 drifts into Evesham from the south with the 8.50 am (Saturdays excepted) Ashchurch to Redditch pick-up goods on 14th June, 1961. This particular service was invariably lightly loaded, as is the case here with just one wagon contributing so far to the line's upkeep. The 1957-built WR signal box is seen in the background. *J.A. Peden*

positioned the small MR two road locomotive shed, capable of housing only two locomotives. Little is known of this structure, which is believed to have been erected around 1870, as water pipes were laid 'to the new shed' in 1870 at a cost of £49. A tank with water crane and gas fittings, costing £47, was installed the following year. On 21st September, 1899 the MR Way & Works Committee considered a replacement shed, but the proposal was 'postponed, so that an alternative plan and estimate can be prepared'. Evidently the original proposal was too expensive, and no further action seems to have been taken. It closed on 14th September, 1931 and was demolished shortly after. The original 42 ft turntable, sited immediately in front of the shed, was replaced by a larger unit (probably of 54 ft) some time after 1930, which continued to be used until the 1960s, particularly as engine crews also continued to be stationed there. The area on the south side of the shed was developed for additional sidings in 1934/35 providing space for a further 97 wagons, and also giving rail access to Espley's sawmills.

At the south end of the up platform was a side- and end-loading dock, which saw much of the fruit traffic, and was linked to the GWR through their own goods sidings for the exchange of traffic. A further connection towards the GWR engine shed had also been installed at an early date, but it is not thought that either saw much use, possibly as they led from Worcester towards the Redditch direction. The connection was installed primarily as the result of the traffic rights enjoyed by the GWR over the route to Redditch, with additional running powers in the event that traffic was not being freely allowed.

Major engineering works were required in Stanton cutting on the Honeybourne to Cheltenham WR line in 1957, involving the removal of thousands of tons of Cotswold clay and slurry, and the subsequent relaying of more than a mile of track on a sounder foundation. This caused the complete closure of the section between Toddington and Honeybourne to passenger services. Local trains continued to run from Cheltenham to Toddington, and a bus service was provided onward to Honeybourne, calling at the intermediate stations. However, through trains such as 'The Cornishman' and the Birmingham to Cardiff expresses were diverted at Honeybourne East to Evesham, where work had begun on an entirely new connection to the Ashchurch line, but on an opposite alignment, i.e. from the Honeybourne direction towards Ashchurch. However, this new connection was not ready for the diverted traffic, which therefore had to continue to Norton Junction, near Worcester. Here spare engines were provided to back on to the trains and haul them down the spur on to the MR main line at Abbotswood Junction and thence to Cheltenham (Lansdown). During May, a Worcester 'Castle' was scheduled to haul 'The Cornishman' over this route. This diversion and the reversal added about half an hour to the running times of the affected trains. Meanwhile, night time freight trains continued to run over the site of the engineering works by way of a temporary crossover for single line working controlled by a small signal box installed at Laverton Halt, as presumably the contractors did not work on the cutting during the hours of darkness. Work began on 18th March and was scheduled for completion on 27th May.

The new connection at Evesham was finally completed during the early Summer, and a further programme of work was proposed for the Honeybourne to Cheltenham line during the autumn. This involved work on the Southam cutting (between Cheltenham Racecourse station and Bishops Cleeve) from 23rd September until 9th November, and on the cutting at Weston-Sub-Edge station from 11th November until 14th December. For the first period, local passenger trains ran from

The former GWR single-road shed at Evesham was situated in the fork of the Worcester and Ashchurch lines, and for most of its life was home for up to half a dozen engines. In this view taken on 26th August, 1956 identifiable locomotives are 0-6-0PT No. 3745 and Collett Mogul No. 6348. *Industrial Railway Society/H. Townley*

The large black-painted corrugated-iron fruit store at Evesham bore the legend 'LMS Railway' until it was demolished in the 1960s. As can be seen here, it was latterly the property of the British Basket & Besto Co. Ltd as their chip basket store. The 'chip baskets ' referred to are actually those containers used for the storage and convenience of soft fruit, such as strawberries. In the Vale of Evesham the necessity for such packaging is obvious.
Almonery Heritage Centre Collection

Looking across the former GWR goods yard and MR loading bank towards Evesham station, as Ivatt class '4' 2-6-0 No. 43033 has arrived with the 10.37 am from Birmingham, and an unidentified classmate rolls in from Ashchurch. The date is 11th June, 1962 and the goods yards are full of traffic as a Swindon-built 204 hp 0-6-0DM busies itself with shunting in the former MR goods depot. *Almonery Heritage Centre Collection*

Collett '2251' class 0-6-0 No. 2246 of Worcester shed is busily engaged in shunting the former MR goods shed at Evesham on 11th June, 1963. Not surprisingly for the time of year, fruit vans predominate in the yard, with some 'conflat' wagons loaded with containers receiving attention in the MR side and end loading bay on the left. *R.K. Blencowe Collection*

'Castle' class 4-6-0 No. 7002 *Devizes Castle* swings into Evesham with the 10.05 am Hereford to Paddington, as Churchward Mogul No. 5358 waits with the empty stock forming the 11.45 am from Evesham to Stratford-upon-Avon. The BR signal box built in 1957 to control the new access between the former MR and GWR lines is visible behind both trains, and the closed GWR locomotive shed in the distance, upper left. *Author*

After leaving Evesham and crossing the River Avon, the line passed through the Evesham suburb of Hampton where the station named as 'Bengeworth' was located. In this 1920s view looking east, the bridge carrying the line over the Pershore road (A44) can be seen, advertising the local newspaper the *Evesham Journal and Four Shires Advertiser*. *Author's Collection*

Honeybourne to Winchcombe, where a connecting bus service was provided onward to Cheltenham. For the second period, local trains ran from Toddington to Cheltenham, with a connecting bus to Honeybourne. The small temporary signal box from Laverton Halt was moved to a position about ¼ mile north of Willersley Halt, and a crossover installed, so as to once again permit the passage of night time freights. 'The Cornishman' and the Birmingham to Cardiff diesels were then able to use the new connection at Evesham and so run direct through Ashchurch to Gloucester, calling at Cheltenham's Lansdown station instead of Malvern Road. This diversion only added 15 minutes to the running time of 'The Cornishman', and this was largely offset by an acceleration between Gloucester and Bristol of seven minutes.

A new signal box was installed at Evesham, opposite the connection and on the up side of the WR main line, to control these movements and to replace the existing GWR signal boxes. Following the completion of the works mentioned above, the connection was thereafter used on a regular basis for through traffic, mainly of ironstone from Oxford to South Wales with the corresponding empty return wagons. These will be examined in the next chapter.

The GWR engine shed was sited in the fork of the Ashchurch and Worcester routes, and was opened in 1901, replacing an earlier shed, described in Chapter One. The shed was a single-road affair, with a steeply gabled, slated roof containing five separate ventilators, and measured 110 ft by 20 ft overall. A small office was positioned on the south side near to the entrance, and two sidings were also on this side, primarily for coaling directly from open wagons, as no coal stage was provided. It was a sub-shed to Worcester. The final allocation here was at 1st January, 1947 when the sole occupant was Dean '2721' class 0-6-0PT No. 2774. It was withdrawn shortly after this date, in April 1948. Thereafter, locomotives were simply outstationed from Worcester, returning for washouts and maintenance, and being rotated on a regular basis. Pannier tanks of both Collett and Hawksworth designs were used for shunting the yards, and were exchanged every 10 days. Evesham had several passenger turns as well as local pick-up freight duties, and the 10.10 am freight to Gloucester. Worcester supplied the shed with a variety of Collett '2251' class 0-6-0s, '56XX' class 0-6-2Ts, and both Collett and Churchward '43XX' class 2-6-0s. However, in 1952 it was noted that a 'Hall' was stabled here each Sunday, for a regular turn of passenger duties, including the 4.33 pm to Stratford-on-Avon. During July 1952 this was often No. 7920 *Coney Hall*. In 1954 BR Standard class '2' 2-6-0s from Worcester's allocation of Nos. 78001/4/8/9/14 were regularly stabled here for passenger turns to Leamington and Stratford-on-Avon, being rotated every three or four weeks. Banking engines from Honeybourne (mostly Collett 0-6-0s) were also sent here for minor repairs. After the shed was closed in June 1961 Swindon-built 204 hp 0-6-0DM shunters of class '03' were sent from Worcester, stabling in the goods yard as necessary.

As the line left Evesham station it still initially faced west, until it crossed the River Avon, on the fine lattice girder bridge of two spans, each of 123 ft 7 in. The central piers were constructed of three iron cylinders placed in line, and the abutments on the river banks were of stone with ornamental cappings. Here the line made another 90 degree arc, this time finishing facing south. At this point, it should be noted that there are several rivers named 'Avon' in Britain, the derivation being from the Celtic meaning river (the Welsh 'afon' is another derivation). Our River Avon, rises near Naseby in Northamptonshire, and flows through Leicestershire, Warwickshire and Worcestershire to join the River Severn at Tewkesbury. However,

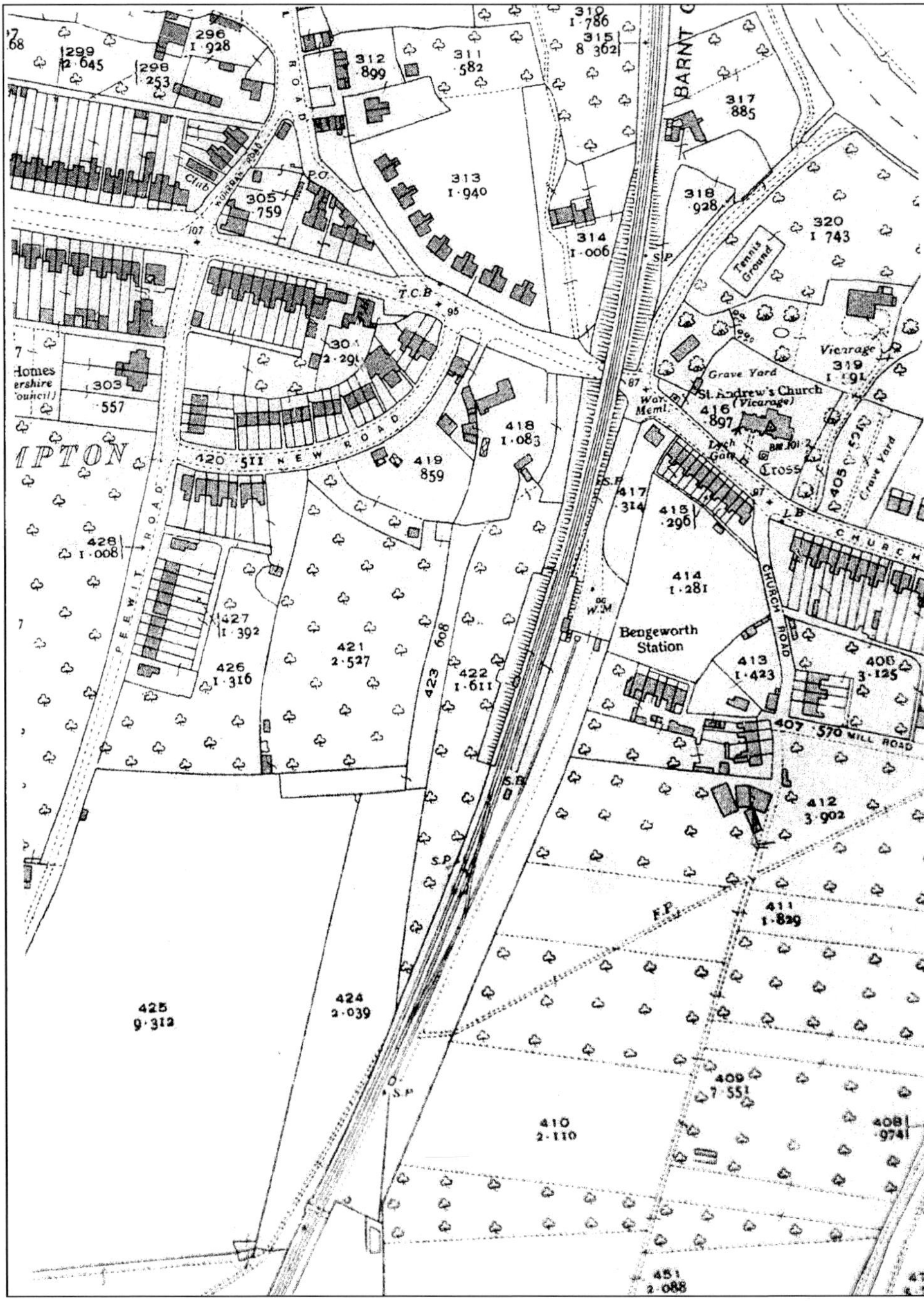

Bengeworth station. *Reproduced from the 25", 1938 Ordnance Survey Map, Crown Copyright*

some misunderstandings have arisen concerning this area, because of another River Avon, which flows through Bristol into the Bristol Channel at Avonmouth, having risen near Tetbury in Gloucestershire.

Having reached the western bank of the Avon, the line then ran alongside it, as the river is describing a large 'U' shape as it passes through Evesham. In the southern suburbs of Evesham, the line arrived at **Bengeworth** (23 miles 20 chains or 23¼ miles). The name adopted by the MR for this station caused more than a little upset, as it is actually located in Great Hampton. However, the MR was concerned that it should not be confused with an existing station of the same name on the Derby line north of Birmingham, let alone others on the LNWR and the London & South Western Railway. The MR were not moved by the pleas of the local population, so the name stayed and the locals just had to get used to it!

The main station building was on the down platform, comprising a single wooden gable-ended affair that included booking office, waiting room and staff room. The up platform contained a small wooden gable-ended waiting shelter, with the typical MR diagonal wooden fencing at the rear of both platforms. Passengers crossed the line by a boarded crossing at the north end of the platforms. Road access to the station and goods yard led from a nearby lane that passed beneath the line north of the station. The goods yard did not open with the line, but nearly three years later on 1st June, 1867. It comprised a single siding of 24 wagons capacity, passing behind the station building, and reached from a short loop that was accessible to both running lines via a crossover. This was a typical arrangement for small MR goods yards served by a double track line. No goods shed was provided, but an old coach body served as a sort of goods store for many years, and a weighbridge was installed in the yard. A hipped-roof MR signal box was opened on 29th July, 1890, being sited at the south end of the down platform. This closed when the goods and passenger services were withdrawn at Bengeworth on 8th June, 1953. The sidings were taken out some considerable time later. By 1962 the platforms were totally derelict and overgrown with weeds, but still discernible.

From here the line ran due south, through fairly flat countryside dotted with the various market gardening establishments for which the area is famous. The River Isbourne was less than a quarter of a mile away, over to the east, and was followed for the next two miles until **Hinton** (24 miles and 76 chains or just under 25 miles) after which the river curved away to its source in the Cotswold hills. The station building was unusually built of local blue lias limestone with Bath facings, with the two-storey gable-ended station master's house featuring a ground floor bay window, positioned at right angles to the platform and adjacent to the road overbridge at the south end of the down platform. A separate single-storey building in the same material was next along the platform, containing the booking hall, waiting room, toilets and staff rooms. On the up platform, a small square, flat-roofed waiting shelter was also executed in the blue limestone. Steps from the lane crossing the line at the south end gave pedestrian access to the down platform, at which point a boarded crossing gave access to the up platform. Although the station nameboards latterly bore the LMS 'hawkseye' signs right up until closure, they were actually mounted on the original MR double staging of a 'V' pattern. The station was downgraded to an unstaffed halt as from 31st August, 1953.

The goods yard was on the down side, comprising a single siding, accessible via a crossover from both running lines, and extending in both directions, with a total capacity of 32 wagons. The small wooden goods shed, painted black, was placed beside the southern siding extension rather than astride it, which extended to the

The entrance to Bengeworth station around 1930, looking west. The railway overbridge has been renewed by the LMS in the plain girder style, compared to the original bow girder. The driveway to the station leads off to the left. *Author's Collection*

LMS Fowler class '4' 2-6-4T No. 2326 calls at the rarely photographed Bengeworth station with the 5.18 pm from Birmingham to Ashchurch on 26th August, 1947. The LMS 'hawkseye' running in board has been attached to the original v- shaped MR framework.

Almonery Heritage Centre Collection

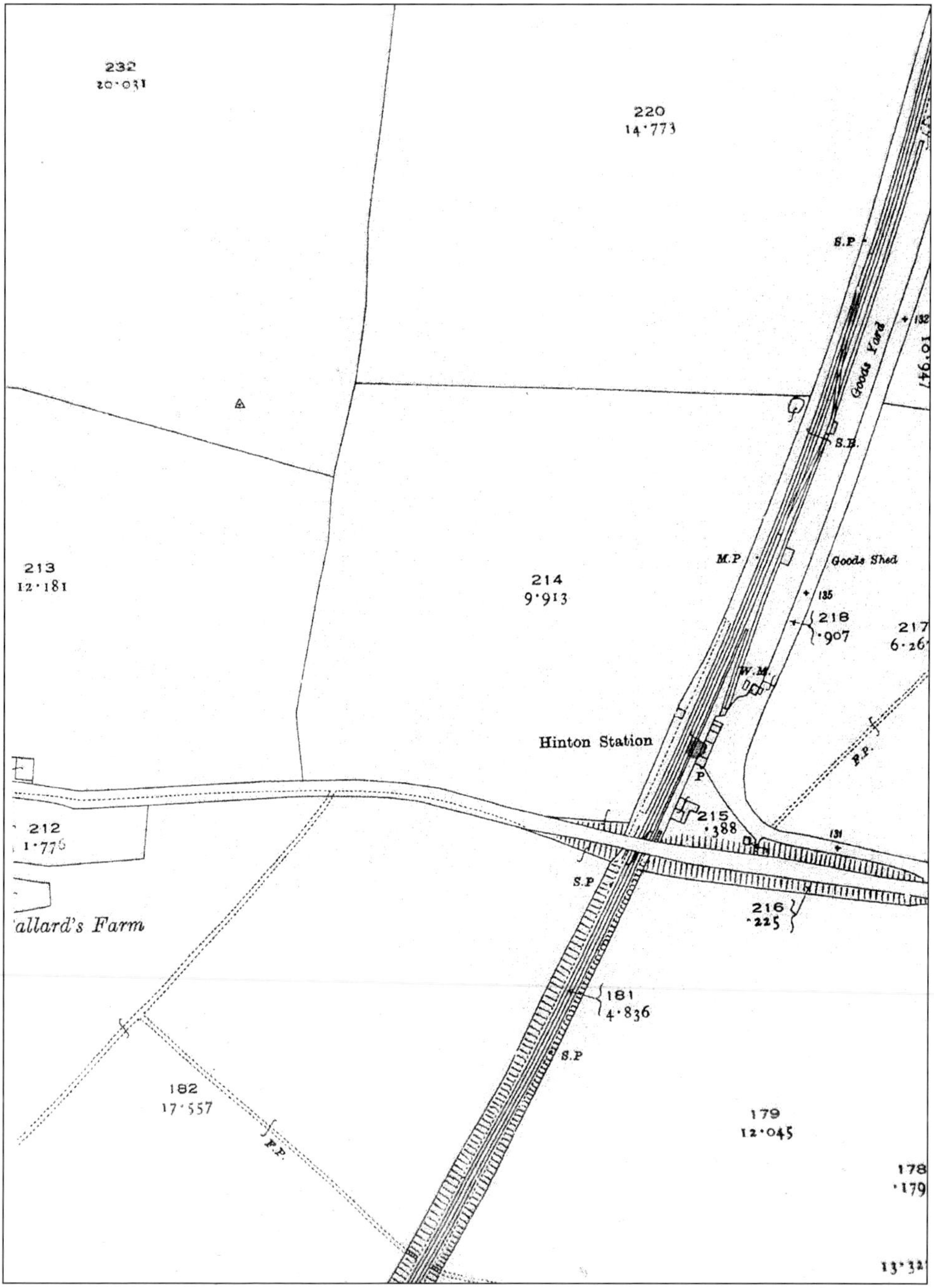

Hinton station. *Reproduced from the 25", 1923 Ordnance Survey Map, Crown Copyright*

A Stanier '8F' class 2-8-0 approaches Hinton station with a southbound freight around 1962. By this time the station had been relegated to an unstaffed halt for some nine years, as reflected in its appearance. *Almonery Heritage Centre Collection*

This view of Hinton station was taken on 31st March, 1962 and is looking southwards towards Ashchurch. The style of architecture used for stations on the Evesham & Ashchuch Railway incorporated much local stonework and differed markedly from those on the line north of Evesham. *G. Parker/Kidderminster Railway Museum*

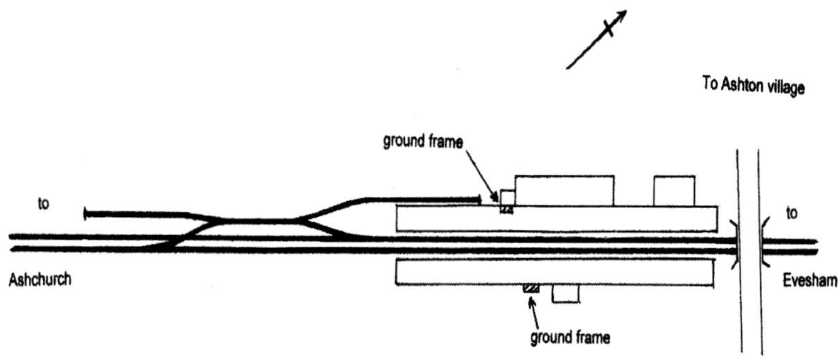

Ashton-under-Hill station diagram *circa* 1914 - not to scale.

station road yard, where a weighbridge was located. An MR hipped-roof signal box was originally provided on 29th July, 1890, on the down side opposite the crossover to the running lines, but was replaced on 8th January, 1924 by a standard LMS gable-ended box. Even though the station was very convenient to the village of Hinton-on-the-Green, it also served the larger village of Sedgeberrow, which despite being only one mile directly to the south, was more like 2½ miles by road.

The line had climbed very slightly since Bengeworth, and after another mile reached a summit after which it descended at an equally easy rate to **Ashton-under-Hill** (26 miles 66 chains or 26¾ miles). The station buildings were identical to those at Hinton, but were a mirror image, being located on the up platform immediately south of an overbridge carrying a lane to the village. Steps from this lane gave pedestrian access to the north end of the up platform, and as at Hinton, a boarded crossing led to the down platform. Once again the MR nameboards with LMS 'hawkseye' signs survived here until closure. This station also became an unmanned halt, but not until 1st March, 1957. The goods yard was also of an identical arrangement to Hinton, but with a slightly larger capacity of 38 wagons, so it is surprising to find that no form of goods shed was ever erected here. The signal box opened on the down side opposite the goods yard on 12th August, 1890 but was closed on 25th January, 1910, being replaced by two open ground frames, one on each of the platforms, which controlled the distant and home signals in each direction, as well as the connections from the running lines to the goods yard.

After cresting a small rise just after the station, the line continued its gradual downhill run, with the two peaks of Dumbleton Hill and Alderton Hill dominating the skyline to the south, and the somewhat larger Bredon Hill on the north side, from which Ashton derived its enlarged name. The line took a change of course to the south-west, and on both sides of the line the activities of the market gardeners and

Ashton-under-Hill station looking northwards to Evesham in the 1950s. The similarity in construction to Hinton station will be observed, although they were mirror images, as the main buildings here are on the up side, whereas at Hinton they were on the down side.

Almonery Heritage Centre Collection

Beckford station retained its glass canopy on the down platform until World War II, which dates this photograph at an earlier date. The goods shed has already been extended, and the goods yard appears to be quite busy. *Almonery Heritage Centre Collection*

apple growers were again quite familiar, as the line entered **Beckford** (28 miles 66 chains or 28¾ miles). Tickets were collected here, as Ashchurch was an 'open' station. This was a somewhat grander station, executed in red brick, with a similar style to Evesham of cream surrounds to the windows, doors and lower string course. Furthermore, it featured one of the MR glass canopies attached to the booking hall and waiting room on the down platform, and supported by cast-iron columns, which with a vaulted central glass section of four bays was both light and airy. This canopy was removed at some time around World War II. Apart from its red brick construction and stone window and door surrounds, the station master's house was similar to the previous two, as indeed was the small square waiting shelter on the up platform. The station name boards were latterly of the standard LMS pattern, with the 'hawkseye' signs, and these too lasted until closure. As well as the usual driveway from the lane passing over the line at the south end of the station, steps for passengers also led from this bridge to the south end of the down platform, where a boarded crossing provided passenger access to the up platform.

The goods yard was more extensive than the previous two, and as we shall see later was the starting point for some northbound goods services during the Summer season, due to its proximity to a large number of orchards. Until Winchcombe received its own line from Honeybourne to Cheltenham, opened by the GWR in 1906, much goods traffic in particular was dealt with here on behalf of that town, despite it being some 10 miles away. There were two loops in the goods yard, and two connections to the main running lines. These led to five sidings with a capacity for 78 wagons, the furthest away being normally used by a local coal and brick merchant, James Taylor & Co. Ltd who had a large depot in the goods yard and a number of their own railway wagons. The next siding led into the large single-road brick-built goods shed, again with cream surrounds to the doors and windows,

This view northwards at Beckford is believed to date from the late 1950s, when the station was still well cared for, as witnessed by the general tidiness, and the exceptional gardens on the up platform surrounding the stone-built waiting shelter. Although it has lost the glass platform canopy, this now better reveals the cream surrounds to the windows and doorways of the red brick building. *J. Tarrant/Kidderminster Railway Museum*

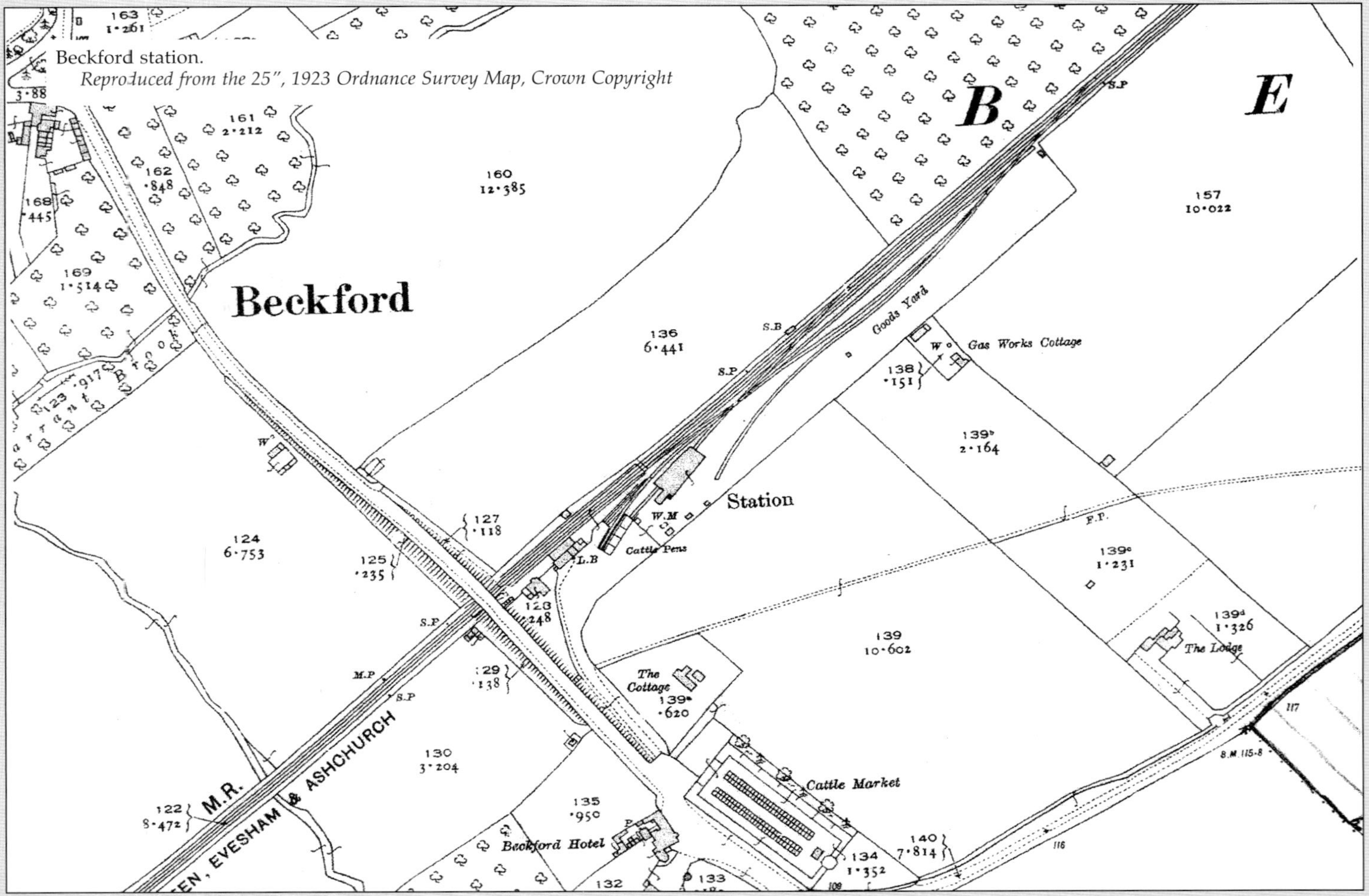

Beckford station.

Reproduced from the 25", 1923 Ordnance Survey Map, Crown Copyright

which around 1924 was extended in plain red brick to approximately double its length and in which a 1½ ton crane was installed. The extended goods shed featured two porches over the unloading decks for road vehicles. Two smaller sidings adjacent to the station buildings led to cattle pens and loading dock, and to an end- and side-loading dock behind the down platform. A large livestock market was located less than a quarter of a mile to the south at the junction of the lane passing over the railway to the village, and the main Evesham to Cheltenham road (A435), which provided a further source of traffic. The fifth siding, installed around 1924, was the most northerly and was generally used as a headshunt.

An MR hipped-roof signal box was opened on 12th August, 1890 on the up side opposite the goods yard and was replaced by a standard LMS gable-ended box on 18th December, 1923 on the same site.

After only half a mile the line passed beneath a minor road bridge that led to the nearby village of Little Beckford, and then after a further mile of generally westerly running crossed into Gloucestershire. To the west there were clear views of the Malvern Hills. The line had been following the course of the Carrant Brook, and shortly after the hamlet of Aston Carrant took a southerly turn to enter **Ashchurch** (32 miles 45 chains or 32½ miles). As the line made its final turn, the large Army Ordnance Depot appeared on the down side, with a trailing junction. The rail connection for this depot was opened on 4th August, 1940 and is still in use today, although to a much lesser extent. War Department locomotives have been used at this site since its opening, and were frequently visible from passing trains. Access to the depot lines was via a separate loop starting at the south end of the station and running to the metal gates across the line, which were controlled by War Department (later Ministry of Defence) personnel. Several additional holding sidings were also put in during World War II alongside the Redditch line, but were removed with the cessation of hostilities. Control over all these sidings was handled by a new signal box, 'Ashchurch East' (not to be confused with the box of the same name referred to below), which came into operation on 13th September, 1942 and remained in use only until 31st December, 1949.

Just after, at the site of Evesham Junction signal box , the double track connection to the Tewkesbury line was visible curving away to the right, and we shall return to this shortly. At the same time, the down running line crossed over to reach the single platform face for branch line trains, which was on the right hand or up side. The Redditch line platform adjoined the down main platform, and opposite, the Tewkesbury line platform adjoined the up main platform. The main station buildings were sited on the up side, and constructed as a single block in a 'V' shape of grey brick with black and grey stone lintels around windows and doors. This contained the Tewkesbury waiting rooms, staff accommodation, with a generous bay window facing the up line, refreshment rooms, the booking hall, up main line waiting rooms and the station master's two-storey house. In front of the booking hall, a three-bay glass canopy led out over the platform, supported by cast-iron columns, with the gable ends at right angles to the line. A large cast-iron drinking fountain with the date '1873' cast therein found later use as a flower bed, but an ornate Victorian post box, with a hinged flap, was retained in its original role. As the Tewkesbury line was constructed at the same time as the station, the opportunity was taken to present a unified and harmonious appearance to the buildings serving both of these lines. The licensed refreshment rooms appear to have been operated by an independent contractor from the outset, and gained a considerable reputation for

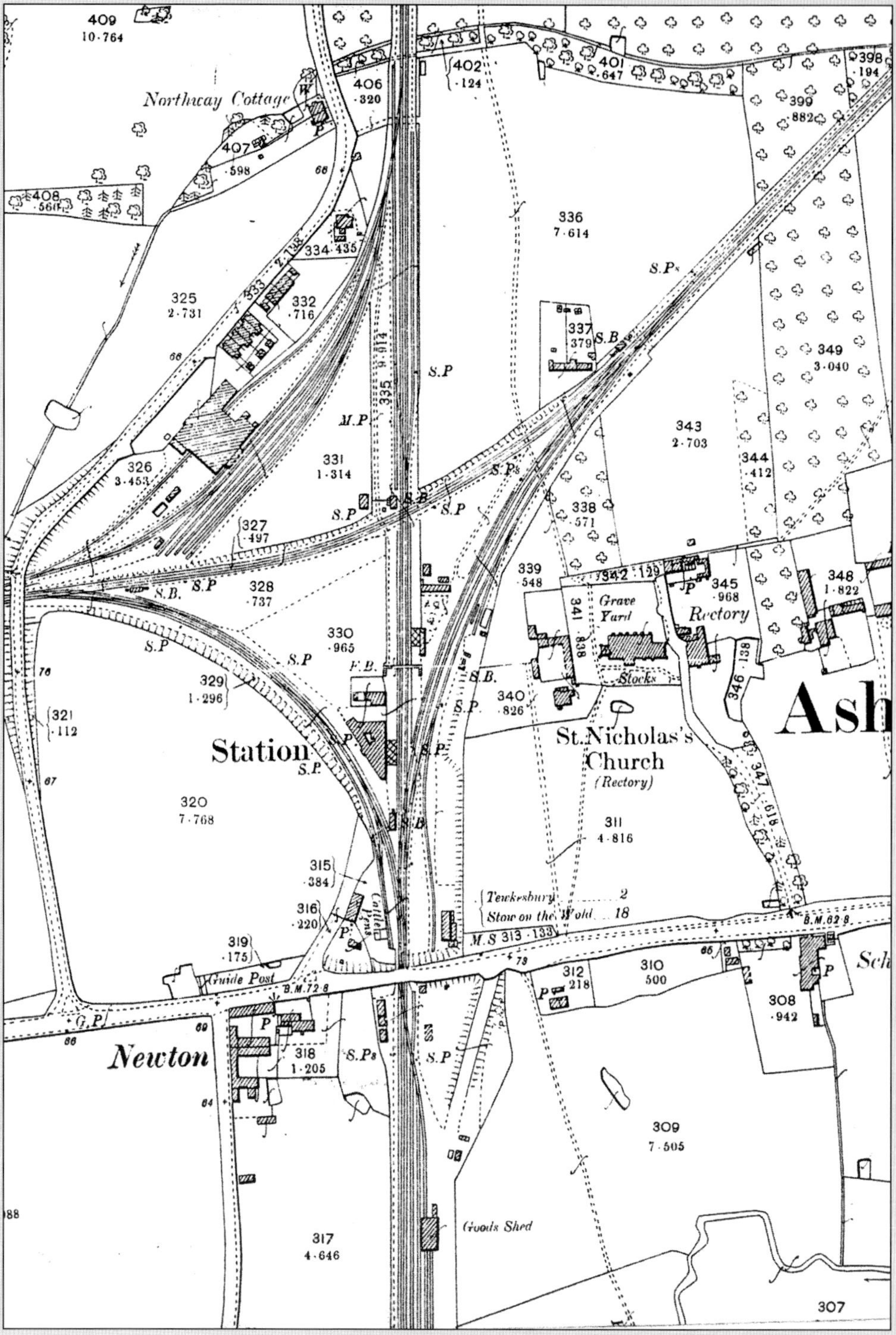

Ashchurch station. *Reproduced from the 25", 1904 Ordnance Survey Map, Crown Copyright*

the quality of their food. In fact, this became a favourite meeting place during World War II for US airmen based locally and their local girlfriends. The only access for both vehicles and pedestrians was to the main station frontage, there being no external access to the down side platforms.

A black lattice iron footbridge was erected around 1883, connecting the up and down platforms. Presumably prior to this date the only means of such access would have been by a boarded crossing - not a particularly good practice here, as main line expresses have always been able to make considerable speed along this stretch of line. A large gong on the station building was sounded when trains were approaching, even if they were not stopping, and this practice may have originated as a warning to passengers in the days before the footbridge. The smaller buildings on the down platform were constructed in a similar style, and formed an uneven 'V' shape between the platforms, but only consisted of waiting rooms for each of the two platforms. The irregular shape of these small buildings reflects their construction at different dates. However, the down main platform was furnished with a smaller version of the glass canopy on the up platform, this time of just two bays, but still very appealing. All of the wooden station nameboards were of LMS pattern with wooden raised lettering and surrounds picked out in cream, and survived until closure. The largest, on the up platform, read 'Ashchurch. Junction for Tewkesbury, Evesham and Redditch'.

The goods yard, with capacity for 100 wagons, was sited south of the station on the down side of the main line, just beyond the overbridge carrying the Tewkesbury to Stow-on-the-Wold road (A438), from which a driveway led to the goods shed. This was a single-road, red brick structure, with rail access directly from the Redditch line, as well as main line connections and a 1½ ton crane.

The connection from the Redditch line to the Tewkesbury line involved a flat crossing, almost at right angles, at the northern end of the main platforms. Originally constructed as a double track line, this was singled in 1927. The signal boxes opened in 1876 and controlling each end of this connection, Ashchurch East (formerly 'Evesham Junction') on the Evesham line, and Ashchurch West (formerly 'Tewkesbury Junction') on the Tewkesbury line were both closed on 16th October 1927. The connection was finally taken out of use as from 5th May, 1957 but not officially closed until 24th May, 1957. The possible uses of this connection will be examined in the next chapter. On the north-western side of this line was a large imposing red brick building, originally constructed as Provender Stores by the MR. Rail access was available from the Tewkesbury line (removed as part of the 1927 track reorganization) and from the up main line. This building was certainly in use by 1876, and reflects the importance of providing horse feed at that time. Bearing in mind that most of the road deliveries by the railway companies were made by horse and cart until well into the 1930s, as well as their use around the many goods yards, it can be seen that feedstuffs were vital. It is not often appreciated that one of the duties of the gangers working on the lines was to cut the grass on embankments and cuttings, which was collected for use as feedstuff. Eventually, when this was no longer required, this building was sold to the Cotswold Packaging Company, who in 1935 were using it for the packing of fruit and other goods. These were packed directly into railway wagons, for onward shipment. The engineering company of Dowty Ltd later put it to use, but it was demolished, possibly in the 1970s. Nearby, a large water tower with a brick built base for stores was located just north of the level crossing, to feed the water column adjacent to the 'Junction' signal box (*see below*) and to supply the station and yards with non-potable water.

Looking north to Ashchurch station at an unknown date prior to the Grouping of 1923, as the wagons on the right are lettered 'M.R.'. The Kirtley 0-6-0 with curved double frames on the right, appears to be engaged in some shunting duties from the Evesham, whilst further along that line a string of passenger stock is stabled. The line and platform for Tewkesbury and Malvern trains curves away to the left, and the 1890 Junction signal box is prominent at the south end of the up main platform. *Roy Burrows Collection*

As a Swindon-built dmu calls at Ashchurch station with a down main line service, Collett pannier tank No. 4614 waits at the branch line platform with a service to Evesham on 1st June, 1963. *W. Potter/Kidderminster Railway Museum*

A hipped-roof 'Level Crossing' signal box to protect the level crossing was installed on the up side of the main line north of the crossing before 1877, but was replaced by a similar box on the same side but south of the crossing on 16th September, 1900. This was, in turn, replaced by a further box on 16th October, 1927 immediately opposite, on the down platform just south of the crossing, which also took over the functions of the two smaller boxes at each end of the connection, mentioned above. Also in 1877, 'Ashchurch Junction' box was opened on the main line on the down side just south of the Redditch line junction, and was replaced by a further hipped roof MR-style box sited at the south end of the up main platform in 1900. This was replaced by a brick and concrete box on the site of the original 'Junction' box, with effect from 27th July, 1958. This closed on 16th February, 1969, control passing to the new Gloucester Panel signal box.

Several sources have speculated about the erection of an early engine shed at Ashchurch. MR records reveal that foundations for a turntable were placed in 1863, and that at the same time orders were given that 'a temporary shed for one engine be erected', which was to be 'a corrugated iron locomotive shed' at a cost of £35. The coal stage received a new roof in 1914 at an estimated cost of £50. An inspection/ash pit was located adjacent to the station near to the water column, and almost opposite the junction of the Tewkesbury line, and may owe its existence to this early engine shed, which had disappeared prior to the Grouping of 1923. However, the engine shed at Tewkesbury which opened between 1859 and 1864, and was only two miles distant, thereafter provided stabling for locomotives whose duties terminated at Ashchurch. After the closure of Evesham shed in 1931, locomotives regularly ran as light engines from there to Tewkesbury. Although the last passenger train to Tewkesbury ran on 14th August, 1961 the shed remained open for the daily goods service to Upton, and for servicing locomotives from the Redditch line until 7th September, 1962.

LMS Compound 4-4-0 No. 1049 has just crossed the Evesham to Tewkesbury chord line, and enters Ashchurch station with a stopping train on 18th April, 1949. The level crossing signal box can be seen behind the tender. *W. Potter/Kidderminster Railway Museum*

MIDLAND RAILWAY.

OPENING OF THE ALCESTER AND REDDITCH SECTION

OF THE

EVESHAM AND REDDITCH RAILWAY.

ON MONDAY NEXT, MAY 4th, 1868, and until further notice, Trains will run between BARNT GREEN, REDDITCH, ALCESTER, EVESHAM, and ASHCHURCH, in connection with the Main Line Trains, as under:—

WEEK-DAYS—DOWN.

	1 2 GOV.	1 2 Class	1 2 Class	1 2 GOV.	1 2 GOV.	1 2 GOV.
	a.m.	a.m.	p.m.	p.m.	p.m.	p.m.
BIRMINGHAM .... dep.	7 0	9 45	1 0	5 5	6 30	7 55
Camp Hill .... ,,	7 11	9 53	1 9	5 13	6 38	8 5
Moseley .... ,,	7 14	9 58	1 13	5 18	6 41	8 8
King's Heath............ ,,	7 18	10 3	1 18	5 23	6 44	8 11
King's Norton .... ,,	7 25	10 10	1 25	5 30	6 51	8 18
Barnt Green .... arr.	7 38	10 22	1 35	5 42	7 2	8 31
Barnt Green .... dep.	7 45	10 24	1 37	5 47	7 5	8 45
Alvechurch	7 51	10 29	1 43	5 53	7 11	8 51
REDDITCH..............	8 0	10 37	1 51	6 2	7 20	9 0
Studley and Astwood Bank..	8 7	10 44	1 58	6 9	..	
Coughton	8 13	10 50	2 4	6 15	..	..
Alcester..............	8 19	10 56	2 10	6 21	..	..
Wixford..............	8 25	11 2	2 16	6 27	..	..
Salford Priors	8 30	11 7	2 21	6 32	..	..
Harvington	8 36	11 13	2 27	6 38	..	..
EVESHAM .... arr.	8 43	11 20	2 34	6 45	..	
G. W. Railway. Evesham.............. dep.	10 33	..	2 50	7 1	..	..
Moreton .... arr.	11 14	..	3 30	7 42	..	..
Oxford.............. ,,	12 25	..	4 40	8 48	..	..
Oxford.............. dep.	.	8 30	11 40	3 10	..	..
Moreton .... ,,	.	9 45	12 45	4 25	..	..
Evesham.............. arr.	.	10 20	1 21	5 3	..	..
EVESHAM .... dep.	8 45	11 22	2 36	6 47	..	..
Bengeworth	8 50	11 27	2 41	6 52	..	..
Hinton	8 55	11 32	2 46	6 57	..	..
Ashton-under-Hill	9 1	11 38	2 52	7 3	..	..
Beckford	9 6	11 43	2 57	7 8	..	..
ASHCHURCH .... arr.	9 15	11 52	3 6	7 17	..	..
Tewkesbury .... arr.	9 34	12 15	4 19	7 43	..	..
Upton.............. ,,	10 10	1 50	4 35	8 0	..	..
Great Malvern .... ,,	10 30	2 10	4 52	8 20	..	..
Ashchurch.............. dep.	9 20	11 59	3 48	7 27	..	..
Cheltenham .... arr.	9 44	12 20	4 7	7 51	..	..
Gloucester .... ,,	9 58	12 35	4 22	8 10	..	..
Bristol.............. ,,	11 55	2 25	5 35	10 10	..	..

WEEK-DAYS—UP.

		a.m.	a.m.	a.m.	p.m.	p.m.
Bristol.............. dep.	..	6 0	8 0	8 45	3 20	4 20
Gloucester..............	..	8 5	9 3	10 40	4 34	6 20
Cheltenham	..	8 23	9 24	10 57	4 50	6 39
Ashchurch .... arr.	..	8 42	9 39	11 12	..	7 2
Great Malvern .... dep.	..		8 30	11 10	2 55	6 35
Upton..............	..		8 47	11 27	3 12	6 53
Tewkesbury	..		9 5	11 45	4 50	7 12
	1 2 GOV.	1 2 GOV.	1 2 GOV.	1 2 Class	1 2 GOV.	1 2 GOV.
	a.m.	a.m.	a.m.	p.m.	p.m.	p.m.
ASHCHURCH.......... dep.	..	..	9 50	12 30	5 22	7 35
Beckford	..	..	9 59	12 39	5 31	7 44
Ashton-under-Hill	..	..	10 5	12 45	5 37	7 50
Hinton		..	10 10	12 50	5 42	7 55
Bengeworth	..	..	10 16	12 56	5 48	8 1
EVESHAM .... arr.	..	..	10 21	1 1	5 53	8 6
G. W. Railway. Evesham .... dep.	..	..	10 33	2 50	7 1	STOP.
Moreton .... arr.	..	..	11 14	3 30	7 42	..
Oxford.............. ,,	..	..	12 25	4 40	8 48	..
Oxford.............. dep.	..	..	8 30	..	3 10	..
Moreton .... ,,	..	..	9 45	..	4 25	..
Evesham.............. arr.	..	..	10 20	..	5 3	..
EVESHAM .... dep.	..	7 15	10 30	1 6	5 55	..
Harvington	..	7 22	10 37	1 13	6 2	..
Salford Priors	..	7 28	10 43	1 19	6 8	..
Wixford..............	..	7 34	10 49	1 25	6 14	..
Alcester	..	7 41	10 56	1 32	6 21	1 2
Coughton	..	7 46	11 1	1 37	6 26	GOV.
Studley and Astwood Bank..	..	7 52	11 7	1 43	6 32	p.m.
REDDITCH..............	7 15	8 0	11 15	2 0	6 40	8 10
Alvechurch	7 23	8 8	11 23	2 8	6 48	8 19
Barnt Green .... arr.	7 30	8 14	11 30	2 13	6 55	8 25
Barnt Green .... dep.	..	8 15	11 32	2 15	7 10	8 44
King's Norton .... arr.	..	8 24	11 42	2 26	7 20	8 55
King's Heath.............. ,,	..	8 31	11 50	2 32	7 28	9 4
Moseley.............. ,,	..	8 35	11 54	2 37	7 32	9 8
Camp Hill .... ,,	..	8 38	11 57	2 41	7 37	9 11
BIRMINGHAM .... ,,	..	8 50	12 10	2 55	7 50	9 25

Third Class Passengers are conveyed by all Trains between Barnt Green and Redditch, also between Birmingham, Alvechurch, and Redditch, only.

This Table shews the Times at which the Trains may be expected to arrive at and depart from the several Stations, but their departure or arrival at the times stated is not guaranteed, nor does the Company hold itself responsible for delay or any consequence arising therefrom.

The Classes of Trains shewn on this Table refer only to Stations between Barnt Green, Alcester, Evesham, and Ashchurch.

Third Class Passengers are Booked Through from Redditch, Alcester, and Evesham, to Tewkesbury, Cheltenham, Gloucester, and Bristol, by Trains leaving Redditch at 8.0 a.m. and 6.2 p.m.

Third Class Passengers are Booked Through from Bristol at 6.0 a.m. and 4.20 p.m.; Gloucester at 8.5 a.m. and 6.20 p.m.; Cheltenham at 8.23 a.m. and 6.39 p.m.; and Tewkesbury at 9.5 a.m. and 7.12 p.m., to Evesham.

NOTICE.—All Time-Tables and Notices of a previous date, respecting the running of Trains between Barnt Green, Redditch, Alcester, Evesham, and Ashchurch, are withdrawn.

Public timetable at opening of the entire line, as published in the *Redditch Indicator*, 2nd May, 1868.

Chapter Seven

Working the line From 1868 to 1964

This chapter covers train operations and methods of working from the opening of the through route in 1868, to the closure of through services south of Redditch to passengers (effective from 15th June, 1963) and goods (officially from 6th July, 1964).

Passenger Services

An opening timetable from May 1868 is illustrated opposite. This shows a very straightforward level of down services, with all such trains starting from Birmingham - four through to Ashchurch and two evening services as far as Redditch. At least three of the Ashchurch services appear to run through to Gloucester, with connections for Bristol. The fourth service, departing Ashchurch at 3.48 pm, is a main line service through to Bristol. The up services show a slightly different pattern, with the first starting from Bristol at 8.00 am and travelling via Redditch, the second and fourth being main line connections, starting from Gloucester. The third does not stop at Ashchurch, begging the question as to why it is included in the timetable as it could not have connected with the Tewkesbury services either, even if it did stop. The fourth service terminated at Evesham at 8.06 pm. In addition, one Birmingham train started from Evesham (at 7.15 am). The two trains starting from Redditch were an early morning service to Barnt Green only, and a late evening return to Birmingham. There were no trains on Sundays. Interestingly, although all trains catered for first and second class passengers, 'Government' or 'Parliamentary' class passengers were not permitted on the two morning down trains and one lunchtime up train. Presumably, working class people would be expected to be just that, at work at that time of day.

Two and a half years later, in November 1870, there was a distinct improvement in the number of services (*see page 138*). The four through down services were still mostly on their previous timings and routes. However, there were two further services for Redditch only, one during the afternoon, leaving Birmingham at 3.55 pm and a further late night service at 10.40 pm, not stopping at Northfield and Alvechurch. A further Mondays-only service was introduced between Evesham (depart 5.20 pm) and Gloucester, for the benefit of persons returning from the market at Evesham. In the up direction, there were additional departures from Redditch at 8.48 am and 4.58 pm, but the early morning service to Barnt Green had ceased. The outward part of the Mondays-only service from Gloucester left there at 1.15 pm terminating in Evesham at 2.15 pm, and giving travellers the opportunity to spend the afternoon at the weekly market. There were still no Sunday trains.

Moving forward to January 1879 the first two down trains ran through to Ashchurch as before, but the 1.00 pm departure from Birmingham ran only as far as Redditch. The next train ran south from Redditch at 2.05 pm on Mondays only to Evesham for the market day, and on Tuesdays and Saturdays to Alcester for their market, but none of these stopped at Coughton. The mid-afternoon service to Redditch was dropped, but the return market train from Evesham to Ashchurch on Mondays still ran. The three evening services to Redditch were slightly retimed, with the final train leaving Birmingham an hour earlier at 9.35 pm. The up services

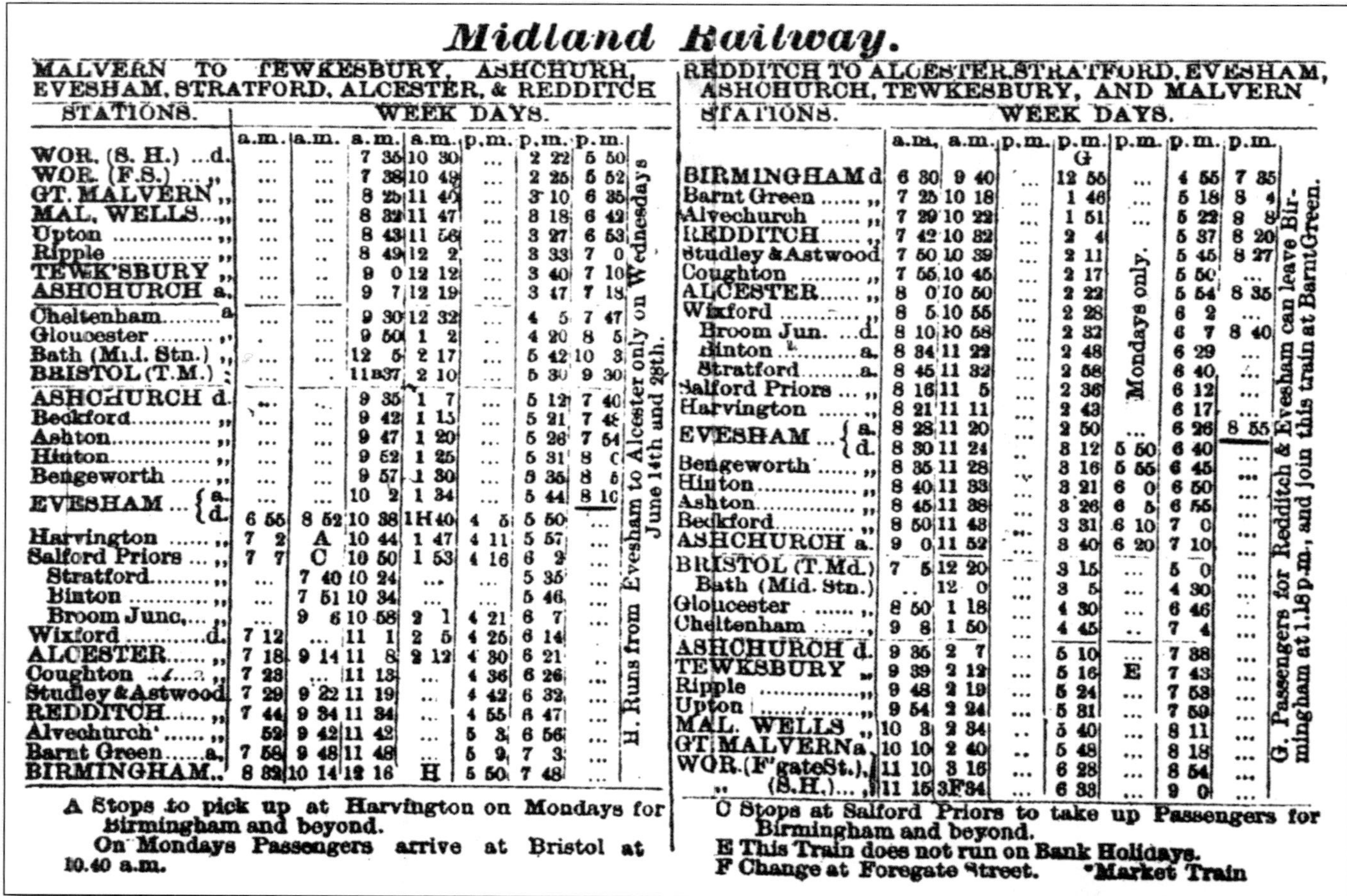

Midland Railway.

MALVERN TO TEWKESBURY, ASHCHURCH, EVESHAM, STRATFORD, ALCESTER, & REDDITCH

STATIONS.	WEEK DAYS. a.m.	a.m.	a.m.	a.m.	p.m.	p.m.	p.m.
WOR. (S. H.) ...d.	...	...	7 35	10 30	...	2 22	5 50
WOR. (F.S.) ... ,,	...	...	7 38	10 49	...	2 25	5 52
GT. MALVERN ,,	...	...	8 25	11 40	...	3 10	6 35
MAL. WELLS ,,	...	...	8 32	11 47	...	3 18	6 42
Upton ,,	...	...	8 43	11 56	...	3 27	6 53
Ripple ,,	...	..	8 49	12 2	...	3 33	7 0
TEWK'SBURY ,,	...	..	9 0	12 12	...	3 40	7 10
ASHCHURCH a.	...	...	9 7	12 19	...	3 47	7 18
Cheltenham a.	...	...	9 30	12 32	...	4 5	7 47
Gloucester ,,	.	...	9 50	1 2	...	4 20	8 5
Bath (Mid. Stn.) ,,	...	...	12 5	2 17	...	5 42	10 3
BRISTOL (T.M.) ,,	...	.	11B37	2 10	...	5 30	9 30
ASHCHURCH d.	...	...	9 35	1 7	...	5 12	7 40
Beckford ,,	...	...	9 42	1 15	...	5 21	7 48
Ashton ,,	...	...	9 47	1 20	...	5 26	7 54
Hinton ,,	...	...	9 52	1 25	...	5 31	8 0
Bengeworth ,,	...	...	9 57	1 30	...	5 35	8 5
EVESHAM ... a.	...	...	10 2	1 34	...	5 44	8 10
EVESHAM ... d.	6 55	8 52	10 38	1H40	4 5	5 50	...
Harvington ,,	7 2	A	10 44	1 47	4 11	5 57	...
Salford Priors ... ,,	7 7	C	10 50	1 53	4 16	6 2	...
Stratford ,,	...	7 40	10 24	...	...	5 35	...
Binton ,,	...	7 51	10 34	...	...	5 46	...
Broom Junc. ,,	...	9 6	10 58	2 1	4 21	6 7	...
Wixford d.	7 12	...	11 1	2 5	4 25	6 14	...
ALCESTER ,,	7 18	9 14	11 8	2 12	4 30	6 21	..
Coughton ,,	7 23	...	11 13	...	4 36	6 26	...
Studley & Astwood	7 29	9 22	11 19	...	4 42	6 32	...
REDDITCH ,,	7 44	9 34	11 34	...	4 55	6 47	...
Alvechurch* ,,	52	9 42	11 42	...	5 3	6 56	...
Barnt Green a.	7 58	9 48	11 48	...	5 9	7 3	...
BIRMINGHAM..	8 32	10 14	12 16	H	5 50	7 48	...

H. Runs from Evesham to Alcester only on Wednesdays June 14th and 28th.

A Stops to pick up at Harvington on Mondays for Birmingham and beyond.
On Mondays Passengers arrive at Bristol at 10.40 a.m.

REDDITCH TO ALCESTER, STRATFORD, EVESHAM, ASHCHURCH, TEWKESBURY, AND MALVERN

STATIONS.	WEEK DAYS. a.m.	a.m.	p.m.	p.m. G	p.m.	p.m.	p.m.
BIRMINGHAM d.	6 30	9 40	...	12 55	...	4 55	7 35
Barnt Green ,,	7 25	10 18	...	1 46	...	5 18	8 4
Alvechurch ,,	7 29	10 22	...	1 51	...	5 22	8 8
REDDITCH ,,	7 42	10 32	...	2 4	...	5 37	8 20
Studley & Astwood	7 50	10 39	...	2 11	...	5 45	8 27
Coughton ,,	7 55	10 45	...	2 17	Mondays only.	5 50	...
ALCESTER ,,	8 0	10 50	...	2 22		5 54	8 35
Wixford ,,	8 5	10 55	...	2 28		6 2	...
Broom Jun. d.	8 10	10 58	...	2 32		6 7	8 40
Binton a.	8 34	11 22	...	2 48		6 29	...
Stratford a.	8 45	11 32	...	2 58		6 40	...
Salford Priors ,,	8 16	11 5	...	2 36		6 12	...
Harvington ,,	8 21	11 11	...	2 43		6 17	...
EVESHAM ... a.	8 28	11 20	...	2 50	...	6 26	8 55
EVESHAM ... d.	8 30	11 24	..	3 12	5 50	6 40	...
Bengeworth ,,	8 35	11 28	..	3 16	5 55	6 45	...
Hinton ,,	8 40	11 33	...	3 21	6 0	6 50	...
Ashton ,,	8 45	11 38	...	3 26	6 5	6 55	...
Beckford ,,	8 50	11 43	...	3 31	6 10	7 0	...
ASHCHURCH a.	9 0	11 52	...	3 40	6 20	7 10	...
BRISTOL (T.Md.)	7 5	12 20	...	3 15	...	5 0	...
Bath (Mid. Stn.)	..	12 0	...	3 5	...	4 30	...
Gloucester ,,	8 50	1 18	...	4 30	...	6 46	...
Cheltenham ,,	9 8	1 50	...	4 45	..	7 4	...
ASHCHURCH d.	9 35	2 7	...	5 10	...	7 38	...
TEWKSBURY ,,	9 39	2 12	...	5 16	E	7 43	...
Ripple ,,	9 48	2 19	...	5 24	...	7 53	...
Upton ,,	9 54	2 24	...	5 31	...	7 59	...
MAL. WELLS ,,	10 3	2 34	..	5 40	...	8 11	...
GT. MALVERN a.	10 10	2 40	..	5 48	...	8 18	...
WOR. (F'gate St.)	11 10	3 16	...	6 28	...	8 54	...
,, (S.H.) ...	11 15	3F34	...	6 38	...	9 0	...

G. Passengers for Redditch & Evesham can leave Birmingham at 1.18 p.m., and join this train at Barnt Green.

C Stops at Salford Priors to take up Passengers for Birmingham and beyond.
E This Train does not run on Bank Holidays.
F Change at Foregate Street. *Market Train

Public timetable for the line, as published in the *Berrow's Worcester Journal*, 24th June, 1870.

saw the return of the early morning 7.05 am service from Redditch to Barnt Green, and the 8.48 am departure from Redditch to Birmingham was retimed to 9.20 am. The two other morning services (from Evesham, and from Ashchurch) ran as before, but the 12.30 pm departure from Ashchurch was retimed to 1.00 pm and ran on Tuesdays terminating at Alcester, for the market. The 1.45 pm market day train from Ashchurch to Evesham was retimed to 2.00 pm running as before on Mondays only. The final three trains of the day, from Gloucester to Birmingham, Ashchurch to Evesham and Redditch to Birmingham ran as before.

By October 1880, the 4.58 pm from Redditch was extended to leave from Evesham at 3.55 pm to Birmingham, but otherwise the services stayed the same. To summarize, the down trains comprised three Birmingham to Ashchurch, one Birmingham to Evesham, four Birmingham to Redditch and the market trains to Alcester and from Evesham. The up services were two Ashchurch to Birmingham, two Evesham to Birmingham, four Redditch to Birmingham, one Ashchurch to Evesham, and the market trains.

It should be mentioned that the opening in April 1876 of the Birmingham West Suburban Railway (BWSR) from a new station at Granville Street through Selly Oak and Bournville to meet the original Camp Hill line at Kings Norton, gave a potential new route for our services. However, this line was at first limited to local trains to Kings Norton, and other services for destinations further south were only gradually moved on to it. In fact, it was not until 1885 that southbound sevices from New Street were able to take this route.

By May 1885 the services were somewhat simplified with four trains from Birmingham at 6.40, 9.40 am, 1.25 and 5.02 pm to Ashchurch stopping at all stations. These departures took over the slots of previous trains, which of course had not all run the entire route. The return market train from Evesham to Ashchurch still ran on Mondays, but those for the Alcester market were incorporated into the daily through services. In the up direction, as before there were two from Ashchurch to Birmingham, two from Evesham to Birmingham, and one from Ashchurch to Evesham, and the return Evesham market train on Mondays. A new daily service from Ashchurch was at 1.20 pm for Evesham, which ran forward on Tuesdays to Alcester for the market. No trains now started from Redditch to Birmingham, and there was still no Sunday service.

June 1894 gave principally the same four through services each way, with the 1.25 pm departure from Birmingham to Ashchurch being retimed to leave half an hour earlier. The only other changes were that the return market train from Evesham to Ashchurch then left nearly an hour later, at 5.50 pm, and one new service was added, being an evening 'express' from Birmingham to Evesham at 7.30 pm, which after Redditch only stopped at Alcester and Broom. This was matched by a new morning departure from Evesham at 8.50 am with the same restrictions and the Alcester and Evesham market trains in this direction were eliminated. All other services continued as in 1885.

The 1894 timetable continued in June 1899 with the only addition being that the 1.07 pm departure from Ashchurch to Evesham was once again extended to run through to Alcester on Tuesdays. The only other change was that passengers at Harvington and Salford Priors were picked up by the limited stop 8.52 am departure from Evesham, as long as they were travelling to Birmingham or beyond. One further item of note is that passengers for south of Barnt Green could catch a 1.18 pm departure from Birmingham, which overtook the 12.55 pm Ashchurch departure, and then join this train at Barnt Green! This, of course, only worked as long as both trains were running on time.

MIDLAND RAILWAY.

TIME TABLE for NOVEMBER, and until further notice.

The Classes of Trains shewn on this Table refer only to Stations between Barnt Green, Alcester, Evesham, & Ashchurch.	WEEK DAYS.—DOWN.							
	1 2 Gov.	1 2 Class	1 2 Class	1 2 Gov.	1 2 Gov.	1 2 Gov.	1 2 Gov.	1 2 Gov.
	a.m.	a.m.	p.m.	p.m.	p.m.	p.m.	p.m.	p.m
BIRMINGHAM ......dep.	6 50	9 40	1 0	3 55	5 5	6 25	8 0	10 40
Camp Hill	7 3	9 48	1 8	4 3	5 13	6 33	8 10	10 43
Moseley	7 7	9 52	1 12	4 7	5 17	6 36	8 14	10 52
King's Heath............	7 11	9 56	1 16	4 11	5 21	6 39	8 18	10 56
King's Norton	7 18	10 3	1 22	4 17	5 27	6 46	8 25	11 2
Northfield	7 23	10 8	1 27	4 22	5 32	6 51	8 30	..
Barnt Green..........arr.	7 32	10 17	1 34	4 29	5 39	6 59	8 41	11 14
Barnt Green..........dep.	7 40	10 22	1 37	4 32	5 43	7 12	9 2	11 16
Alvechurch	7 46	10 28	1 43	4 38	5 49	7 18	9 8	..
Redditch	7 55	10 37	1 54	4 45	5 59	7 27	9 15	11 30
Studley & Astwood Bank ..	8 2	10 44	2 1		6 7	..	..	..
Coughton	8 8	10 50	2 7	1 2	6 13	..	..	..
ALCESTER	8 14	10 57	2 14	Gov.	6 20	..	..	..
Wixford	8 20	11 2	2 20	Runs on Mondays only between Evesham and Gloucester.	6 25	..	..	..
Salford Priors............	8 25	11 7	2 25		6 30	..	..	..
Harvington............	8 31	11 12	2 31		6 35	..	..	..
Evesham ....arr.	8 38	11 19	2 38		6 42	..	..	..
G. W. Railway.								
Evesham ....dep.	10 25	11 48	3 4		7 10	..	..	..
Evesham...... ,,	10 34	..	3 4		7 10	..	..	..
Stratford	11 20	..	5 47		7 54	..	..	..
Warwick	11 55	..	6 33		8 30	..	..	..
Leamington	12 0	..	6 38		8 35	..	..	..
Oxford	11 55	2 2	5 8		9 3	..	..	..
London, Pddngtn., arr.	1 45	3 50	6 50		10 40	..	..	..
London, Pddngtn., dp.	..	6 0	10 0		2 20	..	..	..
Oxford	..	8 27	11 40		4 10	..	..	..
Leamington	..	8 0	10 20		3 40	..	..	..
Warwick	..	8 5	10 25		3 45	..	..	..
Stratford	..	8 38	11 12		4 30	..	..	..
Evesham...... ,,	..	9 20	11 42		5 30	..	..	..
Evesham ....arr.	..	10 18	1 6		5 30	..	..	..
Evesham ....dep.	8 40	11 22	2 40	5 20	6 49	..	..	..
Bengeworth............	8 45	11 26	2 45	5 25	9 53	..	..	..
Hinton	8 50	11 31	2 50	5 30	6 58	..	..	..
Ashton-under-Hill	8 56	11 36	2 56	5 36	7 3	..	..	..
Beckford	9 1	11 41	3 1	5 41	7 8	..	..	..
Ashchurch ....arr.	9 10	11 50	3 10	5 50	7 17	..	..	..
Tewkesbury ....arr.	9 56	12 15	3 20	6 0	7 35	..	..	..
Upton .... ,,	10 11	1 46	5 25	..	7 50	..	..	..
Great Malvern .... ,,	10 30	2 6	5 45	..	8 10	..	..	..
Ashchurch ....dep.	9 18	12 8	3 51	5 52	7 27	..	..	..
Cheltenham ....arr.	9 41	12 23	4 10	6 13	7 49	..	..	..
Gloucester............ ,,	9 56	12 38	4 25	6 30	8 5	..	..	..
Bath (Midland Stn.).. ,,	12 30	2 40	5 50	..	..	..	..	..
Bristol .... ,,	11 55	2 20	5 38	..	10 0	..	..	..

The Classes of Trains shewn on this Table refer only to Stations between Ashchurch, Evesham, Alcester, and Barnt Green.	WEEK DAYS—UP.						
	1 2 Gov.	1 2 Gov.	1 2 Gov.	1 2 Class	1 2 Gov.	1 2 Gov.	1 2 Gov.
	a.m.	a.m.	a.m.	a.m.	p.m.	p.m.	p.m.
Bristol ....dep.	..	6 0	8 0	10 10	..	3 15	4 35
Bath (Midland Stn.).. ,,	..	..	7 40	9 55	..	3 0	4 15
Gloucester .... ,,	..	8 0	9 12	11 22	1 15	4 30	6 33
Cheltenham .... ,,	..	8 21	9 32	11 40	1 29	4 47	6 53
Ashchurch ....arr.	..	8 42	9 47	11 55	1 42	5 2	7 15
Great Malvern........dep.	..		8 30	11 5	..	2 55	6 30
Upton .... ,,	..		8 47	11 23	..	3 12	6 48
Tewkesbury .... ,,	..		9 5	11 50	1 7	5 0	7 5
Ashchurch ....dep	..	..	9 50	12 30	1 45	5 20	7 35
Beckford	..	..	9 58	12 39	1 53	5 28	7 44
Ashton-under-Hill	..	..	10 4	12 45	1 59	5 33	7 50
Hinton	..	..	10 9	12 50	2 5	5 38	7 55
Bengeworth	..	..	10 15	12 56	2 10	5 43	8 1
Evesham ....arr.	..	..	10 19	1 1	2 15	5 47	8 6
G. W. Railway.							
Evesham ....dep.	..	..	10 25	3 4	1 2	7 10	..
Evesham ...... ,,	..	..	10 34	3 4	Gov.	7 10	..
Stratford	..	..	11 20	5 47	Runs on Mondays only between Glo'ster and Evesham.	7 54	..
Warwick	..	..	11 55	6 33		8 30	..
Leamington..........	..	..	12 0	6 38		8 35	..
Oxford ....arr.	..	..	11 55	5 8		9 3	..
London, Pddngtn., ,,	..	..	1 45	6 50		10 40	..
London, Pddngtn., dep.	..	..	6 0	..		2 20	..
Oxford ....arr.	..	..	8 27	..		4 10	..
Leamington....dep.	..	..	8 0	..		3 40	..
Warwick ......arr.	..	..	8 5	..		3 45	..
Stratford ...... ,,	..	..	8 38	..		4 30	..
Evesham ...... ,,	..	..	9 20	..		5 30	..
Evesham .... ,,	..	..	10 18	..		5 30	..
Evesham ....dep.	7 10	..	10 30	1 6		5 53	..
Harvington............	7 17	..	10 38	1 13		6 1	..
Salford Priors............	7 22	..	10 43	1 19		6 6	..
Wixford	7 27	..	10 48	1 25		6 11	..
ALCESTER	7 34	..	10 55	1 32		6 21	..
Coughton	7 39	..	11 1	1 37		6 27	..
Studley & Astwood Bank ..	7 45	..	11 7	1 43		6 33	Gov.
Redditch	7 54	8 48	11 15	1 56	4 58	6 45	8 20
Alvechurch	8 2	8 56	11 23	2 4	5 6	6 53	8 29
Barnt Green..........arr.	8 8	9 2	11 29	2 11	5 12	6 59	8 35
Barnt Green ....dep.	8 9	9 3	11 31	2 16	5 13	7 5	8 57
Northfield	8 16	9 11	11 38	2 23	5 21	7 13	9 5
King's Norton	8 21	9 16	11 43	2 28	5 26	7 18	9 10
King's Heath............	8 27	9 22	11 50	2 35	5 32	7 24	9 18
Moseley	8 31	9 26	11 54	2 39	5 36	7 29	9 23
Camp Hill	8 34	9 29	11 58	2 43	5 39	7 33	9 27
BIRMINGHAM ......arr.	8 45	9 40	12 10	2 55	5 50	7 45	9 43

Third Class Passengers are Booked Through from Redditch, Alcester, and Evesham to Tewkesbury, Cheltenham, Gloucester, and Bristol, by Trains leaving Redditch at 7.55 a.m. and 5.59 p.m.

Third Class Passengers are Booked Through from Bristol at 6.0 a.m., Gloucester at 8 a.m., Cheltenham at 8.21 a.m., and Tewkesbury at 9.5 a.m. to Evesham, Alcester, and Redditch; also from Bristol at 4.35 p.m., Gloucester at 6.33 p.m., Cheltenham at 6.53 p.m., and Tewkesbury at 7.5 p.m. to Evesham only.

Third Class Passengers are Booked Through from Evesham and Redditch to principal Stations in the North by Train leaving Evesham at 7.10 a.m., proceeding from Birmingham at 9.15 a.m. and Derby at 1.10 p.m.

Printed and Published by the Proprietor, EDWARD MOOR WRIGHT, at his Offices, High-street, Alcester, in the County of Warwick,—Saturday, Nov. 5, 1870.

Public timetable for the line, as published in the *Alcester Chronicle*, 5th November, 1870.

By April 1910 the four down services from Birmingham to Ashchurch left at 6.25, 9.55 am, 1.15 and 5.00 pm. The first train ran via Camp Hill, the second and fourth were non-stop to Kings Norton, and the third non-stop to Barnt Green. Passengers at intermediate stations outside Birmingham were catered for by an intensive service, some of which involved a circular New Street-Lifford Curve-New Street route run in both clockwise and anti-clockwise directions. Departures from Birmingham for Evesham were at 12.33 pm (non-stop to Barnt Green), 7.37 pm (non-stop to Kings Norton) and Saturdays only at 11.20 pm (via Camp Hill). There were nine trains to Redditch of which five went via Camp Hill, and one was non-stop to Kings Norton. There was one train from Redditch to Evesham, at 6.58 am, and two from Evesham to Ashchurch at 9.40 am and 1.05 pm, plus the return market train on Mondays at 4.53 pm.

In the up direction, there were three through trains from Ashchurch to Birmingham leaving at 9.40 am (non-stop after Kings Norton), 1.47 pm (stopping only at Kings Norton, after Redditch), and 5.20 pm (via Camp Hill). Evesham to Birmingham trains left at 6.50, 7.52, 8.52 am (not calling at Wixford and Coughton, and non-stop after Kings Norton), 4.00 pm (non-stop after Barnt Green) and 9.40 pm (Saturdays only). There were seven services from Redditch to Birmingham of which four took the Camp Hill line, and one at 2.08 pm which terminated at Barnt Green. Ashchurch to Evesham services comprised departures at 8.45 am and 12.22 pm (both calling only at Beckford), at 7.44 pm, and the Mondays-only outward working for the return market train at 4.00 pm.

Thus the services had been substantially improved and many accelerated, although some of the smaller stations would not have noticed too much change. There were still no Sunday services.

During World War I, the services were changed several times, mainly due to the reduction in available manpower, not only amongst footplate crews, but all the other staff necessary to keep services running. However, there had been little change by 1914/15, when the weekday services were as follows: Birmingham to Ashchurch (four), Birmingham to Evesham (one, plus one more on Saturdays), Redditch to Alcester (one) and Evesham to Ashchurch (one, plus the return Monday market day train). Up trains were Ashchurch to Birmingham (three), Evesham to Birmingham (two, plus one more on Saturdays), Alcester to Birmingham (one) and Ashchurch to Evesham (two, plus the Monday market train). Sunday services had been introduced in 1910, for which there were two each way between Birmingham and Evesham. Undoubtedly, there were further cuts in services as the war continued.

By 1916, the French railway system was in crisis, and unable to perform the vital functions required. To alleviate the situation and thus give our forces the necessary support, the British government introduced restrictions as from 1st January, 1917 which included the curtailment, alteration, and deceleration of passenger services, the discontinuing of seat reservations, a major reduction in the number of sleeping cars, dining cars and through carriages, and the cancellation of cheap fares. Furthermore, passenger fares were increased by 50 per cent, and a number of branch lines were closed so that their tracks could be removed and taken for use in France, which resulted in the closure of 225 stations for the duration of the war. Some were never to reopen, and for some others it was several years before they did, as we have seen on the Alcester to Bearley line. A less extreme fate befell the Evesham to Ashchurch section, which was singled as from 31st January, 1917 between Bengeworth and Beckford so that the track could be used in France. Track remained in position alongside the up platform at Ashton and the down platform at Hinton,

Evesham station viewed from the south, probably around 1900. It is not possible to positively identify the type of locomotive, as it gets its train under way for Ashchurch. The hipped roof signal box at the end of the down platform is Evesham South dating from 1890.

Almonery Heritage Centre Collection

Kirtley '156' class 2-4-0 No. 164A steams into Alvechurch station with a Birmingham train. The date is after September 1894 when it was put on the duplicate list, but prior to December 1907 when it was renumbered as No. 19. Built in 1868, this engine lasted until 1933 when it was withdrawn. The period costumes and advertisements add considerable charm to this scene, and from the goods and containers on the platform, there is an air of prosperity.

Lens of Sutton/R. Carpenter

which were of course where the main station buildings were located. The double track formation was finally restored on 22nd February, 1921.

Despite some changes by the summer of 1934, the overall effect was pretty much the same as pre-war. At Ashchurch there were four departures for Birmingham, one for Redditch, and four for Evesham with an extra one on Saturdays. Evesham had two daily plus two more Saturday departures for Birmingham, and Alcester had three for Birmingham including one Saturday train, and a further one on Saturdays for Redditch. There were no less than a further seven daily departures from Redditch for Birmingham New Street. In the down direction, there were departures from Birmingham for Redditch (five Mondays to Fridays, but two less on Saturdays), Alcester (one daily), Evesham (three daily), and Ashchurch (three daily). From Barnt Green there was one to Redditch each day, and a Saturday service to Ashchurch, operating as an excursion. From Redditch there were two Saturday services to Alcester, and one daily to Evesham, and from Evesham there were four daily to Ashchurch. The market day trains seem to have gone out of favour by this time, although the LMS timetable includes what it describes as 'Motor Trains' on many of the local services from Ashchurch. In reality these were 'push and pull' trains where the locomotive was semi-permanently attached to one end of the usually short train of perhaps no more than two carriages, and could be driven from either the locomotive or from a cab in the leading coach.

Sunday services comprised two trains each way between Evesham and Birmingham, with a further three each way between Redditch and Birmingham.

Three years later, the summer timetable for 1937 revealed an entirely different pattern. At Ashchurch there were now seven departures for Birmingham (plus a further Saturday-only (SO) working), and two for Evesham only. No Birmingham trains originated at Evesham, but Alcester still had three, including one Saturday train, and a further Saturday train to Redditch only. Redditch maintained its seven departures for Birmingham. In the down direction, the departures from Birmingham for Redditch increased (seven Mondays to Fridays, but two less on Saturdays), and Alcester (one daily, and a further one on Saturdays). The revised pattern of Ashchurch up trains was repeated in the down trains, with just one then running from Birmingham to Evesham, but the number for Ashchurch was increased to five daily, plus an extra Saturday service. From Barnt Green there was one to Redditch each day, and a further Saturday service. From Redditch the two Saturday services to Alcester were reduced to one, and one daily to Evesham was extended to Ashchurch. From Evesham the four daily to Ashchurch were reduced to two, and the 'motor trains' withdrawn. It may be concluded that the increased traffic pattern reflected the general air of optimism at the time, as well as increasing numbers of commuters travelling to Birmingham.

The biggest change affected the Sunday services, where the services between Birmingham and Redditch was limited to two each way, but from Birmingham to Evesham were expanded to five each way. In addition, a shuttle service was introduced between Redditch and Barnt Green, with eight trains in each direction. These provided the citizens of Redditch with the opportunity to visit the Lickey Hills, as well as providing connections at Barnt Green for destinations in each direction.

As might be expected there was a considerable curtailment of passenger services during World War II, so that in July 1942 from Birmingham there were two Ashchurch trains, two to Evesham, one to Alcester and none solely between Birmingham and Redditch, nor between Evesham and Ashchurch. Up trains

A passenger service for Evesham and possibly Ashchurch leaves Broom Junction around 1924, double-headed by a Johnson 0-6-0 and a Johnson 0-4-4T - surely a rare event. A further 0-6-0 is waiting in the up goods loop, and in the foreground is the turntable. The SMJR line to Stratford-on-Avon can be seen curving away above the tank locomotive. *R.S. Carpenter*

Fowler class '3' 2-6-2T No. 16 calls at Barnt Green with a Redditch to Birmingham New Street train on 12th July, 1939. The goods yard, goods shed and cattle loading dock are clearly visible in the background, along with a large area of land levelled for future use. The flower beds behind the train were later cleared to enlarge the car parking. *H.C. Casserley/R.S. Carpenter*

balanced these, with an additional one from Alcester to Birmingham. Sunday trains were suspended for the duration. By this time, all scheduled services used the BWSR, although the Camp Hill line was used in emergencies and at times of congestion, for which New Street station had achieved an unenviable reputation, and to this day is still very much applicable.

The nationalization of the railways in 1948 initially caused very little change to the pre-war services, insofar as by 1950 the pattern had changed yet again, but once more the overall effect was little different. The Working Timetable for passenger trains with effect from 25th September, 1950 is shown on page 144. In summary, there were five through weekday services from Birmingham to Ashchurch, four to Redditch (with an additional one on Saturdays), and one from Redditch to Alcester. In the up direction, there were five from Ashchurch to Birmingham, three from Redditch to Birmingham (with an additional two on Saturdays), and one from Alcester to Birmingham. The locomotive from the last train of the day to Ashchurch (8.00 pm ex- Birmingham New Street) ran to Tewkesbury shed for overnight stabling, leaving there the following morning at 6.33 am to work the 7.11 am to New Street. There were two trains each way between Birmingham and Evesham on Sundays.

The only changes in the September 1956 weekday timetable was an additional train at 6.20 pm, except Saturdays, from Birmingham to Evesham, returning from there at 8.15 pm; and the 8.00 pm Birmingham to Ashchurch. Therefore, from Monday to Friday the last arrival at Ashchurch was the 5.10 pm from Birmingham and so it was the locomotive off this train which went on to Tewkesbury shed overnight. Tewkesbury shed also now serviced the locomotive off the 8.27 am from Birmingham, which returned at 1.00 pm to work the 2.17 pm departure from Ashchurch. On Sundays the morning return from Evesham to Birmingham, and the evening Birmingham to Evesham working were suspended during the Winter months from 23rd October, 1955 until 1st April, 1956. To avoid a lengthy layover at Evesham of around 10 hours for the crew, the paths of the suspended trains were used to run the light engine back to Saltley and return in the evening to work the 8.10 pm departure.

The final schedule of services operated fully by steam were in the period from 2nd November, 1959 which should have run until 12th June, 1960. The timetable for this period was similar to 1956, with only minor time changes (*see pages 148/149*). The only additional working was a parcels service from Redditch to Birmingham Central Goods at 9.35 pm running Saturdays excepted (SX).

However, this service pattern did not run for the full season, as diesel-multiple-units (dmus) were introduced as from 25th April, 1960 and transformed the service, with approximately hourly departures in each direction between Redditch and Birmingham New Street on weekdays. Steam was still used on peak hour services, and for those continuing to Evesham or Ashchurch, although these latter were reduced from five to three round trips. To replace these two missing trains, services were introduced between Redditch and Ashchurch, operated by steam locomotives which were outstationed at Tewkesbury shed for this purpose. The trains involved departed from Ashchurch at 10.00 am, 1.15 pm (SO) and 4.30 pm. In the reverse direction there were departures from Redditch at 11.38 am, and 2.55 pm (SO). A further service was operated from Evesham at 8.30 pm to Redditch, but this only had a return working on Saturdays, at 9.30 pm. As might be expected from these rather unbalanced workings, the result was a number of light engine and empty stock movements. Furthermore, passengers travelling through to or from Birmingham

BARNT GREEN, REDDITCH, EVESHAM AND ASHCHURCH.

Miles.	CLASSIFICATION	C	B	B	B	B	B	B	B	B	B	B	B	B	B	B	SUNDAYS. B	SUNDAYS. B
		WEEKDAYS. PARCELS 12.40 a.m. Leicester to Bath.		6.25 a.m. from Birmingham.	8.27 a.m. from Birmingham.	11.50 a.m. from Birmingham.	12.50 p.m. from Birmingham.	1.25 p.m. from Birmingham.	1.4 p.m. from Birmingham.	4.20 p.m. from Birmingham.	5.10 p.m. from Birmingham.	5.32 p.m. from Birmingham.	6.20 p.m. from Birmingham.	8.0 p.m. from Birmingham.	10.20 p.m. from Birmingham.	10.20 p.m. from Birmingham.	7.55 a.m. from Saltley.	6.45 p.m. from Birmingham.
		MX		R		RSO	SX	SO	SO		R	R	SX	R	SX	SO		R
		a.m.	a.m.	a.m.	a.m.	p.m.	p.m.	p.m.	p.m.	p.m.	p.m.	p.m.	p.m.	p.m.	p.m.	p.m.	a.m.	p.m.
0	BARNT GN. ⊕ dep.	2 36		7 5	8 55	12 22	1 23	2 12	1 36	4 55	5 41	6 11	6 53	8 32	10 48	10 48	8 38	7 12
1¾	Alvechurch			7 10	9 0	12 27	1 28	2 17	1 41	5 0	5 46	6 16	6 58	8 37		10 53	8 43	7 17
4½	Redditch Nth. ⊕	2*43		7*15	9* 5	12*32	1*33	2*22	1*46	5* 5	5*51	6*21	7* 3	8*42	10*55	10*58	8*48	7*22
5	Redditch ⊕ arr.			7 17	9 7	12 34	1 35	2 24	1 48	5 7	5 53	6 23	7 5	8 44	10 57	11 0	8 50	7 24
	Redditch dep.	2*45	6 35	7 27	9 12		1 40		1 53		5 58			8 48			8 54	7 26
8¼	Studley & A. B. ⊕	2*50		7 34	9 19		1 47		2 0		6 4			8 55			9 1	7 33
10¼	Coughton			7K39	9 24		1 52		2 5		6 9			9K 0				
12¼	Alcester	2*56	6 50	7 45	9 30		1 58		2 11		6 15			9 6			9 9	7 41
14¼	Wixford																	
15½	Broom Jc ⊕ arr.			7 51	9 36		2 4		2 17		6 21			9 12			9 15	7 47
	Broom Jc dep.	3* 0		7 59	9 37		2 24		2 19		6 22			9 14			9 16	7 48
16	Broom Jc. W. ⊕	3* 2		8* 1	9*39		2*26		2*21		6*24			9*16			9*18	7*50
16¾	Salford Priors			8 4	9 42		2 29		2 24		6 27			9 19			9 21	7 53
18½	Harvington ⊕	3* 7		8 10	9 48		2 35		2 30		6 32			9 25			9 27	7 59
22	Evesham ⊕ arr.	3W13		8 17	9 55		2 42		2 37		6 38			9 32			9 34	8 6
	Evesham dep.	3W18		8 22	10 0		2 47		2 42		6 42			9 37				
23½	Bengeworth	Rep.		8 27	10 5						6 47			9 42				
25¼	Hinton	No.		8 32	10 10		2 54		2 49		6 52			9 47				
27	Ashton-under-Hill	P477		8 37	10 15		2 59		2 54		6 57			9 52				
29	Beckford			8 42	10 20		3 4		2 59		7 2			9K57				
32¾	ASHCHURCH arr.	3*35		8 49	10 27		3 11		3 6		7 8			10 4				

K—Stops to set down only.

K—Stops to set down only.

Miles.	CLASSIFICATION	B	B	B	B	B	B	B	B	B	B	B	SUNDAYS. B	SUNDAYS. B
		WEEKDAYS. To Birmingham.	To Birmingham.	To Birmingham.	To Birmingham.	To Birmingham.	To Birmingham.	To Birmingham.	To Birmingham.	To Birmingham.	To Birmingham.	To Birmingham.	To Birmingham.	To Birmingham.
		R			R		R SO	SO	R					
		a.m.	a.m.	a.m.	a.m.	a.m.	p.m.	p.m.	p.m.	p.m.	p.m.	p.m.	a.m.	p.m.
0	ASHCHURCH dep.				7 11	9 35			2 20	4 30		8 0		
3¼	Beckford				7 18	9 43			2 27	4 38		8 8		
5¾	Ashton-under-Hill				7 23	9 48			2 32	4 43		8 13		
7½	Hinton					9 53			2 37	4 48		8 18		
9¼	Bengeworth				7 30	9 58				4 53		8 23		
10¾	Evesham ⊖ arr.				7 34	10 2			2 43	4 57		8 27		
	Evesham dep.				7 39	10 7			2 47	5 1		8 32	10 5	8 18
14¼	Harvington ⊕				7 47	10 15			2 55	5 9		8 40	10 13	8 26
16	Salford Priors				7 53	10 21			3 0	5 15		8 46	10 19	8 32
16¾	Broom Jc. W. ⊕				7*55	10*23			3* 2	5*17		8*48	10*21	8*34
17¼	Broom Jc. ⊕ arr.				7 57	10 25			3 4	5 19		8 50	10 23	8 36
	Broom Jc. dep.				7 59	10 26			3 5	5 24		8 53	10 24	8 37
18¼	Wixford													
20¼	Alcester		7 5		8 6	10 33			3 11	5 31		9 0	10 31	8 44
22¼	Coughton				8 12	10 39			3 17	5 37		E		
24¼	Studley & A. B. ⊕		7 14		8 18	10 45			3 23	5 43		9 14	10 40	8 53
27¼	Redditch ⊕ arr.		7 21		8 25	10 52			3 30	5 50		9 21	10 47	9 0
	Redditch dep.	6 30	7 24	8 0	8 27	10 57	12 50	2 40	3 31	5 55	7 43	9 33	10 50	9 3
28¼	Redditch Nth. ⊕	6*32	7*26	8* 2	8*29	10*59	12*52	2*42	3*33	5*57	7*45	9*35	10*52	9* 5
31	Alvechurch	6 39	7 33	8 9	8 36	11 6	12 59	2 49	3 40	6 4	7 52	9 42	10 59	9 12
32¼	BARNT GN. ⊕ arr.	6 45	7 39	8 15	8 42	11 12	1 5	2 55	3 46	6 10	7 58	9 48	11 5	9 18

E—Alcester Signal Box arr. 9*1, dep. 9*5 p.m.

Passenger working timetable from 25th September, 1950 until further notice. Services marked 'R' given accelerated timings. Trains only allowed 30 seconds at stations where no separate arrival times shown.

Shortly after nationalization, on 21st May, 1948, Stanier class '3' 2-6-2T No. 117 brings a passenger train from Birmingham around the sharply curved down branch platform at Barnt Green. The locomotive has not yet been repainted into BR colours and received its new number.
H.C. Casserley/Kidderminster Railway Museum

The date is April 1949 and this Fowler 2-6-4T No. 42326 of Saltley shed is just departing from Alvechurch for Birmingham New Street. The locomotive has just passed the hut built to protect the ground frame that gave access to the single siding here. *Millbrook House/R. Carpenter*

The last week of services for Coughton is commemorated here, with LMS Compound No. 41191 calling with an Ashchurch train. The date was 21st June, 1952, just nine days before closure of this station. *R.S. Carpenter Collection*

One of Saltley's Ivatt Moguls, No. 43036, pauses at Studley and Astwood Bank station with a southbound passenger service in April, 1957. The signal box is evidently switched out, as the lower quadrant up home signal is pulled 'off'. *Author's Collection*

For one week in April 1959 LMS Compound 4-4-0 No. 41157 was rostered by Saltley depot to work over the Redditch line. This was arranged at the request of Pat Whitehouse so that it could be filmed as material for his popular *Railway Roundabout* television series. In the upper photograph the locomotive is seen departing from Studley and Astwood Bank on 11th April with the 1.03 pm from New Street to Ashchurch. In the lower photo, it is drifting into Beckford with an Ashchurch train during that period. This engine was actually allocated to Derby at the time, but had been loaned to Saltley.

Millbrook House/R. Carpenter & D. Johnson Collection/Millbrook House

K124

WEEKDAYS — **BARNT GREEN AND ASHCHURCH** — **SUNDAYS**

Mileage M	Mileage C	DOWN	Ruling Gradient 1 in	B	B	B	B	B	B	B	B	B	B	B	B	B	B	B	B (Sundays)	B (Sundays)	G (Sundays)		B (Sundays)
					6.32 a.m. Birmingham	8.27 a.m. Birmingham	11.50 a.m. Birmingham	12.57 p.m. Birmingham	1.3 p.m. Birmingham	1.37 p.m. Birmingham	4.20 p.m. Birmingham	5.10 p.m. Birmingham	5.32 p.m. Birmingham	6.20 p.m. Birmingham	8.8 p.m. Birmingham	8.8 p.m. Birmingham	10.30 p.m. Birmingham	10.30 p.m. Birmingham	7.55 a.m. Saltley	7.55 a.m. Saltley	6.20 p.m. LE from Saltley Shed		6.40 p.m. Birmingham
				2883	2583	2583	2897	2583	2583	2897	2897	2583	2897	2883	2897	2583	2897	2897	2883	2883	0062		2883
							SO	SX	SO	SO				SX	SX	SO	SX	SO					
				am	am	am	PM	PM	PM	PM	PM	PM	PM	PM	PM	PM	PM	PM	am	am	PM		PM
0	0	BARNT GREEN arr			7 4	8 53	12 21	1 28	1 34	2 4	4 50	5 40	6 4	6 51	8 36	8 36	10 54	10 54	8 37	8 37		To work 8.15 p.m. to Birmingham	7 6
		dep			7 8	8 55	12 22	1 29	1 36	2 5	4 52	5 41	6 11	6 52	8 37	8 37	10 56	10 56	8 38	8 38	6 50		7 7
1	60	Alvechurch	74F		7 13	9 0	12 27	1 34	1 41	2 10	4 57	5 46	6 16	6 57	8 42	8 42		11 1	8 43	8 43			7 12
4	40	Redditch North	65R		7 18	9 5	12 32	1 39	1 46	2 15	5 2	5 51	6 21	7 2	8 47	8 47	11 3	11 6	8 48	8 48	6 59		7 17
4	78	Redditch arr	124R		7X20	9 7	12 34	1 41	1 48	2 17	5 4	5X53	6 23	7 4	8 49	8 49	11 5	11 8	8 50	8 50			7 19
		dep		6 35	7 28	9 12		1 46	1 53			5 59		7 8		8 53			8 54	8 54	7 0		7 21
8	12	Studley and Astwood Bank	129F		7 35	9 19		1 53	2 0			6 5											
12	33	Alcester	107F	6 50	7 46	9 27		2 4	2 8			6 13		7 23		9 7			9 6		7 14		7 33
15	7	Broom Jn. arr	125F		7X52	9 33		2 10	2 14			6 19		7 29		9 13			9 12	9 12			7 39
		dep			7 59	9 34		2 20	2 20			6 20		7 31		9 14			9 13	9 13	7 21		7 40
15	55	Broom Jn. West	245F		8 1	9 36		2 22	2 22			6 22		7 33		9 16			9 15	9 15	7 24		7 42
16	39	Salford Priors	370F		8 4	9 39		2 25	2 25			6 26				9 19			9 18				7 45
18	40	Harvington	203R		8 10	9 45		2 31	2 31			6 31				9 24			9 24				7 51
21	77	EVESHAM arr	164F		8 17	9 52		2 38	2 38			6 37		7 44		9 30			9 31	9 31	7‖35		7 58
		dep			8 22	9 57		2 43	2 43			6 41				9 35							
25	17	Hinton	210R		8 29	10 4		2 50	2 50			6 49				9 42							
27	8	Ashton-under-Hill	196R		8 34	10 9		2 55	2 55			6 55				9 47							
29	6	Beckford	210F		8 39	10 14		3 0	3 0			7 0				9 D52							
32	65	ASHCHURCH arr	199F		8 46	10 21		3 7	3 7			7 6				9 58							
																			Until 18th Oct., 1959, and from 1st May, 1960	From 25th October, 1959, until 1st April, 1960	From 25th October, 1959, until 24th April, 1960		Until 18th Oct., 1959, and from 1st May, 1960

SINGLE LINE—Barnt Green Junction to Evesham. Worked by Electric Train Token between Barnt Green Single Line Junction and Redditch North and Redditch South to Evesham.

Sections :

Barnt Green Single Junction to Redditch North.
Redditch North to Redditch South (Double Line Disc Block Telegraph).
Redditch South to Studley and Astwood Bank.
Studley and Astwood Bank to Alcester.
Alcester to Broom Junction North.
*Broom Junction North to Broom Junction West.
Broom Junction West to Harvington.
Harvington to Evesham.

*—When Broom Junction West is not in circuit, a Through Token is operated between Broom Junction and Harvington

Crossing Stations :

Redditch.
Alcester.
Broom Junction.

Auxiliary Key Token Instruments

Broom Junction Station—At Alcester end of Platform.

Passenger working timetable, down trains, from 2nd November, 1959 to 12th June, 1960.

WEEKDAYS

ASHCHURCH AND BARNT GREEN

UP

M	C	Station		Ruling Gradient 1 in	B To Birmingham 2897 am	B To Birmingham 2897 am	B To Birmingham 2897 am	B To Birmingham 2897 am	B To Birmingham 2897 am	B To Birmingham 2897 SO PM	B To Birmingham 2897 SO PM	B To Birmingham 2897 PM	B To Birmingham 2897 SUS PEN DED PM	B To Birmingham 2897 PM	B To Birmingham 2897 PM	B To Birmingham 2897 SX PM	B To Birmingham 2897 SO PM		C To Birmingham (Central) Pcls. 3836 SX PM
0	0	**ASHCHURCH**	dep					7 14	9 41			2 17	2 20	4 25			8 5	H—Alcester S.B. arr. 9*3, dep. 9*8 p.m.	
3	59	Beckford		199R				7 21	9 49			2 24	2 27	4 33			8 13		
5	57	Ashton-under-Hill		210R				7 26	9 54			2 29	2 32	4 38			8 18		
7	48	Hinton		196F					9 59			2 34	2 37	4 43			8 23		
10	68	**EVESHAM**	arr	179R				7 34	10 5			2 40	2 43	4 50			8 29		
			dep					7 37	10 10			2 44	2 47	4 57		8 15	8 34		
14	25	Harvington		104R				7 45	10 18			2 52	2 55	5 5			8 42		
16	26	Salford Priors		297F				7 51	10 24			2 58	3 1	5 11			8 48		
17	10	Broom Jn. West		245R				7 53	10 26			3 0	3 3	5 13		8 24	8 50		
17	58	Broom Jn.	arr	245R				7X55	10 28			3 2	3 5	5 15		8 26	8 52		
			dep					7 57	10 29			3 3	3 6	5 20		8 29	8 55		
20	32	Alcester		125R		7 5		8 4	10 36			3 10	3 13	5 27		8 36	9H2		
24	53	Studley and Astwood Bank		107R		7 14		8 16	10 45			3 19	3 22	5 39					
27	67	Redditch	arr	126F		7X21		8 23	10 52			3 26	3 29	5X46		8 52	9 24		
			dep		6 30	7 26	8 0	8 25	10 55	12 50	2 40	3 29	3 32	5 55	7 31	9 2	9 34		9 35
28	25	Redditch North		126F	6 32	7 28	8 2	8 27	10 57	12 52	2 42	3 31	3 34	5 57	7 33	9 4	9 36		
31	5	Alvechurch		65F	6 39	7 35	8 9	8 34	11 6	12 59	2 49	3 38	3 41	6 4	7 40	9 11	9 43		
32	65	**BARNT GREEN**	arr	74R	6 45	7 41	8 15	8 40	11 12	1 5	2 55	3 44	3 47	6 10	7 46	9 17	9 49		9 51
			dep		6 46	7 42	8 16	8 41	11 15	1 8	2 56	3 45	3 48	6 14	7 47	9 18	9 51		9 52

SUNDAYS

Station		B To Birmingham 2897 am Until 18th Oct., 1959, and from 1st May, 1960	G LE to Saltley Shed 0252 am From 25th October, 1960, until 24th April, 1960		B To Birmingham 2897 PM Until 18th Oct., 1959, and from 1st May, 1960	B To Birmingham 2897 PM From 25th October, 1959, until 24th April, 1960
ASHCHURCH	dep			After working 7.55 a.m. from Saltley		
Beckford						
Ashton-under-Hill						
Hinton						
EVESHAM	arr					
	dep	10 0	10‖ 0		8 15	8 15
Harvington		10 8			8 23	
Salford Priors		10 14			8 29	
Broom Jn. West		10 16	10 16		8 31	8 31
Broom Jn.	arr	10 18			8 33	8 33
	dep	10 19	10 19		8 34	8 34
Alcester		10 26	10 26		8 41	
Studley and Astwood Bank						
Redditch	arr	10 39			8 54	8 54
	dep	10 42	10 45		8 56	8 56
Redditch North		10 44	10 47		8 58	8 58
Alvechurch		10 51			9 5	9 5
BARNT GREEN	arr	10 57			9 11	9 11
	dep	10 59	10 59		9 12	9 12

K125

Passenger working timetable, up trains, from 2nd November, 1959 to 12th June, 1960.

Above: The duties of the Redditch pilot included working passenger services to Ashchurch on Saturdays from 1960 to 1962. As the pilots were supplied from the fleet of Bromsgrove's Lickey bankers, it fell to the remaining two Fowler 'Jinty' 0-6-0Ts to provide this service from to time. Here we see No. 47276 entering Alcester around 1961 with the 1.15 pm return working from Ashchurch.
D. Johnson Collection/Millbrook House

Left: Ivatt class '4' 2-6-0 No. 43049 rounds the curve into Redditch passing the goods depot, with the 1.06 pm (Saturdays only) Birmingham New Street to Evesham on 9th December, 1961. The size of the goods depot can be gauged from the road vehicles parked beneath the awning.
Author

Right: Stanier class '5' 4-6-0 No. 45263 arrives at Alvechurch with a Birmingham train in the summer of 1961. The station was quite evidently well looked after at this time.
Lens of Sutton/R. Carpenter

Ivatt Mogul No. 43047 passes the LMS pattern signal box, and goods yard at Alcester, and runs into the double track formation of the station with a southbound service in 1961.
D. Johnson Collection/Millbrook House

Fowler Class '4' 2-6-4T No. 42327 prepares to leave Broom Junction in July 1960 with a three-coach Evesham train comprising non-corridor stock, although the first vehicle is of Gresley LNER design. In the background, a dmu for Birmingham gets under way from the up side of the island platform. *N. Forrest/Transport Treasury*

Fowler class '4' 2-6-4T No. 42400 runs into Beckford station from the south with the 12.19 pm from Ashchurch on 20th August, 1960, at which time the flowerbeds on the up platform were still tended regularly. *B. Moone/Kidderminster Railway Museum*

Ivatt Mogul No. 43017 runs into Redditch past Abel Morrall's works on the left, with the 1.36 pm (Saturdays only) Barnt Green to Evesham on 24th June, 1961.The goods yard and loading deck are to the right, and in the background is the lengthy footbridge across the goods yard.

Author

In the evening of 27th March, 1962, Ivatt 2-6-0 No. 43046 strides up the grade into Redditch alongside the Clive Road sidings, with the 6.18pm (SX) Birmingham New Street to Evesham.

Author

On Friday 13th April, 1962 Ivatt Mogul No. 43106 pulls out of Redditch with the 11.38 am departure for Ashchurch. To save moving the empty stock, and to leave the down platform clear for a dmu arrival and departure for Birmingham, it was the custom for this train to use the up platform. The locomotive had only recently been transferred from Woodford Halse depot on the GCR section, and so retained the relatively high mounting for its numberplate on the smokebox door, a feature of Eastern Region engines. This locomotive is now preserved on the Severn Valley Railway. *Author*

Fowler 2-6-4T No. 42416 of Saltley shed runs into Broom Junction from the south with the 4.30 pm Ashchurch to Birmingham on 23rd April, 1962. The unused line to Stratford, closed in 1960, curves away to the left. *Almonery Heritage Centre Collection*

and using these trains had waits at Redditch of between 20 and 50 minutes. In contrast, the final train of the day from Redditch to Birmingham was a non-stop dmu service, which covered the 15¼ miles in 26 minutes, the fastest train ever on this line. The dmus were also used on the Sunday trains, which comprised two trips each way between Birmingham and Evesham. The weekday parcels service was retimed to leave Redditch at 6.10 pm for Birmingham Central.

The services for 1961 and 1962 continued broadly as in 1960, and featured 15 weekday dmus from New Street to Redditch and 16 return trips, which involved one empty dmu from Saltley to Redditch, as the dmus were never stabled at Redditch. On Saturdays, there was one less down working, but four down and two up workings travelled via the Camp Hill line. Steam still provided the motive power for the weekday peak hour services to Ashchurch (two) and Evesham (one), with the return workings of one each from Ashchurch, Alcester and Redditch. As part of this diagram, the early morning train from Redditch to Alcester was retained. The two workings to Ashchurch also ran on Saturdays, but the Evesham service from New Street was replaced by one commencing at Barnt Green at 1.36 pm (the empty carriages for this were worked from Kings Norton). As there was no balancing working the engine returned light to Saltley via the Camp Hill line. The remaining up steam workings to Birmingham also ran on Saturday. The services between Redditch and Ashchurch or Evesham also continued to be worked by steam. Parcels workings were steam hauled from New Street at 6.14 am (Monday to Saturday), and from Redditch at 6.10 pm, the engine of which then returned light from New Street to Redditch for stabling overnight. The later 9.50 pm parcels from Redditch to Central Goods did not run on Saturdays.

Sunday services in 1961 and 1962 comprised one morning and one evening return dmu between New Street and Evesham. However, as from 10th September, 1962 these were scheduled to terminate at Redditch, not run at all as from 21st October, 1962 for the winter period, and then recommence on 14th April, 1963. But these planned services were overtaken by other events.

BR had proposed the withdrawal of passenger services from Birmingham to Redditch around this time, but protests from four local MPs indicating that Redditch was about to become a dormitory suburb of Birmingham managed to stave off the closure, although a formal reprieve was not announced until 31st July, 1964. Meanwhile, passenger services from Redditch to Evesham, and goods services from Alcester to Evesham, ceased as from 30th September, 1962 after the WR Civil Engineer had declared the line to be unsafe. Replacement bus services were provided by the Midland Red (appropriately!) between Redditch and Evesham, calling only at the railway stations en route. As the buses continued in the paths of the former through services, a train service from Evesham to Ashchurch continued in the same paths over that section of the journey, usually consisting of just one or no more than two coaches. Consequently, there were departures from Ashchurch at 7.05, 10.00 am, 1.15 (SO), and 4.30 pm, with return workings from Evesham at 8.20 am, 12.24, 3.41 (SO) and 6.47 pm. There were, of course, no Sunday services. After a short consultation, it was decided that the costs of repairing the line were too great, and that it would close. Many local people saw this only as a vindication of their views that BR were just looking for an excuse to close the line anyway, and given the chance would close the remainder. Certainly, the rather odd times of some of the southbound trains did not seem to have been designed to encourage new passengers, let alone retain existing ones. The next chapter will consider events occurring during this period in a little more detail.

A recent shower has washed the down platform at Alcester as Fowler 'Jinty' 0-6-0T No. 47276 pauses with the 11.38 am Redditch to Ashchurch on 14th July, 1962. *P. Kingston/R.S. Carpenter*

Ivatt Mogul No. 43047 runs into Ashton-under-Hill with a train from Ashchurch to Birmingham during 1962, the final year of through running. The platforms are already beginning to look a little unkempt. *D. Johnson Collection/Millbrook House*

During the harsh winter of 1962/63 the newly-introduced dmus suffered a large number of failures. Whilst most such occurrences usually meant the replacement of dmus by steam trains, on this occasion, 19th January, 1963, a Stanier '8F' class 2-8-0, No. 48070, was summoned from its goods duties in Redditch to haul the 12.30 pm dmu set to Birmingham New Street. I only just managed to photograph this incident, and would dearly have loved to have travelled in the front compartment of the dmu to Birmingham. *Author*

A Collett '57XX' class 0-6-0PT calls at Hinton station in 1963 with a shuttle service from Evesham to Ashchurch, unusually loaded to two coaches. *D. Johnson Collection/Millbrook House*

Collett GWR pannier tank No. 4614 stands in the Evesham branch platform at Ashchurch with the single coach shuttle service on 1st June, 1963. The substantial waiting room for branch passengers can be seen on the right. *W. Potter/Kidderminster Railway Museum*

On 1st June, 1963 Collett 0-6-0PT No. 4614 pauses in Ashton-under-Hill with the 12.24 pm Evesham to Ashchurch service. The rundown nature of the station buildings is apparent, as it had been unstaffed since 1957. *Almonery Heritage Centre Collection*

Closure of the Redditch to Evesham section meant that it was inevitable that the Evesham to Ashchurch services could not survive in isolation, and so these too were withdrawn coincidentally. On 15th June, 1963 the last train, the 6.47 pm from Evesham to Ashchurch was worked by Collett pannier tank No. 3745 of Cheltenham (Malvern Road) shed. There had been little in the way of local protest leading up to this day, and patronage on the final day was composed almost entirely of railway enthusiasts.

Goods services

The initial goods services were of a distinctly local nature. In December 1869, there were goods services from Lawley Street in Birmingham to Evesham at 10.20 am, to Redditch (Monday, Wednesday, Friday and Saturday) at 10.40 am, from Redditch to Evesham at 1.56 pm, and from Evesham to Ashchurch at 11.40 am (Tuesday, Thursday, Saturday), 12.30 pm (Monday, Wednesday and Friday) and 3.50 pm (Monday, Wednesday, Friday). The last train ran on alternate days to Gloucester.

Up workings were from Gloucester to Evesham at 8.20 am (which left at 9.17 am on Monday, Wednesday and Friday), Ashchurch to Evesham at 3.10 pm (which left at 3.45 pm on Tuesday, Thursday and Saturday for Beckford only), Evesham to Redditch at 11.49 am and to Birmingham at 4.00 pm. Finally, there was a Redditch to Birmingham working at 2.05 pm on Monday, Wednesday, Friday and Saturday.

By October 1876 there were still only two down goods workings along the line, but only operating as far south as Evesham.The first down working, arriving in Evesham at 10.20 am, still ran, but the next working was retimed to arrive in Redditch some 1½ hours later at 12.15 pm before continuing to Evesham at 1.55 pm, arriving at 2.55 pm and now running daily. The midday services from Evesham to Ashchurch did not appear. The morning up service from Gloucester to Evesham was retimed to run daily arriving at 10.40 am, continuing northwards (except Tuesdays) at 11.30 am with another lengthy layover in Redditch from 1.35 pm until 3.00 pm. On Tuesdays this left Evesham at 1.00 pm, and had its long layover at Alcester between 1.45 pm and 2.40 pm. The only other goods working left Evesham at 5.00 pm and was described as an 'Express Goods', passing Barnt Green at 7.00 pm on its way to Birmingham.

By 1909, there were several trains now operating from additional goods terminii that had opened in Birmingham in the intervening years. There were through services from Lawley Street to Bath and Bristol, as well as from Central Goods to Bristol and Gloucester. The yards at Washwood Heath provided three services of local traffic for Evesham, and there were local services between Evesham and Ashchurch, including some specific fruit traffic, and from Redditch to Broom for onward movement by the SMJR, which had three daily trains from Broom to Stratford. Only one train ran through from the SMJR at this time, onwards to Gloucester, and leaving Broom at 4.45 am. Overall there were 14 down weekday goods workings along the line, with a further two on Sundays, all of the through workings taking place at night.

Up workings for Birmingham from Broom, Gloucester and Evesham were all scheduled to arrive at Lawley Street, with one exception, the 7.15 pm from Evesham which ran to Duddeston. With the local workings there were around 12 such movements each weekday, with two on Sundays.

Mention should perhaps be made of the fruit and vegetable traffic from Evesham and other intermediate stations, particularly Beckford. For although the perishable

A private owner five-plank 8 ton open wagon, as supplied in 1900 by the Gloucester Carriage & Wagon Co. Ltd to James Taylor & Co. of Beckford, who had their own sizeable depot in the goods yard there. *Almonery Heritage Centre Collection*

This seven-plank 10 ton open wagon was built by the Gloucester Carriage & Wagon Co. Ltd for the coal merchant Richard White & Son of Evesham in 1911.

Almonery Heritage Centre Collection

items were themselves individually seasonal, the harvest dates and thus the traffic continued for virtually the whole year, although the volumes did vary. During the springtime and early summer there were many vegetables being harvested such as cabbages, onions and sprouts, with some traffic in flowers, and of course, asparagus for which the Vale of Evesham was rightly famous. Fruit started in the summer, with gooseberries, strawberries, plums and into the autumn with apples, pears, tomatoes, cucumbers, damsons and marrows. Dependent on the volumes much of the produce would go by passenger train, or into vans attached to general goods trains, having been secured into packages specifically designed for each crop, so as to minimize damage. However, the plum traffic in August and September was particularly heavy and so special trains were often scheduled. Sometimes this could reach 1,000 tons in a single week, and it must not be forgotten that the GWR was also handling similar volumes, notably at Littleton & Badsey, as well as at Evesham.

Although the number of general workings did not grow in number, the destinations and points of departure did change, so that by July 1930 there were still around 12 to 14 goods workings in each direction each weekday, with most taking place at night. However, there were by then no workings passing through on Sundays. There were three workings for Bath or Bristol, and one starting from Burton-on-Trent. The Avonmouth Docks to St Pancras 'banana specials' passed through Broom Junction at 4.13 am (Monday to Thursday) and 8.05 am (Monday to Friday), although these only ran 'as required'.

By May 1946 the number of goods workings had increased considerably, to around 21 down and 15 up. These included some new destinations/origins, such as Toton, Water Orton and Bournville, and comprised a more varied mix of fitted, partially fitted, unfitted, minerals and empty minerals trains. The SMJR route was also providing additional traffic, from Bedford, Olney, and Blisworth through to Gloucester and Westerleigh Yard (Bristol). Sunday working had also become important with three from Washwood Heath to Evesham and one return, one each from Blisworth to Gloucester, Gloucester to Bedford, and Broom to Evesham. However, the number had declined before June 1951 with now only 15 down and 11 up workings. Those previously booked to work the entire route of the SMJR had disappeared from the working timetable.

The Working Timetable for freight trains from 17th June, 1956 to 16th September, 1957 (*see pages 164-167*) shows 21 down and 17 up weekday freight workings, with eight down and four up on Sundays. Of particular note are the five mineral trains and return empties workings each way between the former Great Central Railway at Woodford and various points in South Wales. This was mentioned earlier, and started as from 6th June, 1951 utilizing the SMJR and the east to south curve put in at Broom during 1942. These workings became an important feature of the line. The remainder of the workings indicate the usefulness of the line in being able to carry traffic away from the Lickey Incline, which otherwise caused a bottleneck, especially for unfitted and partially fitted trains that had to descend the incline, as well as the considerable time taken for lengthy freight trains ascending the incline. However, this usefulness was somewhat limited by the single line sections, and lack of passing places on our line, that restricted the capacity of the line overall.

In the last year of through working, the Working Timetable for 11th September, 1961 to 17th June, 1962 shows that there were no through down workings, although there were a number of shorter workings. These comprised three from Washwood Heath to Redditch, the first being at 12.03 am (Monday, Wednesday, Fridays only) - although actually the next day, returning with the 1.15 am Tuesday, Thursday,

Alcester station some time shortly after 1905, with a Kirtley 0-6-0 on a southbound freight. The signalman in the box on the right is taking a keen interest in the photographer. This signal box was a replacement of the original on the same site, opening in 1905 and itself replaced in 1932. *Author's Collection*

Two goods trains passing in Redditch station, with the southbound one headed by a double-framed Kirtley 0-6-0. The front numberplate mounted on the smokebox door dates the photograph as after 1907. There is a plethora of advertisements mounted along the up side platform wall. *Chris Jackson Collection*

LMS Fowler '4F' class 0-6-0 No. 4134 pulls out from the down slow line on to the main line at Barnt Green with a lengthy partly fitted southbound goods train. The suspended doll signal on the left was a repeater for the taller signals not visible here, and has been pulled off for a northbound train; 12th July 1939. *H.C. Casserley/Kidderminster Railway Museum*

Churchward '28XX' class 2-8-0 No. 2818 comes off the line from Ashchurch and crosses to the Western Region route to Honeybourne with a heavy class 'H' freight in 1957 during the diversions from the Cheltenham to Honeybourne route. This locomotive is now preserved at the National Railway Museum, York. The new signal box to its right had only just opened.
Almonery Heritage Centre Collection

BARNT GREEN TO ASHCHURCH

WEEKDAYS

DOWN

Mileage M	Mileage C	Station		H	E	H	D	H	H	H	H		H	J	J	H	J	G		J	H	K
				9.50 pm Woodford Halse to South Wales	11.35 pm Washwood Heath to Gloucester	12.55 am King's Norton to Gloucester	1.45 am Washwood Heath to Westerleigh	1.30 am Woodford Halse to South Wales	1.50 am from Washwood Heath	1.35 am Exchange Sidings to Westerleigh	2.15 am Woodford Halse to Gloucester W.R.		3.15 am from Washwood Heath	4.5 am Washwood Heath to Gloucester	5.0 am King's Norton to Gloucester	6.50 am Stratford-on-A. to Westerleigh	9.55 am Stratford-on-A. to Gloucester	9.55 am LE Stratford-on-A. to Gloucester		8.50 am King's Norton to Gloucester	11.13 am Stratford-on-A. to Gloucester	7.55 am from Washwood Heath
				MX	MX	MX	MX	MX	MX	MX	MX		MO	MO	MO			SO				SX
				am	am	am	am	am	am	am	am		am	am	am	am	am	am		am	am	am
0	0	**BARNT GREEN**	arr																			8 51
			dep		12 22	1 10	2 25		2 40	3 20			4 7	4 55	5 20					9X 5		9 15
0	25	Barnt Green Single Line Jn.			12 24	1 12	2 27		2 45	3 22			4 9	4 57	5 22					9 7		9 22
1	66	Alvechurch	arr																			9 27
			dep																			9 38
4	20	Redditch North	arr															After working 3.55 am from Clifford Sdgs.				
			dep		12 34	1 23	2 34		2 54	3 35			4 21	5 10	5 34					9 21		9 48
4	58	Redditch	arr						2 58				4 23	5W15	5W37					9W26		9 53
			dep		12 36	1 26	2 36		3 18	3 39			4 35	5W25	5W42					9W31		10 8
7	54	Studley and Astwood Bank			12 44	1 35	2 44		3 27	3 47			4 47	5 36	5 53					9 45		10 18
12	12	Alcester	arr																			10 30
			dep		12 53	1 45	2 52		3 39	4 2			4 57	5 49	6 6					9 58		11 30
14	67	**BROOM JN. NORTH**	arr						3*48				5* 8							10*10		11 40
			dep		1 0	1 54	2 58		4* 0	4 12			5*20	5 59	6 16					10*40		11 55
15	34	Broom Jn. West	arr								4*22											
			dep	12 12	1 2	1 57	3 0	3 10	4 4	4 15	4*28		5 25	6 1	6 18	7 17	10 28	10 28		10 45	11 39	11 59
16	8	Salford Priors	arr																			12 3
			dep																			12 13
18	19	Harvington	arr																			12 20
			dep	12 21	1 9	2 6	3 6	3 20	4 12	4 26	4 42		5 35	6 9	6 28	7 25	10 38	10 37		10 55	11 48	12 32
21	59	**EVESHAM**	arr	12W33	1W20	2W18	3W15	3W32	4 24	4W36	4W54		5 48			7W35	10W51			11W8	12 2	12 47
			dep	12W38	1W30	2W28	3W20	3*44		4W41	5*10			6 21	6 45	7*50	10W56	10 46		11*20	12 12	
24	76	Hinton	arr																			
			dep																			
26	66	Ashton-under-Hill	arr																			
			dep																			
28	66	Beckford	arr																			
			dep																			
32	45	**ASHCHURCH**	arr				3*43									8 26		11*11		11*58	12 43	
			dep	1 7	2 0	2 53	3*55	4 13		5 10	5 39			6 54	7 21	8 45	11 32	11*30		12*22	1 35	
																		SUSPENDED				

Goods working timetable, down trains, from 17th September, 1956 to 16th June, 1957.

WEEKDAYS																				SUNDAYS
BARNT GREEN TO ASHCHURCH																				
DOWN		G	J	K	H	J	H	H	H			H	E	J	H	H	J	H		J
		LE to Tewkesbury Shed	2.5 pm Stratford-on-A. to Gloucester		1.50 pm Exchange Sidings to Westerleigh	7.10 pm Stratford-on-A. to Gloucester	7.20 pm W'ford Halse to South Wales (SX) Gloucester C. (SO)	8.52 pm from Washwood Heath	8.50 pm Woodford to South Wales			9.50 pm Woodford Halse to South Wales	11.35 pm Washwood Heath to Gloucester	12.15 am King's Norton to Cheltenham	12.50 am King's Norton to Gloucester	1.30 am Woodford Halse to South Wales	1.40 am from Washwood Heath	2.15 am Woodford Halse to South Wales		6.30 am from Washwood Heath
				20																
		SX		SX																
		PM	PM	PM	PM	PM	PM	PM	PM			am	am	am	am	am	am	am		am
BARNT GREEN	arr			When required stops at Beckford arr 5.40, dep 5.45, Ashchurch arr 6.0 pm																
	dep				3 57			9 49					12 22	12 35	1 5		2 31			7 21
Barnt Green Single Line Jn.					4 2			9 51					12 24	12 38	1 7		2 33			7 23
Alvechurch	arr																			
	dep																			
Redditch North	arr																			
	dep				4 15			10 2					12 34	12 52	1 23		2 47			7 37
Redditch	arr							10 7									2W52			7 42
	dep	After working 7.55 am from Washwood Heath			4 20								12 36	12 55	1 28		3W2			
Studley and Astwood Bank					4 29								12 44	1 6	1 41		3 16			
Alcester	arr																			
	dep				4 39								12 53	1 19	1 59		3 29			
BROOM JN. NORTH	arr				4*50									1*31			3*41			
	dep			¶—Stops to take up and set down Signalman	5*35								1 0	1*46	2 11		3*57			
Broom Jn. West	arr		2*32																	
	dep		3*10		5 38	7 40	10 6		11 2			12 12	1 2	1 48	2 13	3 10	4 2	4 22		
Salford Priors	arr																			
	dep																			
Harvington	arr																			
	dep		3 22		5 48	7 50	10 15		11 10			12 21	1 12	1 58	2 25	3 20	4 12	4 31		
EVESHAM	arr		3W33		5W58	8W 3	10W27		11W22			12W33	1W22	2W11	2W40	3W32	4 25	4W44		
	dep	1‖ 2	3W38	5 5	6W3	8W 8	10W32		11W27			12W38	1W30	2W16	2W50	3W37		4*59		
Hinton	arr																			
	dep			5¶19																
Ashton-under-Hill	arr	¶—Level Crossing																		
	dep			5¶29																
Beckford	arr																			
	dep																			
ASHCHURCH	arr	1¶27		5 52		8 46			11*58							4* 6				
	dep	1¶32	4 12		6 35	9 30	11 1		12*15			1 7	1 54	2 49	3 22	4*17		5 28		

Goods working timetable, down trains, from 17th September, 1956 to 16th June, 1957.

ASHCHURCH TO BARNT GREEN — WEEKDAYS

UP

Mileage M	Mileage C	Station		H	F	F	E	F§	F§	K	K	H	H	G	G	D	D
				To Washwood Heath	3.25 pm Empties Cardiff to Woodford Halse	4.20 pm Empties Ely to Woodford Halse	3.10 am Barnwood to Stratford-on-A.	3.50 am Empties Westerleigh to Clifford Sidings	3.55 am Empties Westerleigh to Clifford Sdgs.	To Washwood Heath	To Washwood Heath	7.20 am Empties Barnwood to Clifford Sidings	9.5 am Empties Barnwood to Clifford Sidings	12.0 noon EBV from Barnwood Sidings	12.25 pm EBV from Barnwood Sidings	To Water Orton	To Water Orton
				MX	MX	MX		MO	MX	SO	SX			SO	SX	SO	SX
				am	am	am	am	am	am	am	am	am	am	PM	PM	PM	PM
0	0	**ASHCHURCH**	arr										9*47				
			dep		12 25	2 30	3 54	5 59	5 53			7 55	9*51	12 35	12 56		
3	59	Beckford	arr														
			dep														
	59	Ashton-under-Hill	arr											To work 1.55 pm to Water Orton	To work 2.0 pm to Water Orton		
			dep														
7	49	Hinton	arr														
			dep														
10	66	**EVESHAM**	arr		1W0	3W5	4 18	6W28	6*18			8W35	10W25	12 57	1 20		
			dep		1*22	3*33	4 55	6*52	6*20	8 25	8 25	9* 0	11*10			1 55	2 0
14	26	Harvington	arr							8 35	8 35						
			dep		1 35	3 46	5 6	7 5	6 32	8 50	8 50	9 15	11 23			2 4	2 9
16	27	Salford Priors	arr							8 55	8 55						
			dep							9 10	9 10						
17	11	Broom Jn. West	arr														
			dep		1 45	3 55	5 13	7 14	6 44	9 13	9 13	9 25	11 32			2 11	2 16
17	58	**BROOM JN. NORTH**	arr							9 15	9 15					2*15	
			dep							10 36	10 36					2*19	2 19
20	33	Alcester	arr					§—"H" from Evesham	§—"H" from Evesham	10 46	10 46						
			dep							11 15	11 15					2 27	2 27
24	61	Studley and Astwood Bank	arr							11 33	11 33						
			dep							12 10	12 10					2 42	2 39
27	67	Redditch	arr							12 18	12 18						
			dep	12 40						12 32	1 0					2 53	2 48
—	—	Redditch M.P. Depot	dep														
28	25	Redditch North	arr														
			dep	12 46						12 37	1 6					2 57	2 51
30	59	Alvechurch	arr														
			dep														
32	20	Barnt Green Single Line Jn.		1 0						12 48	1 20					3 10	3 3
32	45	**BARNT GREEN**	arr							12 50	1 23						
			dep	1 2						1 0	1 33					3 13	3 5
										SL	SL						

Goods working timetable, up trains, from 17th September, 1956 to 16th June, 1957.

WEEKDAYS — ASHCHURCH TO BARNT GREEN — SUNDAYS

UP		K	H	H	H	F	F	F	F	H (Sundays)	F (Sundays)	F (Sundays)	G (Sundays)
			3.20 pm Barnwood to Stratford-on-A.	3.35 pm Barnwood Sdgs. to Stratford-on-A.	To Lawley Street	6.35 pm Empties Gloucester W.R. to Woodford Halse	8.40 pm Empties Gloucester D.B.S. to Woodford Halse	12.45 pm Empties Alexandra Dk. Jn. to Woodford Halse	2.0 pm Empties Rogerstone to Woodford Halse	To Washwood Heath	3.25 pm Empties Cardiff to Woodford Halse	4.20 pm Empties Ely to Woodford Halse	LE to Washwood Heath
		20											
		SX	SX	SO	SX		FSO						
		PM	PM	PM	PM	PM	PM	PM	PM	am	am	am	am
ASHCHURCH	arr		4 21	4 33									
	dep	2 50	4 36	4 45	5 0	8 22	9 42	9 42	10 54		12 25	2 10	
Beckford	arr	3 4											
	dep	3 30											
Ashton-under-Hill	arr	3 36											
	dep	3 49											
Hinton	arr	3 54											
	dep	4 8											
EVESHAM	arr	4 20	5W 7	5W16	5 31	8W52	10W13	10W13	11W23		1W0	2W38	
	dep		5W12	5W21	5 55	9*35	10*29	10*29	11W28		1*22	3*33	
Harvington	arr												
	dep		5 25	5 34	6 8	9 47	10 41	10 41	11 41		1 35	3 46	
Salford Priors	arr												
	dep												
Broom Jn. West	arr												
	dep		5 32	5 41	6 16	9 54	10 48	10 48	11 50		1 45	3 55	
BROOM JN. NORTH	arr				6 19								
	dep				6 26								
Alcester	arr												
	dep				6 37								To work 6.30 am Washwood Heath to Redditch
Studley and Astwood Bank	arr												
	dep				6 50								
Redditch	arr				7 2		SUSPENDED						
	dep				9 15					12 1			
Redditch M.P. Depot	dep												4‖45
Redditch North	arr												
	dep				7 20					12 5			
Alvechurch	arr												
	dep												
Barnt Green Single Line Jn.					7 33					12 20			4 57
BARNT GREEN	arr									12*25			
	dep				7 37					12*35			5 4

Goods working timetable, up trains, from 17th September, 1956 to 16th June, 1957.

Fowler class '4F' class 0-6-0 No. 44332 runs through Redditch station and passes the Abel Morrall needle works, with the 1.55 pm (Saturdays only) Evesham to Water Orton partly fitted freight in January 1960. *Author*

Fowler 'Patriot' class 4-6-0 No. 45519 *Lady Godiva* pauses in Redditch with a northbound diverted class 'H' freight on Sunday 2nd July, 1961. The engine has an unusual type of external spark arrestor fitted, which makes the chimney rim appear to be double normal thickness. The appearance of a 'Patriot' on this line was always a cause for celebration. *Author*

Johnson '3F' class 0-6-0 No. 43521 of Saltley shed stands in the down branch line platform at Barnt Green with a brake van on 24th May, 1961. *B .Moone/Kidderminster Railway Museum*

It was a particularly miserable day on 2nd July, 1961 as BR Standard '9F' class 2-10-0 No. 92136 passes Redditch shed with a lengthy diverted northbound haul of mineral empties. Saltley's allocation of '9Fs' were a fairly regular, and impressive sight on through freight workings along the line. *Author*

Fowler '4F' class 0-6-0 No. 43940 rolls the 7.10 pm freight to Lawley Street over Hewell Road and out of Redditch goods yard on 29th June, 1961. *Author*

Fowler '4F' class 0-6-0 No. 44185 struggles with wet rails on an unpleasant day, Sunday 2nd July, 1961, as it passes Redditch North signal box with a southbound diverted haul of mineral wagons. The coaches on the left are stabled in the Gas Works siding until Monday morning. *Author*

BR Standard class '9F' 2-10-0 No. 92115 (of Westhouses shed) trundles its northbound diverted freight past Clive Road, Redditch on 9th July, 1961. *Author*

Fowler '4F' class 0-6-0 No. 44013, with a MR-style tender, restarts its southbound diverted freight in Redditch on 9th July, 1961. It was not popular with engine crews (and goods guards) to restart such trains, as this meant an inevitably slow climb through the relatively close confines of the tunnel. *Author*

Above: Fowler '4F' class 0-6-0 No. 44289 pounds up the grade into Redditch with a diverted southbound freight on 8th October, 1961. It is passing the gasworks, whose sidings can be seen on the left.

Author

Right: Hughes/Fowler 'Crab' 2-6-0 No. 42829 of Burton shed drifts a lengthy northbound diverted freight past Redditch shed, on the right, and approaches the North signal box, from the where the photo was taken on 8th October, 1961. This was one of the five 'Crabs' fitted with Reidinger rotary poppet valve gear that were all allocated to Burton, where the fitters were familiar with this arrangement.

Author

Johnson '3F' class 0-6-0 No. 43680 wheels a diverted northbound train of mineral empties through Redditch station on 3rd September, 1961, which was one of those beautifully soft, warm late summer days. *Author*

Fowler '4F' class 0-6-0 No. 44463 had considerable difficulty in making headway up the 1 in 65 grade into Redditch with its southbound diverted freight on Sunday 17th December, 1961. In fact, this was its third attempt, having already set back a quarter of a mile twice before. From the amount of steam shrouding the locomotive, it is doubtful that the engine crew could have had much forward vision! Meanwhile, the Fairburn 2-6-4T seen outside the shed on the left, which had been steamed especially to assist the diverted workings, was not called out. *Author*

Movements into Dixon's coal siding at Redditch were comparatively rare, but we see here Hawksworth '94XX' class 0-6-0PT No. 8487 in the deep snow of 2nd January, 1962. This was another of Bromsgrove's Lickey Bankers, here doing a spell as Redditch pilot. From this angle, it can be seen how the line curves around the rear of the engine shed, in the background. *Author*

Stanier 'Black Five' 4-6-0 No. 44981 arrives at Redditch North signal box, as the signalman prepares to accept the surrender of the single line token, with the 7.55 am pick-up freight from Washwood Heath on 2nd January, 1962. This was running some two hours late, presumably because of disruption caused by a heavy snowfall during the preceding days. *Author*

Whilst Johnson '3F' class 0-6-0 No. 43593 shunts the yard at Redditch, Hughes/Fowler 2-6-0 No. 42827 leaves with the 12.10 pm class 'K' freight to Washwood Heath on 12th July, 1962. *Author*

The arrival of a number of 'Royal Scot' class 4-6-0s on Saltley's allocation during 1962 resulted in their sporadic appearances on the line. Here, No. 46162 *Queen's Westminster Rifleman,* stands in Redditch yard waiting to leave with the 12.10 pm pick-up freight to Washwood Heath. *Author*

Stanier '8F' class 2-8-0 No. 48351 makes a fine show as it storms through Redditch station with a diverted class 'J' mineral train on 7th January, 1962 and heads southwards for the tunnel. *Author*

Fowler 'Jinty' 0-6-0T No. 47308 shunting the yards at Redditch during a cold, but very sunny day on 19th January, 1963. *Author*

Saturday only departure. The second arrived at 3.16 am Mondays excepted (4.23 am Mondays only and 3.51 am Saturdays only), This continued as a separate working from Redditch at 6.10 am as a pick-up freight to Evesham, continuing on to Ashchurch on Saturdays. The next arrival was at 9.31 am (Saturdays excepted), the engine remaining on shed at Redditch until departure at 12.10 pm for Washwood Heath. A further pick up freight ran at 5.05 pm (SX) from Evesham to Ashchurch. There were four weekday workings from the WR line at Honeybourne joining the line at Evesham: 11.59 pm (Mondays excepted (MX)) Hinksey (Oxford) to Rogerstone (Newport), 6.40 am (SX) Hinksey to Rogerstone, 4.55pm (SX) Yarnton (Oxford) to Severn Tunnel Junction (running on Saturdays as the 4.10 pm from Hinksey), and 7.10 pm (MX) Yarnton to Rogerstone. On Sundays only one down freight traversed anywhere on the line, this being the 11.40 pm (SO) Didcot to Rogerstone.

In the up direction, the 6.10 am pick-up from Redditch returned as the 8.50 am (SX) Ashchurch to Redditch arriving at 1.15 pm, where the engine went on shed until departure with the 7.10 pm (SX) for Lawley Street. On Saturdays, this working started from Evesham at 8.32 am and ran straight through to Washwood Heath. An engine and brake van left Gloucester Barnwood at 12.25 pm (Fridays and Saturdays excepted) (11.35 am Saturdays only) to form the main fruit carrying train on the line, the 2.00 pm (Fridays and Saturdays excepted) (1.55 pm SO) class 'C' from Evesham to Water Orton. The earlier Saturday departure time from Gloucester allowed this engine and brake van to collect additional traffic en route, notably at Beckford, running as the 12.05 pm Ashchurch pick-up freight as far Evesham. The WR Honeybourne line trains continued with seven up weekday workings: 11.45 (SX) Rogerstone to Yarnton (with a departure time of 12.50 am on Saturdays), 11.40 pm (SX) Neath to Yarnton (12.35 am Mondays only), 8.20 am Cardiff to Yarnton, 2.00 pm Rogerstone to Yarnton, 12.05 pm Llandilo Junction to Cambridge, 10.40 am Aberdare to Yarnton, and 6.30 pm Cardiff to Yarnton. Finally, a pick-up freight ran at 3.20 pm (SX) from Ashchurch to Evesham, arriving there at 4.27 pm and returning at 5.05 pm as mentioned above.

As we have seen above, goods and parcels services between Alcester and Evesham were withdrawn as from 1st October, 1962 at the same time as passenger services. The Evesham to Ashchurch section closed entirely to both goods and passengers as from 16th June, 1963 but goods services officially continued between Redditch and Alcester until 6th July, 1964 although there can have been little traffic between these two points during the previous 18 months.

Locomotives and Rolling Stock

Even the earliest passenger services on the line were worked by locomotives of pure MR origin, as those taken over from the Birmingham & Gloucester Railway had almost all been sold or scrapped by the opening of the Redditch Railway in 1859. The three exceptions were two Jones & Potts 0-6-0s broken up in 1860 and 1862, plus McConnell's 0-6-0ST *Great Britain* built as a banker for the Lickey Incline. Similarly, all of the Bristol & Gloucester Railway locomotives had also been scrapped by that date, and those of the Birmingham & Bristol Railway had also been either withdrawn, sold or scrapped by then.

Saltley shed had initially provided the motive power for most of the workings on the line, but when Bournville shed opened on 12th March, 1894 many of the passenger workings were taken over by this new depot.

Passenger services on the Redditch line were often powered by the long-lived 2-4-0s of Kirtley's '800' class right into the 1920s. This example, running as LMS No. 60 on a Gloucester to Birmingham train near Kings Norton in 1930 was eventually withdrawn as No. 20060 in July 1936. *Author's Collection*

Midland Railway Johnson 0-4-4T No. 1386 with a southbound stopping train composed of bogie stock south of Northfield in 1921, probably heading for the Redditch line. Locomotives of the various similar classes introduced from 1875 onwards had a long association with the line. *J.A. Coltas*

At first, the primary passenger locomotives along the line were Kirtley 2-2-2s and 2-4-0s of the many classes introduced from 1847 onwards. Later, it is known that the line was host to several 2-4-0s of the '80' class built at Derby in 1862, the '170' class built by Beyer, Peacock in 1867, and of the '800' class built by Neilson and at Derby from 1870 onwards. The six engines of the '80' class were originally built to run the 1862 Exhibition specials between Leicester and King's Cross, and were regulars on the services from Birmingham to Evesham until withdrawn for scrapping, the first going in 1876 and the last in 1888. No. 182 of the '170' class was allocated to Evesham MR shed in 1880, and Nos. 173 to 177 were at Saltley after 1900. Some of the 2-4-0s survived into LMS days, and were occasionally seen on passenger workings in the 1920s. Even the remaining Johnson 4-2-2s managed to make occasional appearances on passenger workings in the early 1920s.

Until 1876 MR engines were all painted a dark blue/green throughout, including their underframes, with the upper surfaces lined out. But from this date Samuel Johnson changed the colour to a lighter green, and then from 1883 adopted a brick red colour for passenger engines, later to become familiar as 'crimson lake' and eventually adopted by the LMS for its express passenger locomotives. This livery was complemented by lining in black and yellow, with the inside of the frames and the buffer beams in vermillion.

Subsequently, Johnson 0-4-4WTs of the '690' class and 0-4-4Ts of his '6', '1261' and '2228' classes became synonymous with the passenger services, and frequently appeared on some of the local pick-up goods turns. The latter two classes lasted well after the start of the 20th century, with four of the '1261' class outshedded at Redditch in 1892, and Nos. 1386 and 1391 of the '2228' class also recorded as regular performers. These were replaced to a large extent by the new Deeley '2000' class 0-6-4Ts, more affectionately known as 'Flatirons'. Although these were in the familiar red livery, many were not lined out. In 1931 Saltley shed had an allocation of 14, and Bournville had three, Nos. 2014/5/23-33/35/37-9. From these sheds, four were usually outshedded at Redditch. These engines gave a good account of themselves, even if they did acquire a reputation for rough riding, which culminated in the notorious accident at Ashton-under-Hill on 25th February, 1935. The following are extracts from *Berrow's Worcester Journal* of 2nd March, 1935:

EVESHAM RAILWAY FATALITY

TRAIN DERAILED AT ASHTON-UNDER-HILL

Coroner's Inspection of Scene

Disaster overtook the 9.51 am LMS train from Birmingham to Ashchurch shortly after it left Evesham, on Monday morning [25th February].

The train, due out of Evesham at 11.20 am, was approaching Ashton-under-Hill Station when it suddenly jumped the rails, tore up 160 yards of the permanent way and demolished 20 yards of boundary fencing before coming to rest.

The locomotive, after its wild dash, fell over onto its side partly in a field which adjoins the track. As the engine reeled over, part of the uprooted track lengths of line torn up and twisted into fantastical shapes lying strewn about the scene of the accident pierced the boiler, permitting to escape steam which severely scalded and burned:

Alfred William Woolley, the engine driver, aged 60, of 40 Laurel Road, Cotteridge, Kings Norton, Birmingham, and George Lyndon, the fireman, of Lynworth Road, Stirchley, Birmingham.

Both men were removed to the Evesham Hospital, where Woolley died nine hours after his admittance.

One of the Deeley 'Flatiron' 0-6-4Ts, No. 2015 has come to grief near to Halesowen Junction, Longbridge in February, 1922. It has been rerailed, although the coupling rods remain disconnected. Was this another example of unstability at speed? *J.A. Coltas*

Deeley 'Flatiron' 0-6-4T No. 2037 emerges from the erstwhile Cofton tunnel with a down local passenger service on 20th June, 1936. These engines tended to replace the Johnson 0-4-4Ts on secondary passenger work out of Birmingham until, as a result of several accidents attributed to unstability at speed, they were reduced to goods and shunting duties, and an early retirement. *J.A. Coltas*

GUARD'S VIVID STORY

The guard, Mr J. Cuttriss, of Redditch, who suffered from a sprained wrist and an injured right arm and leg, through being thrown about violently in his cabin during the train's mad dash after leaving the metals, ran to the assistance of the driver and fireman, and with the help of the latter, extricated Woolley, who was partially covered by debris.

'It's a wonder we are alive', said Mr. Cuttriss, in an interview with our reporter. 'I was conscious that something was amiss immediately I was thrown across my cabin, but from the time it came to a standstill seemed only a matter of seconds to me. I hurried to the front of the train – I felt little of my injuries at the time – and was surprised to find the driver still conscious, despite the severe injuries from which he was suffering. His hands were skinning while I was helping to get him from under the debris', said Mr. Cuttriss, who has travelled the Birmingham to Ashchurch route for over a quarter of a century, and has never before been in the slightest mishap of any kind.

WOMAN PASSENGER WALKS OFF

There were two passengers on the train - the majority had travelled only to Evesham. A permanent way inspector, Mr T. Waite, of Ashchurch, rendered what assistance he could, but the other passenger - a woman - climbed down from the coach in which she was riding, and, with amazing nonchalance, walked away without even revealing her identity. On Tuesday night, however, after exhaustive enquiries, it was discovered that the passenger was Miss Evelyn Harden, of Great Washbourne. She has since left the district on a holiday, so it is reported.

Neither of the coaches overturned, the wheels having become so deeply ploughed into the track as to prevent them being upset.

Mr. T. Whittle, of Ashton-under-Hill, who was driving his horse and dray over the railway bridge, said he saw the train swinging from side to side of the track for some distance, crash into the fencing and the engine overturn.

There was a dull thud, and then followed the terrifying noise of escaping steam, he said.

Breakdown gangs from Tewkesbury, Evesham and Ashchurch hurried to the scene of the accident, but it was not until a steam crane and a breakdown gang from Derby arrived, late in the afternoon, that any progress was made in clearing the line, which was blocked until Tuesday.

With the aid of a steam crane commissioned from Derby and a gang of fifty men, who worked throughout the night, the obstruction on the line was removed by 9 o'clock on Tuesday morning, and a single line working between Evesham and Ashchurch was made possible.

The inquest opened on Wednesday, 27th February, and after hearing some preliminary evidence was adjourned until 12th April. The official enquiry by the railway eventually attributed the cause to both the poor state of the track, as well as the inherent instability of the locomotive. After a further derailment involving one of this class near Leicester in 1935, the Deeley 0-6-4Ts were thereafter limited to 45 mph, and subsequently scheduled for withdrawal and scrapping, although many survived for a number of years, being relegated to freight and shunting work. The locomotive involved in the Ashton derailment was No. 2023, having been built at Derby in 1907, but was not withdrawn until March 1937.

The duties of the 'Flatirons' were taken over by former London, Tilbury & Southend Railway 4-4-2Ts designed by Thomas Whitelegg, with 10 (Nos. 2098-2101 and 2104-2109) arriving at Saltley and Bournville sheds in April 1935. However, their stay was relatively brief as during 1936/37 the Stanier taper-boiler 2-6-2Ts started to arrive and the Tilbury tanks were sent to the East Midlands. Johnson and Deeley 4-4-0s were also

Above: The introduction of Stanier 2-6-4Ts on to the former London, Tilbury & Southend Railway (LTSR) rendered many of their older types redundant. However, several were given a new lease of life at Saltley and Bournville sheds, which following the withdrawal of its Deeley 'Flatirons' had experienced something of a motive power crisis. Here, one of the former LTSR 4-4-2Ts, No. 2105 is ready to depart from Birmingham New Street with a local train, possibly for Evesham around 1938. *RCTS*

Top right: Kings Norton station around 1931 with Fowler class '3' 2-6-2T LMS No. 15515 on a down stopping train, probably for the Redditch line. These locomotives, based at Saltley and Bournville had a long association with the line, and despite shortcomings found elsewhere, proved adequate for the demands placed upon them here. *R. Carpenter Collection*

Right: Another of the former LTSR 4-4-2Ts, LMS No. 2109 at Kings Norton station with a train for the Redditch line on 2nd August, 1935. This locomotive was built by the North British Locomotive Co. in 1903 to a Thomas Whitelegg design as LTSR No. 68 *Mark Lane*, and it has retained its Westinghouse pump for air braked stock, and had also been fitted with a second dome. It was finally withdrawn in March 1951 not having carried its allotted BR number 41926. *J.A. Coltas*

often seen on the passenger turns, especially Nos. 505 to 512, allocated to Saltley and Nos. 430, 439, and 517 at Bournville. The Johnson 4-4-0 Compounds allocated to Saltley and Bournville also continued to appear, right until the 1950s, but the Fowler 2-6-2Ts and the Stanier taper boiler variants provided the mainstay of passenger motive power until after World War II. There was a sizeable allocation of these at Saltley and Bournville, with individual engines seemingly changing frequently. Whilst the Fowler engines were notoriously poor steamers, the Stanier variety was more than capable of the work required, but was disliked by engine crews for their water capacity, which at 1,350 gallons required frequent replenishment. BR Nos. 40115, 40117 and 40149 are particularly remembered. With an increase in the availability of class '4' tank engines, the Fowler 2-6-4Ts became available from 1947 onwards and were welcomed by crews for their impressive power. Saltley's Nos. 42326, 42327, 42336, 42337, 42340 and 42383 were regulars. The early members of this class were replaced in 1960 by the later variants with side window cabs, apparently as the result of complaints from engine crews concerning draught and cold when working bunker first. One wonders why such complaints took so long to surface, or perhaps the complaints had been ignored for many years. Of this latter class, Nos. 42400, 42416, 42417, 42421, 42422 were frequent visitors, and shared the passenger duties with the Ivatt class '4' 2-6-0s right up until closure. Many of this class were allocated to Saltley and Bournville over the years, and so made regular appearances, such as Nos. 43010, 43012, 43013, 43017, 43027, 43033, 43036, 43040, 43041, 43046, 43047, 43049 and latterly Nos. 43063, 43103, 43106, 43122. The last four were transferred from the Eastern and North Eastern Regions and differed in that they were not lined out, and most carried the larger cabside numbers.

In considering these engines, two stand out as having achieved some degree of notoriety. Firstly, Ivatt Mogul No. 43036 gained an undesirable reputation on 8th October, 1958 when working the 12.30 pm empty carriage stock working from Birmingham New Street to Bournville. It managed to become derailed in the tunnels to the south of New Street, bringing a total stop to all southbound trains from the MR side of the station for over two hours. 'The Pines Express' and a Newcastle-Cardiff express had to wait until Stanier 'Black Fives' could be summoned from Saltley shed to back onto these trains and haul them out through Camp Hill to continue their journeys south. The second of these otherwise humble engines was Fowler 2-6-4T No. 42336 which was probably the first LMR engine to visit Paddington, when on 2nd November, 1959 it arrived piloting Collett 'Grange' class 4-6-0 No. 6839 *Hewell Grange* (appropriately enough) on the 1.58 pm from Banbury, albeit arriving some 80 minutes late.

Of course, various other classes made sporadic appearances. During World War II, several Stanier three-cylinder 2-6-4Ts were allocated to Saltley, so that by early 1943 there were six of this class (Nos. 2505/16/18/29/33/36) available for traffic, and some of these were noted working through to Evesham. Another wartime event was the loan of some Southern Railway 4-4-0s to both Saltley and Burton sheds from 1943. These included Drummond 'S11' class 4-4-0s Nos. 395/6/7 and 404, Drummond 'K10' class Nos. 135 and 137, Wainwright rebuilds of Stirling locomotives of class 'F1' Nos. 1060/2/78 and of class 'B1' Nos. 1441/6. Curiously, they seem to have been put to work mostly on goods duties, but it would appear that they did not distinguish themselves particularly well. One stalled at Broom Junction in October 1943 and managed to foul the points at both ends of the loop, so that the crew had to wait for a following train to arrive, which was able to push it clear. As there is no particular gradient at this point, it is difficult to see how the engine managed to get itself into this predicament. By comparison, some sympathy must go to the crew of No. 396 which stalled on the Lickey Incline on 25th November, 1943 whilst hauling 40 wagons and being banked. Presumably some of the other interlopers would have made appearances on the line during this period. All were returned to the Southern Railway by late spring or early summer of 1945.

The LMS Compound 4-4-0s were frequent visitors during the 1950s, and No. 41157 of Derby shed notably worked on the line for four days from 9th April, 1959. For the first two days it worked the 12.57 pm (Saturdays excepted) Birmingham New Street-Ashchurch, ran light to Cheltenham to turn, and returned with the 4.25 pm from Ashchurch. On Saturday the 11th it worked the 1.03 pm (Saturdays only) to Ashchurch, then turned and worked back as above. On the Sunday, it worked the 8.10 am from Birmingham to Evesham, returning light engine. This working was specially arranged by BR with Patrick Whitehouse so that it could be filmed for the BBC TV programme *Railway Roundabout*, which was transmitted on 5th May.

Saltley had one of the BR Standard class '4' 2-6-4Ts allocated for a short while, No. 80063, which was noted on the line. It had come new to Saltley in 1953, but was exchanged for Fowler 2-6-4T No. 42383 from Kentish Town in October 1954. BR Standard class '4' 2-6-0s Nos. 76085 and 76087 were also familiar, being allocated to Saltley from 1957 to 1959 and again from 1963 to 1965, when further members of the class were moved there. Occasionally, BR Standard class '4' 4-6-0s, Stanier 'Black Five' 4-6-0s, Hughes/Fowler 'Crab' 2-6-0s, and even Fowler LMS '4F' 0-6-0s also powered passenger trains. A notable visitor on 1st May, 1963 was Stanier 'Jubilee' class 4-6-0 No. 45653 *Barham* on the 5.10 pm from Birmingham New Street to Redditch, deputizing at short notice for a failed 2-6-4T. It returned on the booked working, the 9.50 pm parcels to Lawley Street. Only a couple of years earlier the appearance of a 'Jubilee' would have been a major incident, but at this date Saltley had nine others of this class, all having been cascaded down from main line duties.

Up to 1960, one regular 'foreign' working was the 9.41am (Saturdays only) from Ashchurch to Birmingham, which originated at Gloucester, and was worked by a Leicester (15C) engine as part of a two-day diagram. Frequently, this service was powered by one of their BR Standard class '4' 4-6-0s, Nos. 75057 and 75059 being recalled.

During the winter of 1961/62 many dmus were sidelined by the weather, and a number of stored Fairburn 2-6-4Ts, many from Neasden, were loaned to Saltley and Bournville, where they were used on the Redditch services. Although many of them showed a definite lack of care in their external appearance, they performed their duties well until the better weather returned along with the dmus.

From the outset the goods workings were handled by the 2-4-0s mentioned above, but were superseded by the 1870s by a variety of 0-6-0s, notably the many variants supplied to Kirtley from outside builders, and then the numerous classes introduced by Johnson, especially his '1873', '1823', '1357', and '2736' classes. The change in livery for MR engines in 1910 resulted in goods engines being painted plain black, although some had been painted a dark brown in 1905. Many of the early 0-6-0s were rebuilt with different boilers and wheels, and became classified by the LMS as '2F' and '3F', lasting into the 1950s and early 1960s. The standard LMS Fowler '4F' 0-6-0s were staple power along the line from the 1930s until closure, along with Hughes/Fowler 2-6-0 'Crabs', Ivatt class '4' 2-6-0s, and Stanier class '5' 4-6-0s and '8F' 2-8-0s. Many of the through freight workings from the 1950s onwards were seen powered by BR class '9F' 2-10-0s, and the sight of one of these magnificent machines at full cry with a heavy freight is something to be treasured forever. These mighty engines were also often used during 1957/58 on the 8.52 pm Washwood Heath to Redditch local goods, returning at 12.18 am and so rarely seen. Finally, Saltley acquired 11 'Royal Scot' class 4-6-0s in mid-1961, that stayed for about a year, and were occasionally seen on the morning pick-up freight from Washwood Heath to Redditch. This caused some excitement at the time, but the demotion of these express locomotives was not a sight to be relished. However, these engines were also used by Saltley on more appropriate turns, such as holiday extras, for which it had previously been forced to use '9Fs'.

Originally Redditch had a designated allocation of locomotives, which in the first place comprised the 2-4-0s performing shunting, passenger and goods work. By 1880 the allocation was four 0-6-0s of both Kirtley and Johnson designs. These were replaced in the 1890s by a similar number of the Johnson 0-4-4Ts, which were largely replaced by Deeley's 0-6-4Ts when they were introduced in 1907, at which approximate time Redditch lost its designated allocation, and locomotives were stabled here rather than being allocated. The exception was a pilot engine, which had been provided at Redditch at least from the 1880s, when the volume of both incoming and outgoing goods traffic to be sorted was sufficient to warrant the full time attention of a locomotive, and for local goods work to Alcester, Broom and Evesham. The earliest are presumed to have been one of the many Deeley and Johnson 0-6-0s outlined above, and certainly by the 1950s these duties became the preserve of one of the Johnson 0-6-0s as rebuilt by Fowler and given the LMS designation of '3F'.

In 1959 the authorized shunting hours at Redditch were from 6.05 am until 9.30 pm Monday to Friday, and 5.00 pm on Saturday. Both Bournville, then latterly Saltley, provided these engines, which usually were outshedded at Redditch for a two-week turn of duty, until returned to their home depot for a boiler washout. This practice continued until 1960, even though the WR had taken over the administration of the line in February 1958. However, eventually in 1960 a change was made, and locomotives were thereafter provided by Bromsgrove shed. Although Bromsgrove usually had one '3F' on its books, this was required for main line movements into and out of the Wagon Works there, to Birmingham and Gloucester. The only other locomotives, apart from the '9F' banker No. 92079 were its stud of Hawksworth '94XX' class 0-6-0PTs (Nos. 8400-8406) and two remaining Fowler 0-6-0T 'Jinties', Nos. 47276 and 47308. The'Jinties' were used at Redditch from January 1960, and were well up to the job, as might be expected. However, there were several periods when Bromsgrove was short of motive power, and '3Fs' were then supplied from Gloucester (Barnwood) shed, the original MR shed in that city. Nonetheless, even this large shed was occasionally itself short of appropriate motive power, and notably in the last week of June 1962 when called upon to supply a locomotive, produced BR Standard class '5' 4-6-0 No. 73096. This fine engine ended its surprise duties in under a week but was on shed over the weekend of 1st July, in company with the usual branch passenger engine, Ivatt 2-6-0 No. 43106, which it rather dominated. Readers may well be aware that this BR Standard engine has since been restored to main line running condition, and has achieved an envious reputation for its performance and reliability.

One of the Saltley '3Fs' managed to derail itself in the goods yard at Clive Road, Redditch on Thursday 21st August, 1958. This probably occurred during shunting operations, although the *Redditch Indicator* of 29th August reported it as having 'been pulling a goods train at a slow speed'. The interesting aspect of this derailment is the speed with which it was rectified, particularly as it was not fouling any of the through running roads. The initial derailment is reported as having occurred at about 5 pm, the Saltley breakdown crane had arrived by 7 pm, and the rerailing exercise was complete by 8.30 pm. A likely scenario today would almost certainly involve cordoning off the whole area with brightly coloured tape for several days whilst fingertip searches were carried out, this being designated a 'crime scene'.

Returning to March 1960, '94XX' class No. 8404 was tried as the Redditch pilot and after the fitting of continuous blowdown valves, members of this class were used frequently. Almost all of the Bromsgrove engines made appearances at Redditch, and several from Worcester shed, such as Nos. 8426, 8487 and 9493, which had been on loan to Bromsgrove also made their way across. The Bromsgrove engines were replaced each fortnight to permit boiler washouts and routine maintenance. During 1961, both the pannier tanks and 'Jinties' were tried on a Saturday passenger turn, the 11.38 am to Ashchurch and 1.15 pm (Saturdays only) return, often loaded to as many as six vehicles, as they were both permitted up to 260 tons over the line. The remainder of this Saturday diagram was then worked by the usual Saltley class '4' 2-6-0 or 2-6-4T, involving the 2.55 pm (Saturdays only) Redditch to Ashchurch, 4.39 Ashchurch to Redditch, 7.35 light engine Redditch to Evesham, 8.30 Evesham to Redditch, 9.30 Redditch to Ashchurch and empty stock back to Redditch. From Monday to Friday, the class '4' engine would retire to Tewkesbury shed after working the 11.38 am ex-Redditch until required for the 4.39 pm departure from Ashchurch and the rest of the diagram. However, this duty was discontinued with the introduction of the winter timetable for 1962, as some of the timings were altered. The 'Jinties' eventually took over as pilot engines in 1962 and stayed until displaced by a class '08' diesel shunter from Saltley after the closure of the shed as from 1st June, 1964. The diesel was stabled in the goods yard at Redditch on a weekly turn until around 1968. After this time, such goods trains that did run were shunted by their own locomotives. From 1961 to 1963 some Redditch 'enthusiasts' were often to be found on Sundays in an otherwise deserted Redditch shed, cleaning at least one of the locomotives, particularly the pilot engine. Some of these received very unofficial liveries, No. 8487 being finished with polished copper-capped chimney and brass safety valve bonnet (normally painted black), and with a red background to its polished side numberplates, a blue background to its front numberplate, and silver painted smokebox hinges. The buffers had too much grease on them to clean off, otherwise we would have painted them silver too. Incidentally, No. 47276 was used in the Bath area for the making of the Peter Sellers film, *The Wrong Box* in 1965, being painted apple green and its number altered to '727' for the purpose.

One short-lived experiment was the use of an Ivatt class '2' 2-6-0 as Redditch pilot during April 1962. The intention was that it would provide more appropriate motive power for the Ashchurch working, which indeed it did, but it was not at all suitable for the majority of the work which involved long hours of shunting. Actually, two engines were involved, Nos. 46526 and 46527, both being green liveried and loaned from Gloucester Barnwood shed.

Evesham was not provided with a pilot engine by the MR, LMS or BR (LMR), as far as is known. Instead, the train engine of any goods workings performed such shunting as was required, until the WR at Worcester furnished a locomotive for shunting work as required at Evesham, which by 1954 certainly included work on the former MR goods sidings as well as the former GWR up and down yards. This engine was due off the former GWR Evesham shed at 6.45 am each day, returning at 8.00 pm (2.00 pm on Saturdays). The locomotives supplied by Worcester shed for this work were invariably pannier tanks of the '57XX' and '94XX' classes, changed over every 10 days. However, after the shed closed in June 1961 a Swindon-built class '03' 204 hp 0-6-0 diesel-mechanical shunter was sent out from Worcester on a daily 'trip' basis to work the yards.

The introduction of dmus from 25th April, 1960 seriously curtailed the activities of steam locomotives, to the extent that only one passenger engine was stabled at Redditch from Saturday night to Monday morning, instead of three previously. One other locomotive was still stabled overnight at Tewkesbury, having worked the 5.10 pm from Birmingham to Ashchurch, and it returned the following day with the first train from Ashchurch at 7.14 am. At first the dmus were of the two-car 'Derby Lightweight' class (later class '108'), often worked in multiple, but were soon joined by the designs from Park Royal (later class '103') and Gloucester Railway Carriage & Wagon Co. (later class '100'), until eventually most services were undertaken by the Metro-Cammell units (later class '101'). The dmus were based at Monument Lane depot in Birmingham, and also included some transferred from Walsall at the commencement of the services, including the later Derby-built twin set units in the series M51416/56271. Diesel locomotives were otherwise very infrequent visitors at this time, although it is reported that the 8.00 am Redditch to Birmingham, and 5.32 pm Birmingham to Redditch services, which were normally steam turns, were occasionally worked by a Birmingham Railway Carriage & Wagon Co. Bo-Bo, later to become class '27'. Presumably these were new and being run-in prior to being allocated to Scotland.

The service between Evesham and Ashchurch during 1962/63 was operated by Collett '57XX' class 0-6-0PTs from Cheltenham shed, with Nos. 3745, 4614 and 8743 being regulars. The only other locomotives believed to have then visited this part of the line were Collett '2251' class 0-6-0s from Worcester shed engaged in track removal after the closure of the line.

The first passenger stock on the line would undoubtedly have been of the four-wheeled variety, but by 1880 the six-wheeled stock designed by Thomas Clayton and built at Derby was being used. The older carriages and third class stock were painted a dark green, but these were eventually repainted in the familiar claret, and their replacements followed in the new colour. In 1876 the MR had introduced 54 ft carriages carried on two six-wheel bogies, containing first and third class compartments, which were the first bogie vehicles in this country. These were the forerunners of many bogie carriages that earned the MR an enviable reputation for having the best rolling stock in the country. Its commitment to the comfort of its passengers was reinforced by its unilateral abolition of second class travel as from 1st January, 1875. Eventually bogie stock found its way onto secondary services, and its use was virtually complete by the early 1920s. Subsequently, both MR and LMS carriages of corridor and non-corridor stock were used on the line, with LMS and BR standard stock being used up until cessation of locomotive haulage. Frequently, in the 1950s and 1960s trains would be composed of a mixture of corridor and non-corridor suburban carriages, with a mixture of carmine and cream, and maroon lined liveries.

Locomotives on the GWR Alcester to Bearley branch

The origins and services of this line have been discussed in earlier chapters. So it is pertinent here to look at the locomotives appearing at Alcester.

The line saw very little variety in locomotives, with Armstrong '517' class 0-4-2Ts being the mainstay from the outset. No. 1156 was allocated to Alcester shed in 1901 and No. 537 in 1926. Otherwise, engines of the same class visited periodically, with Nos. 203 and 523 being noted in the 1920s, and 569 and 1157 in the 1930s. Finally, some of Collett's '48XX' class 0-4-2Ts became regulars, such as Nos. 4801 and 4848. These engines were ideal for the line, as they could work in the 'Auto-train' mode, with the engine semi-permanently attached to one end of the train, which the MR described as a 'Motor Train'. Often passenger services were made up as a 'mixed' train with the single coach supplemented by one or two goods vehicles and a brake van. It is possible that other locomotives such as the Dean 0-6-0s and the various GWR 0-6-0STs and 0-6-0PTs allocated to Stratford-upon-Avon GWR shed may have visited the line on special goods workings, but none have been recorded, and there were no through workings on to the Redditch line beyond Alcester.

Ticketing, and Special Workings

The standard third class fare from Redditch to Birmingham was 1*s*. 4*d*. single in 1863, which had risen to 2*s*. 1*d*. in 1949, although the day return was 3*s*. 3*d*. By the mid-1950s this had risen to 3*s*. 6*d*., becoming 3*s*. 10*d*. in 1962. Other day return fares from Redditch in 1962 were 1*s*. 6*d*. to Alvechurch, 1*s*. 11*d*. to Barnt Green, 2*s*. 7*d*. to Northfield, 3*s*. 0*d*. to Kings Norton, 3*s*. 3*d*. to Bournville, 3*s*. 8*d*. to Selly Oak, 1*s*. 6*d*. to Studley & Astwood Bank, 2*s*. 7*d*. to Alcester, 3*s*. 0*d*. to Broom, 3*s*. 6*d*. to Salford Priors, 3*s*. 10*d*. to Harvington, and 5*s*. 1*d*. to Evesham. At this time the standard single fare, now second class, to Birmingham New Street was 4*s*. 0*d*. It is also worthy of note that BR were offering special five-day tickets from Redditch to Birmingham, valid Monday to Friday, and six-day tickets, valid Monday to Saturday. These permitted one return trip on each day, and were available at a cost of 19*s*. 2*d*. and 23*s*. 0*d*. respectively. However, a little arithmetic shows that these were exact multiples of the day return fares, and so offered no discount incentive to the traveller at all!

Notwithstanding the very reasonable fares charged, certain persons did, and for that matter still do, attempt to travel without a ticket. The following report from the *Worcester Herald* of 2nd May, 1868 describes one such, very early, incident:

> DEFRAUDING THE RAILWAY COMPANY – At the Public Office, on Friday, before LMS H. Milward and E. Holyoake, a respectably-dressed young man, who gave the name of Harcourt, and stated that he was a Birmingham jeweller in search of work, was charged with riding in a railway carriage, on the 23rd. inst., with intent to defraud the Midland Railway Company. It appeared that he arrived at Redditch by the 6.0 p.m. train, and on being requested to produce his ticket said he had lost it. He also stated that he had booked at Camp-hill; but when asked by the station master (Mr Diggles) as to the amount of money he had paid for his fare at that place, his answer showed that he had stated a falsehood; and his replies to other questions put to him being very suspicious, he was handed over to the police. At the police station, after some prevarication, he stated that he had done it on purpose to get locked up, as he had been out of work for three months, and had nothing to eat nor any money. Fined £1 and costs, but in default of payment was sent to gaol for 21 days' hard labour.

If this sentence seems harsh, this is only because such a crime was not considered in those days to have been 'victimless'.

Excursions were an important part of the railway's revenue right from the very start, and we have seen that excursions were run on the opening days of the line. Another such was advertised in the *Worcester Herald* of 22nd September, 1866 for a day trip to take place on the following Tuesday, 25th September, from Alcester to Bristol, departing at 7.00 am, and returning from Bristol at 7.15 pm. The first class fare was 6*s*. 0*d*., and the 'covered carriage' was 3*s*. 0*d*.

Another in the *Alcester Chronicle* of 10th August, 1872 was for an excursion from Alcester to Malvern on the following Tuesday, 20th August. The train left Alcester at 7.34 am and Wixford at 7.40 am, returning from Malvern at 7.05 pm. It is likely that this excursion began at Redditch, or perhaps even further north, and would almost certainly have been one of the rare through workings to use the level crossing over the main line at Ashchurch. A week later, another excursion was to be run from Alcester on 22nd August, this time to the 'Grand Horse Show' at Bingley Hall, Birmingham. It was to leave Alcester at 7.34 am and Coughton at 7.39 am, returning from Birmingham at 5.05 pm. In both cases the advertisements did not disclose the excursion fares, simply advising 'for fares and further particulars see handbills to be had at stations'.

Throughout the life of the line, excursions were run for similar such events, and increasingly as compulsory weekend work became less commonplace, for trips to the seaside resorts of North Wales, Blackpool and Weston-super-Mare. Such excursions inevitably started from the south end of the line if travelling to a northern destination, and from the north end, or even Birmingham if travelling south, so as to call at as many stations as possible in order to maximize the number of passengers. Taking a northerly route often meant calling at all stations to Kings Norton, then following the Camp Hill line, on towards Castle Bromwich, then calling at further stations on the line towards Walsall, before starting on the journey proper. It often seemed that half of the day was spent in these meanderings, and then it all had to be done again on the way back. Nonetheless, the excursion fares were so cheap that it was always worthwhile. The other consideration was that much of the rolling stock was from a reserve that was infrequently used, and often of a considerable age, thus providing somewhat questionable comfort.

Excursions advertised in the *Redditch Indicator* for both Easter and Whitsun holidays in 1895 mostly comprised day and half-day trips to Alcester, Salford Priors and Evesham, but there was also a half-day excursion to Birmingham. Special excursion fares were offered for breaks in London of one, three, five or eight days duration, although these entailed the use of scheduled services. Several seaside destinations were served during the August bank holiday period, and several special trains were run in this connection. Bookings at Redditch for this period were reported as follows:

Saturday, 3rd August	London 15, West of England 72
Monday, 5th August	London 20, Tewkesbury and Evesham 160
Tuesday, 6th August	Weymouth and Bournemouth 90, Scarborough 116, Malvern 112, Birmingham 240, Evesham 33
Wednesday, 7th August	Matlock 316, Weston-super-Mare 59, Birmingham 212, Evesham 90

It was reported that on the Saturday 'all trains were somewhat late', but on Monday 'fairly good times were kept'.

Cook's advertised a number of excursions run in conjunction with the MR, and in 1906 it is of interest that they were running regular half-day excursions to Cheltenham, Gloucester, Bristol and Weston-super-Mare leaving Redditch at 12.40 pm on Wednesdays 15th and 29th August, 12th and 26th September. On 18th August there was an excursion for Blackpool, but earlier, on 11th June, an innovation was in the form of an excursion to Sharpness followed by a sea trip to Ilfracombe and return.

Cook's influence gradually expanded, so that they regularly offered special fares to horse race meetings around the country, and by 1911 these had included Colwall (near Hereford), Lincoln, Nottingham, Warwick, Leicester, Haydock, Uttoxeter, Wolverhampton, Stratford, and Worcester. One further excursion was for the Grand National at Aintree, advertised as a 'Restaurant Express', departing at 8.35 am. Many of these trains were through excursions, picking up at other stations en route, but some were simply special fares, joining scheduled services or the special workings particularly at Birmingham New Street.

Special fares were on offer to Birmingham for the FA Cup Semi-Final on 25th March, 1911 for which 'various' timings were possible. In the same vein, an excursion left at 5.35 am on Saturday 22nd April for the Cup Final at Wembley, although it is most likely that this special only ran as far as New Street, where the passengers changed trains. The day and half-day excursions to Cheltenham, Gloucester, Bristol and Weston-super-Mare continued to be offered as popular destinations, one such being run on 5th June in the Whitsun period, and departing at 12.40 pm from Redditch. The regular excursion fares offered to stations en route to Evesham also continued at this time. The Cook's trip to Sharpness was again available on 21st August, departing at 6.40 am. However, even this early morning start was eclipsed by that of a very enterprising trip to Bournemouth, Weymouth and Cherbourg, which left at 1.18 am!

At this time Cook's continued to advertise a host of special excursion rates involving several nights accommodation to destinations in the North, West and South of England, the Channel Islands, the Isle of Wight, Scotland and the Eastern Counties - but again these mostly relied on scheduled services.

As the country got back on its feet after World War I and then the effects of the depression, so the excursions were offered to more destinations and more frequently too. In 1927, the trips to horse race meetings continued to be offered, now also including such meetings during Easter as at Rolleston (on 16th April at 8.48 am for 9*s*. 11*d*.) and Bromford Bridge (Birmingham) for a mere 2*s*. 8*d*., although the latter used scheduled trains. There were two excursions to Weston-super-Mare; on Sunday 17th April at 11.00 am for 5*s*. 0*d*., and on the following day at 7.27 am, but costing 11*s*. 6*d*. Evidently, you paid for the extra time to be enjoyed at the seaside.

Special fares were promoted to Marston Green, Hampton-in-Arden, Berkswell, Coventry, Kenilworth, Warwick and Leamington on Easter Monday, 18th April - but once again these involved the use of scheduled services.

Whitsun 1927 saw the familiar two excursions to Weston-super-Mare, on Sunday 22nd May at 11.40 am, and on Wednesday 25th May at 11.20 am, but this time the fares at 5*s*. 6*d*. were identical. Special rate fares of 12*s*. 0*d*. to London were again offered during this period, as they had been at Easter, and were to be during August.

The holiday period for August 1927 had expanded somewhat beyond the initial bank holiday period. On 8th and 9th August two specials for Nottingham Races were advertised at 8*s*. 4*d*., but unusually a first class fare was also given, of 13*s*. 11*d*. The usual destinations of Weston-super-Mare, London and Ilfracombe via Sharpness were once again promoted, with the departure time for the latter now being shown as 6.50 am. The LMS were evidently determined to popularize Blackpool, as two excursions were run: on Sunday 14th August at 11.55 am (7*s*. 0*d*.), and on Saturday 20th August at the extreme hour of 2.15 am (priced at 13*s*. 0*d*.).

Peter Turner recalls that such trips during the 1930s were also made to such far-flung destinations as Scarborough, and that these not only involved a very early start but also a very late return. Typically, the excursionist would return home nearly 24 hours after departure!

The London day excursion rate of 12*s*. 0*d*. was still offered 10 years later in 1937 at many dates during the year, but particularly this was promoted in connection with the Ideal Homes Exhibition at Olympia on 21st, 22nd, 24th and 29th April, departing at 7.15 am. This was, of course, a normal service to Birmingham, where the excursion would be picked up, and it is noted that on Wednesday 21st April this ran to Kensington (Addison Road) which was adjacent to the show venue.

A special rate of 2*s*. 0*d*. was offered to Worcester races on 17th and 19th May, but these used normal service trains. However, a special service was run on 1st May for the FA Cup Final (Preston North End versus Sunderland) at Wembley, departing at 5.25 am and as it terminated at St Pancras, this must have involved an interesting route. The fare was the usual 12*s*. 0*d*.

During August 1927 concessionary rates were offered every Sunday (and also on Tuesday and Wednesday 3rd and 4th August) from Redditch to stations further south on the line, travelling on the 8.50 am scheduled service as follows: Alcester 1*s*. 0*d*., Wixford 1*s*. 3*d*., Broom 1*s*. 4*d*., Salford Priors 1*s*. 6*d*., Harvington 1*s*. 6*d*. and Evesham 2*s*. 0*d*. A half-day excursion rate was also available, on Tuesday 3rd August only, by travelling on the 1.39 pm service, and giving further savings to Salford Priors and Harvington (both 1*s*. 3*d*.), and Evesham (1*s*. 6*d*.). A further concessionary fare was offered on any train after 9.00 am from Redditch to Barnt Green on Monday and Tuesday, 2nd and 3rd August for the sum of 9*d*., for those wishing to enjoy the delights of the Lickey Hills. A special train on Sunday 1st August at 7.35 am to Birmingham gave connections to London, Coventry, Crewe, Runcorn, Liverpool, Stafford, Stoke, Macclesfield, Stockport and Manchester for which various fares were available. On the same day an excursion for Weston-super-Mare (5*s*. 6*d*.) departed at 9.45 am, as usual calling at Cheltenham (3*s*. 0*d*.), Gloucester (3*s*. 6*d*.), and Bristol (5*s*. 0*d*.). The following day another excursion for this destination left at the earlier hour of 6.05 am, calling only at Bristol (7*s*. 6*d*.) and Weston (8*s*. 6*d*.). This was a busy day at Redditch station, as by using the 7.29 am to Birmingham, passengers could connect with an excursion for Blackpool (10*s*. 6*d*.) which returned at 8.35 pm. Later, a special working departed Redditch at 10.50 am for Ashchurch, Tewkesbury (both 3*s*. 0*d*.), Upton-on-Severn (3*s*. 6*d*.), Malvern Wells (4*s*. 0*d*.) and Great Malvern (4*s*. 6*d*.). On the same day, Bidford (1*s*. 6*d*.), Binton (1*s*. 8*d*.) and Stratford-on-Avon (2*s*. 0*d*.) were accessible by using the departures at 11.35 am, 1.38 or 2.13 pm and changing at Broom Junction.

The special rates for all stations between Marston Green and Leamington were again offered by using the 8.32 or 10.04 am services to New Street on 2nd August, and also on the 11.37 am service on the following day. A special train left Redditch at 5.00 am on Wednesday 4th August for Rhyl (9*s*. 6*d*.), Colwyn Bay (10*s*. 0*d*.) and Llandudno (10*s*. 6*d*.), and was followed by a departure at 11.35 am for Weston-super-Mare (5*s*. 6*d*.) with the usual calls en route. However, there was another departure for Weston at 11.00 am on each of the following two days, at the same fares.

Following World War II, the demand for excursions was at a much higher level, as many people had experienced a degree of travel never before thought possible. Unfortunately, their personal mobility was severely limited by the continuing rationing of many goods, and the amount of personal transport available was restricted by the national need to export as much as possible in order to pay for the war. It was earlier mentioned that excursion fares were often advertised using scheduled services at weekends, but one notable, and in some ways a surprising, through excursion was from Redditch to London Euston on 19th June, 1953 for the celebrations continuing following the coronation of our Queen. This was hauled throughout by Saltley 'Black Five' No. 44666.

We move forward to the summer of 1955 to present a good example of the specials available. On Sunday 17th July an excursion ran from Redditch at 9.10 am to Bristol

Broom Junction station on 14th May, 1960 as an SLS special comprising a dmu calls at the station on its varied route from Evesham to Stratford-on-Avon, during which it traversed all of the routes at Broom. *Author's Collection*

The restored LMS Compound 4-4-0 No. 1000 traversed the whole of the line on 27th May, 1961 with a Gloucester Railway Society special to Derby works open day, and is seen here heading up the grade into Barnt Green station. *B. Moone/Kidderminster Railway Museum*

(10*s*. 0*d*.) and Weston-super-Mare (12*s*. 3*d*.). On Sunday 14th August, an excursion called at Cheltenham Spa (5*s*. 3*d*.), Gloucester (5*s*. 9*d*.), Newport (11*s*. 0*d*.) and Cardiff (12*s*. 3*d*.), leaving at 9.55 am. The following Sunday, 21st August, saw a departure from Alvechurch at 8.30 am, Redditch at 8.40 am and Studley at 8.45 am, to Exeter (19*s*. 0*d*.), Dawlish (20*s*. 6*d*.), Teignmouth (20*s*. 9*d*.), Newton Abbot (21*s*. 3*d*.), Torquay and Paignton (both 22*s*. 0*d*.). Two weeks later on Sunday 4th September, a much more adventurous excursion departed Redditch at 9.20 am, picking up at all stations on the line, with the twin destinations of Portsmouth and Ryde, Isle of Wight. Prices varied according to the stations, as follows: Alvechurch and Redditch (18*s*. 0*d*. to Portsmouth, 20*s*. 10*d*. to Ryde), Studley (17*s*. 6*d*. and 20*s*. 4*d*.), Alcester, Broom, Salford Priors and Harvington (16*s*. 0*d*. and 19*s*. 0*d*.). An optional road tour of the Isle of Wight was available for an inclusive price of 23*s*. 9*d*. from Redditch, for example.

Another excursion was run to Bristol and Weston-super-Mare on the same day (fares as for 17th July) leaving Redditch half an hour later at 9.50 am. These two excursions must have given the station staffs an unaccustomedly busy Sunday.

On a more local note, a special working was made available for the Redditch Carnival on Saturday 17th September, leaving Barnt Green at 3.15 pm and calling at Alvechurch. The return special left Redditch at 10.15 pm, and the fares for this event reflected some concession to the local celebrations, being only 1*s*. 0*d*. from Barnt Green and 9*d*. from Alvechurch.

The Blackpool Illuminations were always a favourite destination for Midlanders, and these were the subject of excursions on two weekends, on Saturday, 1st October and Sunday, 9th October. The Saturday trains left Redditch at 11.10 am (Alvechurch 11.20 and Barnt Green 11.27 am), and the Sunday train at 9.30 am (Alvechurch 9.40 and Barnt Green 9.48). In both cases the fares were 16*s*. 6*d*. from Redditch, 16*s*. 0*d*. from Alvechurch and 15*s*. 9*d*. from Barnt Green.

Special fares were also available to Blackpool using ordinary service trains, when Weekend Excursion tickets were on offer at 27*s*. 6*d*. for outward travel on the Saturdays of 10th and 17th September, returning on any train after 2.40 pm on the following Monday.

Moving forward to 1958, there was an excursion on Easter Sunday (6th April) featuring a cafeteria car to Weston-super-Mare at 10.00 am from Redditch (fare 13*s*. 6*d*.), although one on the following day at 7.55 am to the same destination cost 16*s*. Fares were the same from Alvechurch, but 6*d*. cheaper from Studley and 9*d*. cheaper from Alcester. Special fares of 4*s*. from Redditch at 8.54 am and 11.42 am to Evesham were available on Whit Sunday (25th May), and further excursions departed to Blackpool (18*s*. 0*d*.) at 9.30 am and to Gloucester (6*s*. 0*d*.), Bristol (11*s*. 0*d*.), and Weston-super-Mare (13*s*. 6*d*.) at 10.15 am.

A frequent service of half-day excursions to Evesham was run on the Whit Monday, with departures from Redditch at 9.12, 10.20, 11.37 am, 12.35, 1.40 and 2.40 pm for 4*s*. 0*d*., although Tewkesbury could be reached for 5s. 0*d*. This service, originating at Birmingham New Street proved popular, such that it was extended later in the year with the novelty of a dmu providing enhanced lineside views, and operated on 15th June, 29th June, and 13th July. Steam returned to the frequent service of half-day excursions on 3rd, 4th, and 5th August (Bank Holiday Weekend), and later a single return service was offered on Sunday 17th August.

Excursions to the seaside destinations continued with departures to Weston-super-Mare on Sundays 31st May, 22nd June, 31st August, and on Wednesday 6th August, most of which also called at Gloucester and Bristol. Prestatyn (16*s*. 0*d*.) and Rhyl (16*s*. 6*d*.) were reached by a 9.30 am departure from Redditch on Sundays 15th

The winch wagon attached to the rear of Ivatt Mogul No. 43013 is in use, and the cable has been attached to a used length of rail (out of sight) lying in the 'four foot', so that it can be winched aboard the carrying wagon, 18th June, 1961. *Author*

The brake van has been detached from the train, and used rails are winched from the 'four-foot' over the roller at the end of the carrying wagon. When all have been loaded, the brake van will be reattached to enable the permanent way train to return. *Author*

June and 10th August, whilst a 7.26 am departure for Poole and Bournemouth (both 24*s.* 6*d.*) left on Bank Holiday Monday 4th August. Sunday 24th August saw an excursion to Blackpool (18*s.* 0*d.*) from Redditch at 9.30 am. The individual departure times from other stations have not been mentioned here, but there was a difference about 15 minutes from Barnt Green, nine minutes from Alvechurch, five minutes from Studley and 10 minutes from Alcester, depending on the direction being travelled. Finally, although not involving any special workings along the line, it is worth recording that Holiday Runabout Tickets were available from all stations on the line during August giving unlimited travel in the Midlands Area for 27*s.* 0*d.* for one week. Additionally, special weekend rates of 27*s.* 6*d.* were available for visits to the Blackpool Illuminations during September and October, involving departure on Friday or Saturday, and return on Saturday, Sunday or Monday using any normal service train.

As we have seen above, from the mid-1950s a frequent service of half-day excursions were run from Birmingham to Evesham. These occurred at the Easter and Whitsun Bank Holiday weekends and at some August Bank Holiday weekends, when the normal timetable was suspended. There was a maximum of eight such trains run in each direction, and usually loaded to a maximum of six coaches. This stretched the platform capacity at many stations, and indeed some of the trains had to be double headed. These trains were still hauled by the same locomotives normally seen on the line, although in later years there was a tendency to borrow BR Standard class '4' 4-6-0s from Gloucester Barnwood shed for these duties.

During the early 1950s regular unadvertised trains ran on most Sundays during the period from June to March, from Birmingham New Street to Evesham for the benefit of anglers. The trains left New Street at around 6.30 and 8.15 am calling at most stations to Redditch, where they left at around 7.00 and 9.00 am. Anglers left the trains at Wixford (until it closed), Broom and Evesham. George Blewitt recalls that at one time the service continued to Ashchurch, where the anglers would cross to the Tewkesbury platform and be conveyed on open flat wagons for the short journey to Tewkesbury. This latter trip was clearly very unofficial in its practice, and was known as 'The Ferry' for obvious reasons. The return trains are believed to have left Broom at around 4.00 and 7.00 pm. On one such trip George Blewitt was returning to Redditch, but fell asleep after a very long day's fishing, only to wake up in New Street station!

The usefulness of the line as a purely diversionary route was illustrated during 1960, and more particularly, during 1961, when the main line south of Barnt Green was closed for major permanent way work on several successive Sundays. It would appear that most of the passenger trains were still able to use the main line, as there were only a few occasions when expresses were noted passing along our line. One incident is recalled when a 'Jubilee' 4-6-0 paused for water in Redditch with a northbound express, so that its lengthy train reached way back into the tunnel!

When freights were diverted the operations along the line often required considerable ingenuity, in the pathing, and passing of these heavy trains. Furthermore, many required banking assistance between Redditch and Barnt Green, especially over the 1 in 74 rising gradient at the end of the single line section and the start of the double line, and so one of the passenger engines stabled at Redditch shed during Sunday had to be prepared for this duty. Then a further complication arose, that is hardly even considered these days: fog.

In those days the fogs (sometimes, it was of the most unpleasant yellow/green colour and known as 'smog') were so thick that people were known to have walked

Right: Two of the line's well known characters - on the left driver Arthur Laight, and on the right fireman Billy Davies in the cab of Ivatt Mogul No. 43013; 18th June, 1961.

Author

Below: Ivatt class '4' 2-6-0 No. 43036 has just arrived at Evesham with a southbound Whitsun extra on 11th June 1962, and already the engine crew are refilling the tender with water. The five-coach train is made up entirely of suburban non-corridor stock.

Author

past their homes without realising it! Trying to run a railway in such circumstances was extremely difficult, not to say dangerous. Because all freights were reduced to a walking pace, they were unable to make headway towards sections of more adverse gradients, and to offset the risk of becoming stalled, were almost entirely double headed. This made for some powerful combinations of Stanier '8Fs', 'Black Fives', Fowler '4Fs' and BR '9Fs', which would have made for some great photographs, but for one unavoidable difficulty - it was impossible to photograph in fog! Such missed opportunities also included the passage of Stanier 'Jubilee' 4-6-0 No. 45685 *Barfleur* on a down freight on Sunday 1st July, 1962, and on the following Sunday Thompson LNER 'B1' class 4-6-0 No. 61317 powered a similar working, also in heavy fog. Although 'B1s' had been seen periodically on the Birmingham to Bristol main line since at least October 1959 this is the only one known to have passed along the Redditch line. Whilst these operating conditions were not at all pleasant for the engine crews, they certainly made viewing at the lineside most interesting.

Shortly before the final closure of the SMJR at least four enthusiasts' specials are known to have worked over the line. On 29th April, 1956 a Stephenson Locomotive Society special worked over the line. This had originated at Kings Cross behind former GER 'D16/3' class 4-4-0 No. 62605 which hauled the special to Hitchin, where Johnson '3F' 0-6-0 No. 43222 took over to run through Bedford, Olney, Towcester and Stratford to Broom then north through Redditch to Birmingham New Street. Here BR Standard class '5' 4-6-0 No. 73099 returned the special to London via Coventry, Leamington and Rugby to Euston. The others are believed to have come from the south, via Evesham to Broom and thence over the SMJR. One was a Railway Enthusiasts Club special on 24th April, 1955, headed by GWR 'Dukedog' 4-4-0 No. 9015, and the other a special on behalf of the Gloucestershire Railway Society on 7th May, 1957, hauled by a Midland '2P' 4-4-0 No. 40450. Another comprised an Stephenson Locomotive Society dmu special on 14th May, 1960 which arrived at Evesham from Honeybourne, then crossed over to the MR side and ran to Broom, where it managed to traverse all of the three routes, before proceeding on to Stratford and the remainder of the SMJR route.

The Gloucestershire Railway Society also sponsored a further special on 27th May, 1961, hauled by the restored Midland Compound No. 1000 which ran the entire length of the line, having started in Gloucester, and was destined for a Derby works open day.

Operating Systems

The line was divided into sections, so that individual trains could be worked in each section, even where these were wholly single line. This method of working permitted a greater utilization of the line by reducing the headway between trains travelling in the same direction. The original section from Barnt Green to Redditch was initially worked by telegraph and the time interval system, but by 1873 the whole line was worked by the Train Staff system, whereby a staff was issued for each section which was the driver's authority to pass into that section. Block telegraph control at this time was limited to the section from Redditch to Studley, as the Board of Trade had insisted on this as a means of control over trains passing through the tunnel. The introduction of block working on all lines had been required in The Regulation of Railways Act, 1889 and electric tablet working was gradually introduced along the remainder of the line, being completed in 1892. Block sections

Far left: During the spring of 1962 two Ivatt class '2' 2-6-0s were tried out as yard pilots at Redditch, with the expectation that they would also be more suitable for the Saturday passenger duties. Here we see green-liveried No. 46527 standing alongside Redditch shed, with the MR-built hipped-roof Redditch North signal box in the background on 30th April, 1962. *Author*

Left: The Midland Railway hipped-roof Barnt Green Single Line Junction signal box in 1931. The box dated from 1883, but was moved to the present site in 1894. A guard rail at rail level was provided for the signalman when leaning out to exchange the single line tablets, and the large lamp was to facilitate this exchange during the hours of darkness. The signalman, Harry Wood, is standing in the doorway of the box. *D. Powell/Kidderminster Railway Museum*

Left: Bristol Barrow Road's Fowler 'Patriot' class 4-6-0 No. 45504 *Royal Signals* approaches the MR style Redditch South signal box with a diverted northbound string of mineral empties on 9th July 1961. At this moment, the signalman, about to accept the single line token, is out of sight on the right.
Author

Below: Redditch North MR signal box was refurbished by BR after the line southwards was closed, as freight services were still using the goods yard. This view of the structure dates from around 1968, shortly before its closure.
Author's Collection

were established for the following sections of line, where tablets would be issued, except for the Redditch North to Redditch South double line section:

Barnt Green Single Line Junction to Redditch North	20th September, 1891
Redditch North to Redditch South	
Redditch South to Studley & Astwood Bank	11th October, 1891
Studley & Astwood Bank to Alcester	11th October, 1891
Alcester to Broom North	7th August, 1892
Broom North to Broom South (later Broom West)	9th October, 1892
Broom South (later Broom West) to Harvington	24th July, 1892
Harvington to Evesham	24th July, 1892

It should be noted that Broom was not originally a 'block station', and so staffs or tablets were not exchanged there until 1892, some 13 years after the opening of the SMJR line. Prior to this time, both lines here operated as individual single lines with their own staffs, even though they actually crossed. A further block section was then also introduced, between Broom North and Broom South.* The changes to signalling and methods of train operation in that year rectified what had been a potentially dangerous situation. Broom West was, of course, a later addition, and when switched out a 'Through Token' was operated from Broom North to Harvington. Because of the distance between Broom North signal box and the north end of the loop, an auxiliary key token instrument was located at the Alcester end of the platform.

The section between Redditch North and Redditch South was worked by the Double Line Disc Block Telegraph system.

As the line south of Evesham was double track, it continued to be worked by the time interval system as far as Beckford and telegraph bells on to Ashchurch, until block telegraph working was introduced in July and August 1890.

In 1959 signal boxes at Barnt Green Single Line Junction, Redditch North, Redditch South, Alcester, Broom North, Broom West, Harvington, and Evesham were open continuously Monday to Saturday, and on Sunday until 6.00 am, then from around 8.30 am to 11.00 am dependent on location, and again from around 6.40 pm to 8.30-9.00 pm. Beckford box was only open from 6.20 am until 8.50 pm weekdays, and was switched out on Sundays, whilst Studley box was slightly more limited, being open on weekdays from 7.00 am until 2.50 pm, and Hinton only open for 15 minutes each weekday, from 3.55 pm to 4.10 pm.

There were a number of permanent speed restrictions on the line, the most severe being of 10 mph on the goods loop linking to the Honeybourne line at Evesham, and over the occupation crossing south of Redditch tunnel. Further restrictions to 15 mph were in force from the single line into the loops at Barnt Green, Redditch, Alcester, Broom and Evesham.

Miscellanea

Mention was made in the previous chapter of the practice by American servicemen stationed during World War II in the area to gather at Ashchurch station and enjoy the licensed refreshment rooms, along with the girlfriends that they had

* Between 1892 and 1934 this short section was probably double line absolute block. The LMS Appendix for 1931 shows the tablet sections ending at Broom North and restarting at Broom South.

been able to recruit locally. Apparently, this became so well known that one Saltley driver, often rostered to work the evening Bristol to Newcastle mail train, decided to put on a show for them. So each evening, after leaving Cheltenham at 7.20 pm, he worked his engine up to its maximum, and absolutely flew through Ashchurch. On the first occasion, with a 'Patriot', he held on to the whistle for about a quarter of a mile as it approached, and was reckoned to have passed through at about 85 mph. The promenaders on the platform scattered for their lives ! The following night they were ready for him, and thereafter relished this performance, with one visiting officer remarking to a local railwayman that this was the fastest train he had ever seen. Thus the reputation of British railways, and the LMS in particular was enhanced across the Atlantic.

Peter Turner lived in Birmingham Road, Redditch where his house backed on to the 30 ft high embankment at the north end of the single line from Barnt Green. At this point the line southwards consisted of a severely rising gradient, with a maximum of 1 in 65. Needless to say, every effort was made to ensure that loose coupled goods workings in particular were given a through road to the summit, which was just past the Hewell Road overbridge. However, events did not always conspire to permit this, and there were several occasions when the locomotive had to reverse all the way back down to take another run at the gradient - just as often occurred to heavy diverted goods workings. However, he recalls that on more than one occasion, the driver had managed to restart rather jerkily and so broke one of the wagon couplings. The guard would be seen frantically trying to apply his brake as the rear half of the train ran back towards Barnt Green!

Replacement of rails on a single track railway had always been a lengthy task, involving closure of a section of line for occupation by permanent way staff. This had required the initial depositing of new rails alongside the line at some previous time, then the removal of old rails and their replacement with the new ones was made at a later date. Subsequently, another occupation was required so that the old rails could be retrieved from the side of the line. All this involved considerable amounts of manual effort. Eventually, a more efficient means of depositing and collecting rails was devised, and photographs of such an operation are shown on page 194. The permanent way train consisted of a locomotive, next to which was marshalled a 'winch wagon' containing a winch, powered by an onboard stationary internal combustion engine. Following this were the bogie wagons for the rail lengths, which were equipped with rollers at each end of the wagon, and finally the brake van. To discharge new rails, the train was brought to the appropriate point, and the locomotive and winch wagon were separated from the rest of the train. A cable was paid out from the winch to the first rail wagon, and attached by hooks to the eyes in the end of each rail length. The winch was operated, pulling out each rail length, over the rollers on the end of the wagon, and dropping them into the 'four foot' between the running rails. This operation was repeated until rails had been left in position for the required replacement. To retrieve the old rails, the locomotive and winch wagon were reattached to the rail wagons, leaving the brake van separated. The cable from the winch wagon was then paid out across the rail wagons so that it could be attached to the first rail lying in the four foot. When attached to the eyes in the old rail, the winch was operated, and the rails hauled over the end rollers into each rail wagon successively.

Ashchurch station looking north on 9th November, 1968. Although the station buildings remain intact, the trackwork for both the Evesham and Tewkesbury lines have been removed. The former MR provender store, prominent on the skyline to the left, was then in use by Dowty Ltd. A train of army vehicles is parked on the line passing behind the 1958-built signal box, which itself was closed only three months later. *RCTS*

After the cessation of regular freight workings into Redditch, the goods yard and depot were left untended, until the commencement of stone traffic in connection with the rebuilding of the town centre for its role as a 'New Town' during the 1970s. In this view, dated 8th November, 1973 piles of stone can be seen on the right, whilst a shovel loader is filling a lorry on the left. The extensive footbridge remained in use, whilst the goods depot was left to become derelict. This photograph shows up the wooden extension (in white) to the depot, that was added after its initial construction in 1926/27, and probably during the 1930s. *Author's Collection*

Chapter Eight

Modern Times

Events leading up to closure

The previous chapter briefly mentioned the closure of the line south of Redditch, and here we shall look at the events leading to the closure, and some of the after effects.

Competition between rail and buses for passengers from Redditch to Birmingham started as early as 4th April, 1914 when the 'Midland Red' bus services, operated by the Birmingham & Midland Motor Omnibus Co. began a service between Birmingham, Redditch and Astwood Bank. This developed into their route '147', and ran via the Pershore Road, Cotteridge and Hopwood. A variation was introduced on 12th June, 1954 when their route '142' commenced from Birmingham along the Bristol Road, via Selly Oak, Longbridge and Barnt Green to Redditch. This new service provided a link for those persons living in Redditch and working at the Austin Motor works at Longbridge, something that BR could not offer as it did not then have a station at Longbridge. Nonetheless, the bus services had little overall effect on the number of passengers travelling by rail, until the late 1950s when the roads had improved to the point that the duration of both road and rail services were almost identical, and the frequency of buses was such that there were around 60 per day between Redditch and Birmingham. Admittedly, each of the buses could not carry the same number of passengers as a train, but the frequency, and so the convenience, persuaded many persons to use them. A personal viewpoint is that the times of arrival and departure are more usually the ruling factor in deciding on the mode of transport to be used, rather than the oft quoted saving of 10 or 20 minutes on the length of the journey.

By 1959 there was already a general movement away from rail travel, and BR were certainly looking at their loss making services. On 14th January, 1959 a WR track testing vehicle left New Street and traversed the line. The following day, a three-car Cravens dmu set made test runs over the whole line. These events helped to fuel local rumours of the introduction of an hourly dmu service from Birmingham to Redditch, two-hourly service to Evesham, and closure of the line from Evesham to Ashchurch. Local opinion was of both concern at the possible closure, and delight at the prospect of enhanced services, but these were rebutted by the district passenger manager, New Street in June 1959 stating that possible alterations to services on the line were only in the 'exploratory stage'. Predictably, a submission for closure of the line southwards from Redditch to Ashchurch was made to the local Transport Users' Consultative Committee shortly after the introduction of almost hourly dmu services from Birmingham to Redditch on 25th April, 1960, and so predating the Beeching Report of March 1963. This move may be seen as coincidental to the complete closure of the Stratford-on-Avon to Broom Junction line as from 13th June, 1960. Thus the lines south of Redditch were seen as having no future for freight traffic, little potential passenger traffic and BR would appear to be offering the improved service with dmus as a trade-off for this anticipated closure. However, this didn't quite have the effect that BR expected, as the popularity of the new dmu services spawned fresh ideas. Instead, local pressure groups were soon pressing for the service to be expanded southwards, as only the Sunday services from Birmingham to Evesham were operated by the dmus. It was argued that if complete dmus could not be provided there was a case for a railbus to be utilized, and even more audaciously, it was suggested that the stations at Coughton and Wixford could be reopened as unstaffed halts. Furthermore, as Sambourne had no public transport other than on Saturdays, a further halt was suggested there. Another location earmarked for development as a halt was a large housing estate near to the southern end of Redditch tunnel, at Lodge Farm. Nothing came of these proposals, and it is significant that nothing new was being promoted for the Evesham to Ashchurch section.

The hourly dmu service had indeed increased the number of passengers between Birmingham and Redditch, up from 285,000 in 1955 to 352,000 in 1961. Even though this represented a 25 per cent increase, it only applied to a small part of the line, and in any case the additional costs were much greater. So it was perhaps inevitable that all of this activity had not only come to nothing, but was reversed with the proposal by BR announced on 6th March, 1962 to close the 28 mile section from Redditch to Ashchurch to passenger traffic. The stations at Harvington and Ashton-under-Hill were to close completely, but all other stations would remain open for goods traffic, except for a restriction at Hinton which would only be available for full wagon loads. Unfortunately, the report from the WR Civil Engineer in September 1962 that the line south of Redditch was in an unsafe condition for passenger trains, led to the immediate closure as from 30th September, 1962. As we have seen, a temporary bus service was introduced between Redditch and Evesham from this date, calling only at the railway stations en route. Freight services were still permitted to Alcester, which at the time amounted to only one train, running as required, from Washwood Heath, and which generally terminated at Redditch anyway. The service between Evesham and Ashchurch continued, but the last passenger train on this section ran on 15th June, 1963 with the official closure date for passengers as two days later. Goods services were officially withdrawn from 1st July 1963, and track lifting began here in April 1964.

The survival of the remnants of the line

Strong representations were made locally for the retention of passenger services south to Studley and Alcester, but eventually the Transport Users' Consultative Committee were persuaded that the costs of repairing the line were too great, and that adequate bus services would be provided, and so agreed on 17th June, 1963 to the closure. With this agreement, the temporary bus services from Redditch to Evesham were discontinued from that date. Goods and parcels facilities were withdrawn from Alvechurch, and all stations south of Redditch were closed completely as from 6th July, 1964 (although not officially until 1st October for goods south of Alcester). However, on 10th April, 1964 Redditch had been designated by the government as the site of a 'New Town', which would require considerations for the future of local transport facilities. Nonetheless, rumours abounded locally that BR would soon withdraw the remaining services between Barnt Green and Redditch, and so in July 1964 BR announced that they had no such plans. Indeed, the timetables for September 1963 to September 1964 continued with the improved service introduced in 1960, which then comprised 16 up services (Monday to Saturday), starting with departures at 6.30, 7.26, 8.00, 8.25 am then almost hourly until the last train of the day at 11.15 pm, which was non-stop to Birmingham New Street, arriving in 26 minutes instead of the usual 39 minutes. Somewhat unusually this last service ran into the Western division side of New Street station on Saturdays only, even though its next movement was as empty carriage stock to Saltley. The down services totalled 19, and there were two each way on Sunday (reintroduced for the Summer only). After arrival at Redditch with the steam-hauled 1.12 and 5.10 pm services from New Street on Saturday, the locomotives returned as light engines to Saltley. All Sunday trains, and most trains after 6.30 pm did not stop at Selly Oak and Bournville. The two down and three up peak hour services, previously operated by steam, were taken over by dmus from 1st April, 1964 when the locomotive shed at Redditch was closed, although occasionally diesel locomotives powered some peak hours trains. One such unusual event was on 15th September, 1965 when Brush type '4' (later class '47') Co-Co No. D1561 of March (31B) shed worked the 4.22 pm Washwood Heath to Redditch freight, and then ran back to Birmingham New Street with the 7.24 pm local passenger. This particular locomotive had been travelling from March to Crewe for repairs, and had been borrowed at Saltley because of an acute shortage of diesel locomotives in the area at the time.

The parcels services continued with the 6.14 am from New Street (Monday to Saturday), and 9.50 pm from Redditch to Central Goods (Monday to Friday). The 6.10 pm parcels to New Street was withdrawn, as this entailed a light engine working back to Redditch, and in any event was usually only loaded to one vehicle!

Trust in BR was shattered in October 1964 when it announced that it planned to withdraw passenger services to Redditch as from 4th January, 1965. Meanwhile, track lifting had begun between Redditch and Evesham, one of the first moves being to sever the track at the northern mouth of Redditch tunnel, although it was noted that track was being lifted at Coughton as late as January 1965. However, almost certainly because of its status as a New Town, Redditch clung on to its rail service, and so in August 1965 the closure was refused by the Minister of Transport, although he did agree to 'modifications' to the services. These were soon revealed, when from 3rd January, 1966 the frequency was slashed to six trains each way, running in peak hours only. There were no Sunday services after this date.

It is noteworthy that the Midland Red introduced a new 'limited stop' service designated 'X7' from Birmingham to Redditch in December 1966 that took only 35 minutes; four less than by train. Meanwhile, the 'Master Plan' for the New Town was published in March 1967 and this was approved by the Government in June 1968.

Further shrinkage of the system at Redditch occurred when the up line was made into a siding, and the down line became the single running line for up and down services, this change coming into effect from 29th January, 1967. As a result, Barnt Green Single Line Junction signal box was no longer needed as a block post, so it was closed from 7th September, 1969 when the new power signalling centre at Saltley came into use and took over these functions.

The timetable from March 1967 to May 1968 gave only five workings in each direction, with an extra up service on Saturday. Although peak hour services appear to have been covered, there was an air of desolation at Redditch station in between the last morning arrival at 8.59 am, and the next arrival at 5.13 pm. Furthermore, this last morning arrival ran empty back to Birmingham, as did the last arrival of the day at 7.00 pm. The parcels service had changed, with the opening of the new parcels facility at Curzon Street, from where such trains ran in future, with one departure from there at 6.05 am and a return working at 8.35 pm.

The old station at Redditch (the second) was demolished in 1971 to make way for the redevelopment of Redditch town centre. The Kingfisher Centre now protrudes over this original station site and the railway cutting was infilled to provide a new

Right: A Metropolitan-Cammell class '101' dmu accelerates away from Redditch station in 1967, framed by the unusual loading gauge that stood in front of the loading bank and cattle dock.
Author's Collection

Below: A class '101' dmu stands in the second Redditch station with an RCTS 'Reunion Railtour' on 22nd November, 1969, as members examine the trackwork. Buffer stops have been installed at the end of the two lines, adjacent to the former Redditch South signal box.
RCTS

bus station at first, although that was subsequently removed as the Kingfisher Centre was extended. The use of the title 'Kingfisher' goes back to World War II years, when Redditch adopted HMS *Kingfisher,* which was an experimental anti-submarine corvette, built in 1935 and broken up in 1947. The Temperance Hall in Worcester Road was taken over during the war as a 'British Restaurant' and renamed Kingfisher Hall. After the war it became the Kingfisher Civic Centre, and when the new shopping centre was built on its site, the name was perpetuated.

A new station (the third) opened in January 1972 on the other, northern side of the Bromsgrove Road bridge, almost on the site of the original goods shed, latterly the parcels depot. It consisted of a single platform with two faces, and very basic passenger facilities. The line southwards to the previous station site was officially closed as from 7th February of that year. By 1972 passenger traffic was almost non-existent, with only around 200 passengers per day reported at Redditch and Alvechurch. The May 1973 to May 1974 timetable of three weekday trains each way was only slightly improved by May 1977 which comprised only three up services, Monday to Saturday, with three down services, Monday to Friday and four on Saturdays. There were no services on Sundays or on Bank Holidays. It was noticed during 1976 that services had sunk to new levels as some were being worked by the former WR single-car units of the W55000 series. It is surprising therefore, to learn of a survey for the possible doubling of the line from Barnt Green to Redditch during 1974/75, although nothing ever came of it. The line was only saved by the planning and funding produced by the West Midlands Passenger Transport Executive (WMPTE), which proposed a major revision of railway services, with Lichfield to Redditch serving as a primary axis across Birmingham. Work began on this project in 1976, and three new stations were opened south of Birmingham, at Five Ways, University and Longbridge in May 1978. The service on this line was worked by ageing former WR dmus with a hugely-improved frequency of around four per hour for much of the day.

One concession to rail travellers during 1982 was that passengers could use their rail tickets on Midland Red buses after the departure of the last service from New Street station, Birmingham.

Single train working on the line was introduced as from 5th September, 1986 with the result that the second Redditch platform face was no longer needed, as the line had effectively become a siding from Barnt Green. The timetable for October 1987 to May 1988 showed that all services from Redditch ran through to either Lichfield or Four Oaks. There were 20 up and 19 down services Monday to Friday with 18 up and 17 down on Saturday. No trains ran on Sundays.

Finally, the 'Cross City' line was electrified in 1993. A new station, often referred to as the fourth station, was constructed at Redditch. In reality, this was a rebuilding of the third station, by eliminating the second platform (on the eastern side), extending the remaining platform, and providing more passenger facilities and a proper booking hall. It is with some relief that this can be described as a modest brick-built single-storey station with a tiled roof and gable ends. Even some of the station fencing reflects its origins by being of the traditional MR diagonal wooden type. This small effort has gone some way to replacing the many designs based on bus shelters, airports and office blocks that not only look cheap and discouraging, but display a bankruptcy of ideas by the designers. The new station was opened by the BBC television newsreader Kay Alexander on 28th May, 1993 just two days before the line was energized.

A new station had also been erected at Alvechurch, costing some £232,000 for a basic platform and waiting shelter, which had opened on 19th March, 1993. The

A Metropolitan-Cammell class '101' dmu stands in the third Redditch station with an RCTS 'Reunion Railtour' on 22nd November, 1980. The second platform face can be just seen on the left. *RCTS*

Tyseley-based class '108' dmu set No. T302 stands in the fourth Redditch station on 1st August, 1994. This was built on virtually the same site as the third station, but dispensed with the second platform, and better passenger facilities were provided. The dmu is presumably deputizing for an emu, as these had many problems with reliability from soon after their introduction, which have since been solved. *RCTS*

goods yard was converted into a car park. Fortunately, the interior of the booking office was rescued, and has been reconstructed inside Kidderminster Railway Museum, adjacent to the Severn Valley Railway station.

Electric train services started as from the following 12th July, but there were many teething troubles with the new rolling stock, and for many months the old dmus were reintroduced. It must be said that having settled in, these electric trains have once again transformed the services, with extremely smooth riding and rapid acceleration. Following privatization in 1994 the services were operated by Centro, but since 2007 have been operated by London Midland and run at around 30 minute intervals during the day. At the time of writing these comprised 36 up and 35 down trains Monday to Saturday, with just a fraction less, 29 up and 28 down on each Sunday. The apparent imbalance is the result of one empty coaching stock working first thing each day.

The freight services

Freight services gradually declined after 1964, there being at first just two daily services from Washwood Heath with others run 'as required'. A Saltley class '08' diesel-electric shunter was outstationed at Redditch from 1964 to perform yard shunting duties.

From October 1965 the first of the two daily weekday inward freight workings (reporting No. 8G35) left Birmingham Lawley Street goods depot at 4.22 am and arrived in Redditch at 5.53 am. The second was from Washwood Heath West End yard at 8.10 am (reporting No. 8G37), arriving at 9.32 am. The return workings were 5G10 leaving at 1.11 pm arriving at Lawley Street at 2.05 pm, and 8G42 (Saturdays excepted) departing at 7.10 pm and arriving at Washwood Heath Up Sidings at 8.18 pm.

By 1968 there was just one scheduled daily freight service, and when this was withdrawn as from 8th September, 1969 Redditch goods shed and yard closed. This was in line with current BR policy which, realising that it could not compete with road transport, required only complete wagon loads as a minimum, and preferably complete block trains. However, coal concentration traffic and services for British Aluminium Company's private siding continued to be run on an 'as required' basis, even if this did not continue for much longer. The large goods shed stood for a number of years, not being demolished until 1983.

The yard remained disused, until during the 1970s when the construction of Redditch town centre and the many projects in the surrounding area began in earnest, and it was reopened for inward stone traffic. The stone trains consisted of 20 to 30 bogie wagons from Associated Roadstone Company's quarry at Tytherington, Gloucestershire and arrived at 6.30 am, where the wagons were left for unloading by cranes on to lorries. The locomotive went to Saltley at around 9.00 am, this movement having to wait until the first passenger services had cleared the line. It returned to collect the empty wagons for departure at 7.20 pm to Kings Norton, where they were left until the following day for return to Tytherington. Initially, pairs of type '2' Bo-Bo diesels (later classes '20', '24' or '25') worked this duty, but these were later replaced by a single type '3' (later class '37') or type '4' (later class '47') Co-Co diesel. These workings continued until around 1980, since when no freight trains have been seen on the line.

One final note here concerns a local group of railway enthusiasts who formed the 'Redditch Steam Locomotive Preservation Group', with the intention that should BR

The original station buildings at Alvechurch are now in use as a private residence, suitably segregated from the running line, 15th May 2004. *Author*

A roadside view of Studley & Astwood Bank station buildings, in use as a private residence in May 2004. The former goods shed and weighbridge office remained extant, but unused at the time. *Author*

close the line from Barnt Green, they would take it over. They acquired space on the site of the former Dixon's Siding, at the rear of what had become the Enfield Industrial Estate. An 80 hp Fowler 0-4-0DM shunter (Works No. 410013 of 1948) named *Plant No. 1301* that had been donated by Garringtons Ltd, of Bromsgrove, was obtained in April 1982 and stored at this site. Unfortunately for this group, the line remained open and they were unable to fulfil their aims. The locomotive was eventually moved to the Chasewater Railway, at Brownhills, Staffordshire on 23rd April, 1994.

The Line Today

The story of the line would not be complete without a look at the present status of the line, and what remains of the original structures. Starting at Barnt Green, the station still retains the up and down branch platforms as well as the main line platforms. Regrettably, all of the station buildings have gone, only to be replaced by the ubiquitous steel and glass 'bus shelters'. Gone too, are the signal boxes, and the main line north of the station has been reduced to double track from the previous quadruple track formation, the sidings have been taken up, and the junction with the Redditch line remodelled. However, one new item of equipment is of interest. Due to the severe curve of the branch platform, excessive wear was always caused to the flanges of rolling stock wheels, made most audible as the trains squealed round the curves. This has been somewhat alleviated by the installation of flange lubricators, which spray an oil based mixture on to the rails automatically, at the approach of a train. This operation is not, of course, visible from the train, but it is worthwhile to stand on the platform and observe it in use.

Up to 2014 the line to Redditch remained single, just as it always was, but after electrification was treated as a single siding, with 'one train operation' being the rule. At Alvechurch the new station sits to the north of the old station, which is still extant. The only missing building is the wooden waiting room, but the station master's house is now a private residence. Even the crumbling platform edging is a reminder of earlier times. However, further construction work here is changing the whole appearance of this formerly sleepy wayside station. The final section in this chapter ('Major New Works') amplifies the work in progress.

The approach to Redditch reveals nothing of the gasworks, that site now being entirely covered by housing development. Redditch North signal box and engine shed are but a distant memory, whilst the sidings alongside Clive Road are now covered by commercial development. The sidings at the main goods yard were removed entirely and the large goods shed demolished, so that most of the goods yard remained largely derelict for many years, although the part nearest to the station was converted into a car park. Finally, during 2005 work started on building dwellings on the remainder of the former goods yard. As a result, the 'Birdcage' footbridge was also removed, and replaced with a much shorter one linking Bridge Street to this now completed development. The fourth station marks the terminus of the line, but the Bromsgrove Road overbridge still remains. Southwards, beyond the infilled station area now once again serving as a bus station, the remainder of the cutting has been infilled right up to the tunnel mouth, this area being used as a garage and maintenance area for the buses.

Studley & Astwood Bank station is substantially complete, and in use as a private residence. Happily, the former goods shed and even the weighbridge office are also complete. But southwards from here there is at first no indication of the route of the

The former station buildings at Salford Priors were in use as offices and storerooms in May 2004 by Bomford & Turner, successors to Bomford & Evershed whose original site here has expanded over the former trackbed. This view is of the former rail side of the station. *Author*

The former goods shed at Beckford is now in commercial use, as we see here in August 2005. It was not possible to photograph the existing station buildings here, nor at Hinton and Ashton-under-Hill, because of encroaching vegetation. *Author*

The view northward at Ashchurch on 15th May, 2004. The station has reopened after being rebuilt, and new trackwork has been laid on the right into the Ministry of Defence storage facility. *Author*

The second Alvechurch station as seen on 15th May, 2004, looking south. This fairly basic station opened in March 1993, two months before the electrified line was energized. Remains of the old station can be seen in the distance. *Author*

Class '323' emu No. 323212 takes the Redditch line at Barnt Green on 28th May, 2005. Noticeable changes here include the removal of the goods yard, signal box, and the down slow line.
Author

The view southwards on the main line at Barnt Green. The original station building on the down platform has disappeared, as has the bookstall and waiting room on the up platform. The latter has been replaced by the modern 'bus shelter' type of basic passenger accommodation, although the MR footbridge is pleasingly still fulfilling its function, 15th May, 2004. *Author*

line, until nearer to Coughton, where a number of overline bridges mark it out. Coughton station has also been redeveloped into a private residence, and further additions have changed the shape of the building, which was admittedly rather small.

The approach to Alcester reveals nothing of the goods yard and divergence of the GWR branch, as these have all been covered by housing and commercial development. The station master's house and the adjacent porters' lodge have been rebuilt as a large private dwelling, and the owner has gone to the trouble of retaining a portion of the up platform, with suitable MR pattern diagonal wooden fencing. One of the brown enamelled WR station signs was found in a recess beneath the platform and has been replaced on the up platform.

At Wixford, the course of the line can be traced, although heavily overgrown, and there are no remains of the small station. South of Wixford the route through Broom has been partly used in that of a new A46 trunk road, alongside which the wartime Broom West signal box still stands on the eastern side, being increasingly overgrown by saplings and other vegetation. This is the only evidence that a railway ever ran at these places, all other traces having reverted to agricultural use.

The station building and goods shed at Salford Priors remain complete, and in commercial use by the agricultural equipment firm of Alamo Manufacturing, successors to the Bomford and Evershed business that originally operated on the site opposite the station. Harvington station is also complete, being another example refurbished for use as a private residence.

As might be expected the bridge over the GWR line north-east of Evesham station has long gone, and the area north of, and around, the MR station has been redeveloped as a housing estate. However, the original booking hall remains complete, albeit minus the elegant platform canopy. After closure in 1964, the station building was eventually utilized as a permanent way depot, which function it still performed in 1976. It is now in commercial use.

South of the station, the spans of the bridge over the River Avon have been dismantled, and the area of the abutments is heavily overgrown. Proceeding on to Bengeworth, once again the whole area has been redeveloped as a housing estate and no trace remains of its railway origins. At Hinton the road overbridge remains alongside the station master's house, which is complete but now surrounded by farm buildings.

The trackbed to the north of Ashton-under-Hill is clearly discernible, but the road overbridge on the north side of the station has been almost entirely flattened. The station building, now standing in virtual isolation, is a private residence.

The area covering the goods yard at Beckford has been converted into commercial premises, including the goods shed, which is still remarkably complete. The booking hall has gone, but the adjacent station master's house is in private use, almost entirely obscured by the growth of trees over the last 40 years. The road overbridge alongside remains as a landmark.

At Ashchurch, the lines to the Ordnance Depot still curve away towards Redditch from the main line, and after a number of years of disuse, now once more see occasional use. The station was unstaffed as from 14th September, 1970, closed completely as from 15th November, 1971 and was thereafter demolished. However, a new station was constructed some 20 years later on the same site, but in the modern basic style, and opened in 1995. It comprises the familiar 'bus shelters' on the new up and down platforms, which are connected to the car park by a substantial footbridge. All other traces of the goods yard and Tewkesbury line have been eradicated. A new roadbridge at the southern end of the station completes the transformation of the scene.

Looking along the branch platforms towards Redditch on 15th May, 2004, with the ubiquitous modern 'bus shelter' accommodation for passengers on the down platform. Pipes for the flange lubricators can be seen between the up side running rails. *Author*

The fourth Redditch station on 15th May, 2004, with emu No. 323005 having recently arrived on a 'Cross City' service. Since electrification, this service has proved immensely popular, as witnessed by the number of passengers in this view. The additional facilities are evident, and the expanded car park used part of the former goods yard. Although the remainder was undeveloped at that time, it is now covered by housing. *Author*

Major new works

A scheme was approved by the Secretary of State for Transport on 31st October, 2013 for Network Rail to improve the flexibility and frequency of services on the existing line, by the introduction of an entirely new running line totalling 1.8 miles. This line will run from just south of the canal bridge north of Alvechurch, to just north of the bridge over Weights Lane, to the north of Redditch, and is sited on the west side of the current running line. Control over this extended loop will be from the West Midlands Signalling Centre at Saltley. Presumably it was not deemed practical to extend the doubling for the whole length of the line, due firstly to the canal bridge and subsequent deep cutting and embankment towards Barnt Green. Secondly, at the Redditch end, the lengthy embankment and bridge over Windsor Road were only constructed for a single line, and so present unacceptable challenges. Further encroachment has also occurred on to the original trackbed approaching Redditch town.

Work began on this section in November 2013, and is expected to be completed by December 2014. As might be expected, the works entailed some disruption to services such that the line from Barnt Green was closed entirely during July and August 2014, with an alternative bus service being offered to passengers from Redditch. Alvechurch station will gain a second platform, alongside the new ('up') line to the west of the present one.

The new services are expected to be operated by six-car sets (possibly class '350' units, being manufactured in Germany by Siemens) at an improved 20 minute interval. Meanwhile, on the main line, electrification work from Barnt Green to Bromsgrove is due to be completed by summer 2016. It is not anticipated that this will cause any lessening of the Redditch services, rather the present 'Cross City' services that terminate at Longbridge will continue to a new station at Bromsgrove.

So far, no changes have been announced for the station facilities at Redditch, but whilst these are at present 'adequate', surely some improvements could be made. Nonetheless, this investment and the popularity of the services, seem to point to an assured future for this remnant of an historic and useful line.

Work for the new 1.8 mile running line was well under way at Alvechurch on 13th April, 2014. Earthworks were being excavated and the land profiled ready for the new platform to be added here on the 'up' side, opposite the 1998 platform. In the background, the original station house can be seen beyond the later platform. *Author*

Chronology

1857 Plans deposited for Redditch Railway (30th November)
1858 Act passed authorizing Redditch Railway (23rd July)
The 'first sod' turned of the Redditch Railway (7th August)
First shareholders' meeting held of the Redditch Railway (20th October)
1859 Redditch Railway inspected by Captain Galton (8th September)
Official opening of the Redditch Railway (19th September)
Alvechurch station opened (10th October)
1860 MR plans for Ashchurch to Evesham line deposited (30th November)
1861 Act passed authorizing MR Ashchurch to Evesham line (7th June)
1862 MR appointed Brassey & Ballard to construct Ashchurch to Evesham line (28th August)
Work began on construction of Ashchurch to Evesham line (September)
Plans deposited for Evesham & Redditch Railway (29th November)
1863 Act passed authorizing Evesham & Redditch Railway (13th July)
Act passed empowering transfer of the Redditch Railway to the MR (21st July)
First shareholders' meeting of Evesham & Redditch Railway (14th October)
1864 Ashchurch to Evesham line opened to goods traffic (1st/6th July)
First inspection of Ashchurch to Evesham line by Captain Tyler (8th July)
Second inspection of Ashchurch to Evesham line by Captain Tyler (16th September)
Ashchurch to Evesham line opened to passenger traffic (1st October)
1865 Contract for Evesham & Redditch Railway awarded to Brassey & Ballard (10th March)
1866 Evesham to Alcester section opened for goods traffic (16th June)
Captain Yolland inspected Evesham to Alcester section (24th July)
Transfer of Redditch Railway to MR completed (14th August)
Evesham to Alcester section opened for passenger traffic (17th September)
1867 Evesham & Redditch Railway Directors inspected finished Redditch tunnel (1st August)
Bengeworth goods yard opened (1st June)
1868 Colonel Hutchinson inspected Alcester to Redditch section (13th March)
Board of Trade approved opening of Alcester to Redditch line (30th March)
Alcester to Redditch line opened for goods and passenger traffic. First Redditch station closed and second station opened (4th May)
1873 Act passed authorizing Evesham, Redditch & Stratford-on-Avon Railway, for Broom to Stratford line (5th August)
Redditch Gas Works expanded, new sidings added
1874 MR empowered to absorb the Redditch Railway (30th July)
1875 MR Board meeting approved absorption of Redditch Railway (11th February)
1876 BWSR opened for passenger traffic from Granville Street to Kings Norton (3rd April)
Alcester Railway, from Bearley Junction to Alcester opened to all traffic (4th September)
1878 Major-General Hutchinson inspected Broom to Stratford line (10th October)
1879 Broom to Stratford line opened to goods and passengers (2nd June)
1880 Broom Junction status changed to a public station (1st November)
1882 Act passed empowering MR absorption of Evesham & Redditch Railway (12th July)
1883 Alcester Railway absorbed by GWR (1st July)
1885 Bidford station opened (22nd February)
BWSR extended to New Street, line doubled, and Granville Street station redeveloped into Central Goods Depot (1st July)
1886 Evesham, Redditch & Stratford-on-Avon Railway in hands of Receiver (2nd June)
Act passed permitting dissolution of Evesham & Redditch Railway (25th June)
1887 LNWR goods service from Blisworth to Broom inaugurated (15th March)
1888 LNWR goods service from Blisworth to Broom terminated (31st October)

1891 MR London to Avonmouth goods service via SMJR and Broom inaugurated (13th April)
1892 Broom Junction station changed from two single lines to a loop (October)
1908 Act passed enabling Evesham, Redditch & Stratford-on-Avon Railway to be absorbed into SMJR as from 1st January, 1909 (1st August)
1910 Bomford & Evershed sidings opened at Salford Priors (July)
1912 MR London to Avonmouth goods service routed away from SMJR (30th September)
1915 Alcester GWR shed closed (1st November)
1917 All services suspended on GWR Alcester to Bearley Junction line (1st January)
Bengeworth to Beckford section singled (31st January)
Track removed from Alcester to Bearley Junction (25th March)
1921 Double track reinstated from Bengeworth to Beckford (22nd February)
1923 MR and SMJR absorbed into LMS (1st January)
Services reinstated on GWR Alcester to Bearley Junction line (1st August)
1925 Church Road station closed (1st January)
1926 Redditch goods yard remodelled, double line section extended
1927 New large goods shed opened at Redditch, old shed afterwards used as parcels depot
Ashchurch connection to Tewkesbury line singled
1930 Somerset Road station closed (28th July)
1931 GWR and LMS stations at Evesham worked as one joint station
Evesham LMS shed closed (14th September)
1935 Major derailment to passenger train at Ashton-under-Hill (25th February)
1939 All services suspended on GWR Alcester to Bearley Junction line (25th September)
1940 Connection to Ashchurch Ordnance Depot installed (4th August)
1941 Selly Oak, Bournville and Camp Hill line stations closed 'for the duration' (27th January)
Workmen's trains introduced from Bearley Junction to Great Alne (July)
1942 East to South spur at Broom opened (17th May)
Broom West signal box opened (27th September)
1944 Workmen's trains from Bearley Junction to Great Alne withdrawn (3rd July)
Five Ways station closed (2nd October)
1946 Camp Hill line stations closed permanently. Selly Oak and Bournville reopened. (27th November)
1948 LMS nationalized (1st January), line became part of London Midland Region
1950 Wixford station closed entirely (2nd January)
1951 Through mineral trains from Woodford to South Wales began via Broom (4th June)
Alcester to Bearley Junction line closed officially (1st March)
1952 Coughton station closed to all traffic (30th June)
1953 Bengeworth station closed entirely (8th June)
Hinton downgraded to unstaffed halt (31st August)
1957 Ashton-under-Hill downgraded to unstaffed halt (1st March)
Ashchurch connection to Tewkesbury line officially closed (24th May)
New connection at Evesham, from Ashchurch to Honeybourne installed (Summer)
1958 Barnt Green to Ashchurch operations passed to BR Western Region (1st February)
1960 Bromsgrove shed commenced supply of Redditch pilot engine (January)
Birmingham to Redditch dmus introduced on almost hourly service (25th April)
Lines from Broom to Stratford closed to all traffic (13th June)
Alcester to Bearley Junction track removed, Alcester GWR shed demolished (July)
1961 Passenger services from Ashchurch to Tewkesbury withdrawn (14th August)
1962 Goods traffic to Tewkesbury withdrawn and engine shed closed (7th September)
Redditch to Evesham passenger services withdrawn (1st October)
Alcester to Evesham goods services withdrawn (1st October)

1963 All services withdrawn from Evesham to Ashchurch (15th June)
1964 Track lifting commenced, Evesham to Ashchurch (April)
All Birmingham to Redditch steam services transferred to dmus (1st April)
Redditch designated as a 'New Town' (10th April)
Redditch locomotive shed closed (1st June)
Redditch to Alcester goods services withdrawn (6th July)
Line from Evesham to Ashchurch officially closed (6th July)
BR proposed closure of Barnt Green to Redditch line from January 1965 (October)
1965 BR closure notice refused by Minister of Transport (4th August)
1966 Birmingham to Redditch passenger services drastically reduced (3rd January)
1968 'Master Plan' for Redditch New Town approved by Government June)
1969 Scheduled goods services suspended. Redditch goods yard and goods shed closed (8th September)
1971 Ashchurch station closed (15th November)
Second Redditch station demolished (December)
1972 Third Redditch station officially opened (January)
1978 New stations opened at Five Ways, University and Longbridge opened (8th May)
New intensive DMU service introduced with backing of WMPTE (8th May)
1983 Redditch goods shed demolished
1991 New Ashchurch station opened
1993 Fourth Redditch station officially opened (28th May)
Birmingham to Redditch EMU service inaugurated (1st June)
1994 Birmingham to Redditch services privatized, and operated by Centro (London Midland)

The curvature of the line as it approached Evesham is evident in this view of Ivatt Mogul No. 43047 as it runs in with a passenger service from Birmingham in October 1962. It has travelled over the track leading off to the top left, and just passed over the GWR Oxford-Worcester line, the bridge parapets being visible behind the first carriage.

Author's Collection

Bibliography and Acknowledgements

Primary documentation has been accessed at the following locations – Public Record Office (now The National Archives (TNA)), Kew - Minutes and records of the Redditch Railway, the Evesham & Redditch Railway, the Evesham, Redditch and Stratford-on-Avon Junction Railway, the East & West Junction Railway, the Stratford & Midland Junction Railway, the Alcester Railway, and selected records of the Midland Railway and the Great Western Railway.

TNA references: RAIL 6/1-10, 168, 199/1-9, 491/277, 580/1, 777/1, 781/411, 793/9, 793/68, 793/88, 1057/2833, 1065/2833, 1066/15-17, 1075/89, 1075/185, 1110/4-5.
MT 6/20/2, 6/20/8, 6/32/5, 6/44/3, 6/51/3, 6/58/1, 6/58/3, 6/162/14.
BT 285/52, 285/360.
MFQ 1/694/7.

The National Railway Museum, York - Working timetables of the Midland Railway, and the London Midland and Western Regions of British Railways.
Midland Railway Study Centre, Derby - Working timetables of the Midland Railway
Warwickshire County Archives - Deposited plans, Parliamentary Acts, *Alcester Chronicle* and Ordnance Survey maps.
Worcester County Archives - Deposited plans, Parliamentary Acts and Ordnance Survey maps.
Worcester Heritage Centre - *Evesham Journal, Berrow's Worcester Journal, Worcester Herald, Worcester Chronicle* and Ordnance Survey maps.
Alcester Library - *Alcester Chronicle.*
Almonery Heritage Centre, Evesham - Photographic collections.
Evesham Library - Photographic collections and *Evesham Journal.*
Redditch Library - Photographic collections, *Alcester Chronicle* and *Redditch Indicator.*
Author's collection - Photographs, public timetables, working timetables, and sectional appendices.

The following secondary sources of information have been consulted:

Locomotive and Train Working in the Latter Part of the Nineteenth Century by E.L. Ahrons (W. Heffer & Sons, 1952)
Encyclopaedia of British Railway Companies by C. Awdry (Guild Publications, 1990)
British Locomotive Catalogue, 1825-1923, Part 3A, Midland Railway by B. Baxter (Moorland Publishing, 1982)
The Railways of Salford Priors by A. Boston (1994)
A Hundred Years of Alcester by J. Bunting (K.A.F. Brewin Books, 2000)
Directory of Railway Stations by R.V.J. Butt (Patrick Stephens, 1995)
Locomotives at the Grouping- No. 3 London Midland and Scottish by H.C. Casserley and S.W. Johnson (Ian Allan, 1974)
Railways of the West Midlands, A Chronology, 1808 to 1954 by C.R. Clinker (Stephenson Locomotive Society, 1954)
A Regional History of the Railways of Great Britain, Vol. 7 The West Midlands by R. Christiansen (David & Charles, 1983)
Postal History of Alcester (website) by J. Donaldson, Alcester & District Local History Society, 1988.
The Stratford and Midland Junction Railway by J.M. Dunn (Oakwood Press, 1977)
An Illustrated Review of Midland Locomotives from 1883 by R.J. Essery and D. Jenkinson (Wild Swan, 1984)
An Illustrated History of the Ashchurch to Barnt Green Line by R.J. Essery (Oxford Publishing Co. 2002)

Industrial Railways and Locomotives of Warwickshire (Preliminary Draft) by R. Etherington (Industrial Railway Society, 2003)
Birmingham New Street - The Story of a Great Station by R. Foster (Wild Swan, 1997)
The Birmingham and Gloucester Loop by C.T. Goode (1998)
The Midland Railway - A Chronology by J. Gough (Railway & Canal Historical Society, 1989)
The Canals of the West Midlands by C. Hadfield (David & Charles, 1969)
GWR Shed Allocations for 1921 by I. Harrison (Wild Swan, 1984)
LMS Engine Sheds, Volume 2, The Midland Railway by C. Hawkins & G. Reeve (Wild Swan, 1981)
Steam on the Birmingham-Gloucester Loop by P.K. Jarvis (K.A.F. Brewin Books, 1988)
The Oxford, Worcester and Wolverhampton Railway by S.C. Jenkins and H.I. Quayle (Oakwood Press, 1977)
The History of Redditch and the Locality by N. Land (K.A.F. Brewin Books, 1984)
The Birmingham and Gloucester Railway by P.J. Long and Revd W.W. Awdry (Alan Sutton, 1997)
An Historical Survey of Great Western Engine Sheds, 1837-1947 by E. Lyons and E. Mountford (Oxford Publishing Co., 1979)
An Historical Survey of Great Western Engine Sheds, 1947 by E. Lyons (Oxford Publishing Co., 1985)
Branch Lines of Worcestershire by C.G. Maggs
The Redditch Railways by D.R. Morgan (Redditch College of Adult Education, 1980)
Redditch Railways Revisited by D.R. Morgan (University of Birmingham, Department of Extramural Studies, 1983)
GWR Shed Allocations for 1934 by N. Pocock and I. Harrison (Wild Swan, 1987)
A Gazeteer of the Railway Contractors and Engineers of Central England 1830-1914 by L. Popplewell (Melledgen Press, 1986)
Locomotives of the GWR - Part Three - Absorbed Engines, 1854-1921 (RCTS, 1956)
The Railway Station - A Social History by J. Richards and J.M. MacKenzie (Oxford University Press, 1986)
A History of Redditch by J.G. Rollins (Phillimore, 1984)
Industrial Railways of the West Midlands by R.A. Shill (Industrial Railway Society, 1996)
'Happy End' by G. Skelsey, *Backtrack,* Vol. 16, No. 3, March 2002.
Industrial Railways and Locomotives of Worcestershire (Preliminary Handbook) by A.C. Smith (Industrial Railway Society, 2005)
'Birmingham to Gloucester Loop' by J.M. Tolson, *Railway Magazine*, Vol. 110, Nos. 763/4 (November/December, 1964)
Alcester - A History by G.E. Saville (K.A.F. Brewin Books, 1986)
George Furness: Willesden's Greatest Resident? by C. Wadsworth (CAW Books, 1996)
Thomas Brassey: Railway Builder by C. Walker (Frederick Muller, 1969)
'Brassey and Ballard - An Anomaly' by Bob Yate, *Industrial Railway Record,* No. 174, September 2003.
B&R Video No. 5 *Midland around Worcestershire* (Vol. 76)
Contemporary traffic reports from various issues of *Railway Magazine, Trains Illustrated, Modern Railways and Railway Observer.*

I should like to record my thanks to the many individuals who provided information, help and advice. In particular, to local residents and former railwaymen George Blewitt, Harry Dawson, John Dudley, John Hickman, Chris Jackson, David Johnson, Graham King, and Peter Turner. Also to Vic Bradley, Ray Shill and Russell Wear. Mention should also be made of the help provided by the staffs of the museums, libraries and archive centres mentioned above. Finally, to my wife Sandra for her understanding and patience whilst I buried myself in detail or absented myself in search of further items of interest.

Index